# Learning Together with Young Children

**Other Redleaf Books by Deb Curtis and Margie Carter**

*Reflecting Children's Lives: A Handbook for Planning Your Child-Centered Curriculum,* Second Edition (2011)

*The Visionary Director: A Handbook for Dreaming, Organizing, and Improvising in Your Center,* Second Edition (2010)

*Designs for Living and Learning: Transforming Early Childhood Environments* (2003)

*The Art of Awareness: How Observation Can Transform Your Teaching* (2000)

*Spreading the News: Sharing the Stories of Early Childhood Education* (1996)

*Training Teachers: A Harvest of Theory and Practice* (1994)

# Learning Together with Young Children

## A Curriculum Framework for Reflective Teachers

Deb Curtis and Margie Carter

Redleaf Press®
www.redleafpress.org
800-423-8309

Published by Redleaf Press
10 Yorkton Court
St. Paul, MN 55117
www.redleafpress.org



First edition 2008
Cover design by Percolator
Cover photograph by LaTisha Pearson
Interior typeset in Utopia and designed by Percolator
Printed in the United States of America
18 17 16 15 14 13 12 11 4 5 6 7 8 9 10 11



Library of Congress Cataloging-in-Publication Data
Curtis, Deb.
Learning together with young children : a curriculum framework for reflective teachers / Deb Curtis and Margie Carter.—1st ed.
p. cm.
Includes bibliographical references and index.
ISBN 978-1-929610-97-6 (alk. paper)
1. Early childhood education—United States—Curricula. 2. Early childhood education—United States—Activity programs. 3. Reflective teaching—United States. I. Carter, Margie. II. Title.
LB1139.4.C876 2007
372.210973—dc22

2007022589

Printed on acid-free paper

Jocelyn (Barbarin) Myres
1951–2001

Jocelyn's leadership in the early childhood field inspired us on many levels.

We first met her as a colleague doing community college field instruction in child care programs across the Seattle area. Wanting to be more closely involved with the lives of children, she took a job as a child care director, and a few years after that, returned to the classroom as a preschool teacher. Jocelyn's unusual career path inspired Deb to return to work directly with children herself.

Jocelyn led by example. Her classroom is prominently featured in our video, *Children at the Center: Reflective Teachers at Work.* Through this window into her thoughts and actions, Jocelyn has inspired early childhood educators across the United States and Canada. Her untimely death is a tremendous loss to the Seattle early childhood community. Her memory and contributions live on as a powerful reminder for what is possible in our work with children and families.

# Learning Together with Young Children

## Chapter 4: Bring Yourself to the Teaching and Learning Process 86



## Chapter 5: Coach Children to Learn about Learning 111



## Chapter 6: Dig Deeper to Learn with Children 139



## Chapter 7: Adapt the Curriculum Framework for Different Settings 174

# Acknowledgments

As always, our families and friends have been incredibly supportive of us during the writing of this book.

Our editor, Beth Wallace, supported us through difficult cuts in a manuscript that was far too long, and offered valuable feedback for the structure of the text.

The staff of Redleaf Press with whom we worked, particularly Sid Farrar, Ryan Scheife, Mara Miller, JoAnne Voltz, Laurie Herrmann, Emily Nesheim, and Tom Owen, were receptive and responsive to our perspectives. They had the challenging task of balancing our fierce advocacy for early childhood educators in the trenches with their publication guidelines, production standards, and marketing agendas. We appreciate the principles that guide Redleaf's publishing efforts and their assurance of fair labor practices in this global economy where the only affordable way to produce a full-color book is to have it printed in a developing country.

Every book we write is a collaborative process, not only between the two of us, but also including a wide range of early childhood educators who generously welcome us into their lives, minds, family child care homes, classrooms, and program cultures. People contributed far more stories and photos than we were able to use in this book, but their contributions have made their way into our thinking and will no doubt appear as examples in the workshops, presentations, and consultations that are central to our professional lives. We are enormously grateful for the engagement and generosity extended to us across North America, Australia, New Zealand, and Italy.

We want to specifically acknowledge the following individuals and organizations and apologize for any unintended omissions:

- Evie Lieberman opened her home to us for our initial writing retreat to launch this book.
- Pauline Baker and the Tucson Children's Project hosted a wonderful gathering of colleagues and loaned us a copy of *The Power of Protocol: An Educator's Guide to Better Practice* by Joseph P. McDonald to stimulate our thinking.
- During that gathering, Teresa Acevedo thrilled us with her courageous act of resistance against bureaucratic mandates that would undermine her Head Start program.
- During our year of writing, Tom Hunter sang and collaborated with us to come up with the concept of taking responsibility for living fully and teaching well.
- Ann Pelo, Kristin Brown, Cindy Hayertz, and Donna King let us interrupt their busy lives again and again with visits or requests to track down a relevant story, photo, or permission slip.
- Special thanks to Rukia Rogers, LaTisha Pearson, Elma Horton, and Michelle and Julie Garrett, who responded to our last-minute requests for photos.
- Children in all kinds of early childhood settings have welcomed us with open hearts and genuinely allowed us to learn alongside them.
- We appreciate the following family providers, teachers, directors, and teacher educators who took time from their other commitments to

answer questions and share experiences, observations, and a multitude of photographs:

*in Australia*: Jenny Dwyer, Trinity Preschool; Fran Bastion and Nicole Tytherleigh, Earlwood Children's Centre; Diane Duvall, Lady Gowrie Child Centre, Gillian McAuliffe, Bold Park Community School

*in Aotearoa/New Zealand:* Chris Bayes, Ministry of Education; Lorraine Manuela and Fran Paniora, Tots Corner

*in Canada*: Lorrie Baird and Sheila Olan-MacLean, Kawartha Child Care Services; Carole Anne Wien, Annette Coates, and Bobbie Lynn Keating, Peter Green Hall Children's Centre; Terry Bussey, Ron Blatz, and Bev Onysko, Discovery Child Care

*in the United States*: Amy Piersol and Lynn Schintzer, Clifton School; Betsy Kempter and Sarah Cornette, Sunflower School; Kate Thegen with Quality Circle; Mona Jackson, Dawna Nifong, Brett Engisch, and Jenifer McKee, Coordinated Child Care in Pinellas County; Jacky Howell and Debbie Lebo, Montgomery Child Care Association; Susan Stacy and Katie Lugg, New Hampshire Technical Institute; John Nimmo and Rebecca New, University of New Hampshire; Karen Opstad; Janelle Clemensen, St. Charles Community College Child Development Center; Brenda Sottler, Bobbie Jones, Jill Baker, Northland Head Start; Kelly Matthews, A Place for You; Billie Ognenoff, Heart and Home Family Child Care; Gabriela Kocian, Sophia, Miss B., Hattie White, Barry Swartwout, Shannon McClellan, and Marcela Clark, United Way Bright Beginnings; Cleta Booth, University of Wyoming Child Development Center; Marsie Habib, Marta Marin, Manzo PACE Program; Rosemary Hooper, Paradise Valley Community College Child Development Center; Judy Poggi; Linda Jimenez, East LA Community College Child Development Center; Kathryn Ingrum, Grossmont Community College Child Development Center; Gregory Uba and Kisha Williamson; Alise Shafer, Evergreen School; Carline McGrue, Erika Flores, Neda Gilson; Rhonda Iten, Cathedral Oaks School; Will Parnell and Ellie Justice, Helen Gordon Child Development Center; Nancy Gerber; Erin Robb and Kathleen Tracy, Lakewood Co-op Preschool; Carol Wroth, Mother's Quality; Deadru Hilliard, Michael Koetje, and Christina Aubel; Vanessa Maanao, Wanda Billheimer, and Charling Chow, Puget Sound ESD; Deb Walrath, Every Voice; Tom Drummond, North Seattle Community College; Janie Castiliano, Sheila Carrigg, Sedro Woolley Head Start; and our colleagues, Marilyn Chu and Jean Kasota.

Margie extends a special appreciation to colleagues at José Martí Child Development Center: Hilda Magana, Martha Diaz, Luz Casio, and Laura McAlister; and to colleagues at Hilltop Children's Center: Sandra Floyd, Sarah Felstiner, Myrna Canon, John Benner, Emily Viehauser, Kendra PeloJoaquin, Ilene Stark, Ann Pelo, and Susan Alexander. Against the persistent barriers inherent in full-time, not-for-profit child care, their remarkable dedication to working with children and families in the manner described in *Learning Together with Young Children* is truly inspiring and reminds us all that another way is possible.

Deb is especially grateful to her coworkers at the Burlington Little School: Cindy Hayertz, Carrie Waterworth, Kirsten Thompson, Cathy Bamba, Linda Henning, Rebekah Mills, Amber Crane, Kami Manley, Marlys Vollegraaf, Victoria Thulman, Ted Wellander, Lindsey Carlson, MaryAnn Nurkiewicz, and Sarah Bishop. In a small farm valley community, they keep alive some of the best practices of progressive education.

This long list of acknowledgments confirms that the notion of "teacher as researcher" is being practiced on a daily basis by an ever-growing cadre of dedicated early childhood educators. Surely *Learning Together with Young Children* qualifies as a research-based curriculum!

# Introduction

*Education is an arena of hope and struggle—hope for a better life and struggle over how to understand and enact and achieve a better world. We come to believe that we can become makers of history, not merely the passive objects of the great human drama.*

**BILL AYERS**

Never has there been a more important time for us to ask ourselves what we believe the purpose of education to be. The future of American democracy may well depend on it. Do schools and early childhood programs primarily exist to produce compliant workers for economic function? Or is the goal to help children grow into their full potential as informed, engaged citizens eager to make a contribution to their communities? Do educational goals narrowed to test scores prepare children to be successful in an increasingly complex world? Should early education focus solely on children's futures or does providing enriched childhood experiences give them a better future?

The answers to these questions determine the approach to curriculum in early childhood education programs. Should teachers design curriculum to remediate children's needs and deficits, or should they focus on children's inherent competencies, ideas, and questions? Can stronger policies and curriculum mandates really improve learning outcomes? Or should the emphasis be on improved working conditions, salaries, and teacher education to support the role of teachers in children's learning? What are your views on these questions?

Education always represents a philosophical and political point of view and serves a particular agenda. The task for educators is to know our history, probe deeper, ask critical questions, and find the ground we want to stand on. Engaging in this critical thinking process has brought us to stand with the voices for progressive education. We first came to the teaching profession in the 1970s, a time of great upheaval, but also of great promise. Ordinary people, such as ourselves, our friends, our fellow teachers, and our neighbors, were engaged in lively debates about where we wanted to take our country. We saw ourselves as makers of history, not passive citizens giving up on America's failure to live up to our democratic ideals. It was an exhilarating time—a time of rage, joy, determination, dancing, and singing—a time of great hope. A fierce sense of possibility first brought us to work with young children and here we are, many years later, clamoring again at the gates of hope.

Perhaps you, like us, came to work in the early childhood field because you wanted to secure the future for young children, and because you wanted to be reminded of the joy and passion for living that young children offer nearly every minute. But in the United States today, childhood, early childhood education, and the teaching profession are under siege, with so much conspiring to diminish our dreams. Educational policies are taking us away from the joy we once felt. Educational authorities want us to believe education should be about teacher-proof, mandated curriculums, high stakes testing, and conformity. The energies of teachers and administrators are pulled toward an avalanche of regulations and accountability systems.

We say, "*¡Basta!*" We can do better than this for our children and ourselves.

## QUESTIONING CURRENT THINKING AND APPROACHES

We know this problem is complex, and simple solutions do not exist. A number of factors contribute to problems in current approaches to early curriculum for children. Here's what we think is currently wrong with the way early childhood education is being conceptualized in the United States:

- Definitions of quality are inadequate.
- Factories serve as a model for education.
- Teachers lack philosophical foundations.
- Authorities view children as needing to be "readied" and fixed.
- Play is not considered a viable source of curriculum.
- Child-directed and teacher-directed approaches are presented as opposed and mutually exclusive.
- There is no infrastructure to support teachers' reflective practice.
- Teachers and programs are required to adopt quantifiable "research-based" curricula.

### •PROBLEM•
### Definitions of Quality Are Inadequate

In the United States, decade upon decade of research, professional efforts, and advocacy have attempted to demonstrate and put into place the components of good experiences for young children. Despite the substantial body of research demonstrating that quality early childhood experiences are directly related to healthy brain development and to social, emotional, and cognitive maturity, the status of early care and education in the United States is a national crisis, and should be a national shame. As policy makers begin to recognize the links between early education and academic success, they have marginalized our professional knowledge and decision-making power, and directed quality reform efforts toward measurable outcomes and high stakes testing. And, as is the custom in U.S. culture, commercial interests then swoop in with quick-fix, easy solutions—so-called teacher-proof curricula, time-saving literacy strategies, tools that take the guesswork out of assessment. "No need to worry or trouble yourself with thinking too hard about all this," is an appealing message for distraught educators. It is also a big source of our problems.

If teachers are to take charge of the direction of early care and education, they must begin to ask, "What is quality?" and the more important question, "Who gets to decide?" What assumptions, values, and agendas do you want to guide efforts to revamp early care and education in the United States? Each community and early care and education organization must undertake an open discussion of its purpose, and the values, philosophy, and theoretical frameworks it wants to guide everyday program practices.

### Stone Soup

*Family provider Donna says she considers "layers of value" when choosing what curriculum ideas to pursue. "We are so ambitious for the children and for ourselves! Because we have a relatively small amount of time with the kids and want that time to be meaningful, I strive for what I call at least 'three layers of value' in everything we choose to take up. By this I mean, when our goals for children are self, community, nature, skills, and dispositions about work and play (such as risk-taking, persistence, passion, curiosity, and joy), then anything we plan must relate to at least three of these areas. For instance, we once made Stone Soup with the children and invited the children's families to the feast. Reflecting back on the activity, we decided it had so many layers of value that we wanted to keep it as a tradition. The process and tradition of making Stone Soup includes working with food in its raw, natural form; the connection between story and the lives we actually live; developing skill with paring knives for work that would be appreciated by the people we love the most in the world; integrating food that came from each person's home into one big pot of soup we all eat together; and there was even singing, math, writing, and drawing. It was rich. Worth our time, worth the children's time. The curriculum we pursue and traditions we adopt help define our program culture. They have to resonate with our values at a high level of detail."*

Children First

As we've traveled across our own country, Canada, Europe, Australia, and New Zealand, we've been enormously inspired to see dedicated early childhood professionals reminding us that something else is possible. In many places we have seen what deep respect for children can look like, what securing the future for our children can look like, what an educational system based on wonder, curiosity, joy in learning, focusing on relationships, and engaged investigation looks like. Sadly, most of these models are not visible to the everyday early childhood practitioner, or they are dismissed because they have privileged resources and are viewed as elitist. We are particularly impressed with the strong government support for progressive-minded early childhood education some nations offer. New Zealand, in particular, shows us how a country can face a history of injustice with a serious refocusing of resources toward a bilingual, bicultural early childhood education system.

## •PROBLEM•
## Factories Serve as a Model for Education

Despite the lip service to individualized learning (and in some cases the genuine efforts of programs to be child-centered), most child care and Head Start settings in the United States resemble a factory model with a culture of compliance, schedules, and mandated curriculum components. Monitors focus on paperwork and crunch numbers to ensure accountability. Teachers move children through the day as if they are cars on an assembly line. Neither the teachers nor the children are afforded time to ponder, wonder, and make meaning out of the day's activities. Increasingly, teachers are given scripts to follow. Some early childhood commercial curricula even market themselves like one-minute managers proclaiming, "This lesson will only take five minutes of your day." You should question why that might be a good thing. If it's worth learning and adding to your program, doesn't it deserve more time? What about the learning that comes from really slowing down and paying attention to what you are undertaking?

Perhaps there is no greater influence in the teaching and learning process than how time is viewed and used (Phillips and Bredekamp 1998). We live in an era shaped not by the rising and setting of the sun and moon, as in eons ago, but in an era when technology and a sense of urgency speed up everything we do. This cultural reality slips into early care and education programs with policies and mandates that fragment our time into little boxes on a schedule. Carole Anne Wien (2004) suggests that because we are so removed from the rhythms of the natural world, we approach time with a linear, not cyclical, mindset. Examining the use of time and allocating it closer to your values and human development knowledge is one of the most important undertakings for early childhood educators.

An unhurried pace fosters a sense of security and possibilities, while a rushed one creates stress, fragmentation, and a sense of discouragement and resignation. When you slow down, you see more; you allow more time for relationships to grow and thinking to deepen. Research has shown that children need at least thirty minutes to engage fully and reap the benefits of their play and exploration (Johnson, Christie, and Yawkey 1987). If teachers want children to be learning social skills in group times; acquiring language and nutritional knowledge during eating times; developing coordination, strength, and neurological connections while outside; and expanding their knowledge of materials, others, and themselves in their play activities, why are they continually rushing children on to something else? It isn't mere exposure to these things that heightens the possibilities for development and learning. Rather, children need time to really immerse themselves in these areas if meaningful learning outcomes are to arise.

## •PROBLEM• Teachers Lack Philosophical Foundations

In the United States, most teacher education efforts within the early childhood realm happen in the in-service, instead of pre-service, arena. Directors feel fortunate if they can hire a teacher with an associate's degree. In-service training for teachers is typically focused on "how-to" skills, at best attached to some understanding of child development. Seldom do these teacher education efforts raise philosophical concerns or challenge teachers to question the purpose of education.

We believe that teaching strategies should flow from a consciously defined belief system, not a set of regulations, a series of activity books, or a bag of tricks. Your curriculum and teaching behaviors reflect a set of assumptions about your view of children and your role as a teacher, whether or not you have examined these underpinnings. Taking the time to understand and clarify your own values and understanding of education, and those of your coworkers, will form a more thoughtful, effective teaching practice. When you are clear about the ideas and values you want to guide your teaching, you will be less likely to drift down a side stream or jump on a runaway train headed somewhere you don't really want to go. With this clarity, you will find more intellectual vitality and heart energy in your work.

*Learning Together with Young Children* derives its philosophical orientation in the tradition of progressive educators such as Jerome Bruner, Carol Brunson Day, John Dewey, Maxine Green, Asa Hilliard, Jonathan Kozol, and a host of other important voices. We believe, as they do, that the purpose of education is to live into a true democracy, to flourish in our humanity, and—as the educators of Reggio Emilia remind us—to find depth, meaning, and joy in the teaching and learning process. The pedagogy we champion is strongly influenced by our study of Jacqueline Grennon Brooks, Lisa Delpit, Eleanor Duckworth, Erik Erikson, Paulo Freire, Friedrich Froebel, Howard Gardner, bell hooks, Elizabeth Jones, Loris Malaguzzi, Maria Montessori, Jean Piaget, Carlina Rinaldi, and Lev Vygotsky. We mention these names to acknowledge some of those who have inspired and taught us, but there are many others, too numerous to mention. We suggest you take it upon yourself to learn more about these pioneers, and the related approaches to education with names like "social constructivism," "empowering or participatory education," "critical pedagogy," "multiple intelligences," and "inquiry-based learning." Grounding yourself philosophically is essential to developing a pedagogy and curriculum approach that reflects your beliefs and goals for living and learning with children. (See the appendixes for tools that will help you with this process.)

## •PROBLEM• Adults View Children as Needing to Be "Readied" and Fixed

The concept of school readiness is full of complexity. On the one hand, whatever their circumstances, children are born eager to learn. However, failing to recognize this, adults immediately impose their wills, perspectives, and agendas on children, in some cases inflicting neglect or abuse. Traditional approaches to education have viewed children as empty vessels to be filled instead of recognizing the existing knowledge they bring to learning opportunities. When children fail to thrive in our educational settings, educators think children need remediation or, even worse, some punitive action. In most cases, it is the curriculum or pedagogy that needs fixing, not the children.

Fortunately, a number of teachers embrace a strength-based approach to education. Educators from Reggio Emilia in Italy, among others, challenge us to see the competency of each child, to believe in children, and to commit ourselves to helping them reach their potential.

## •PROBLEM• Play Is Not Considered a Viable Source of Curriculum

In today's world, play-based curriculum approaches are increasingly viewed with skepticism. In part, this is because children's play is often not what it used to be. Consequently, there are good reasons not to trust it as the natural purveyor of learning for a range of domains—dispositional learning, language and literacy, math and science, and so on. Unfortunately, television, electronic media, and commercial toys have invaded young children's play, often supplanting it with commercial scripts and agendas. Children have limited time to acquire play skills because their lives are scheduled from the time they wake until they go to bed, with very little freedom or time outdoors (Louv 2005). No wonder so many children don't learn how to independently investigate, invent, or problem solve with any complexity.

Teachers, too, have contributed to a mistrust of children's play as a vital source of learning. When children engage in self-initiated play, teachers don't always recognize the learning possibilities unfolding or know how to facilitate play for deeper learning. They lack confidence in articulating learning outcomes embedded in children's play. Furthermore, their own education hasn't prepared teachers to recognize cultural differences in how children learn through play (Neugebauer 1999).

However, the early childhood profession has long recognized that play is important for children's growth and development. In "Chopsticks and Counting Chips," Elena Bodrova and Deborah J. Leong (2004) cite a body of research on the value of play, concluding, "Studies show the links between play and many foundational skills and complex cognitive activities, such as memory, self-regulation, distancing and decontextualization, oral language abilities, symbolic generalization, successful school adjustment, and better social skills." In particular, they delineate the study of Daniel Elkonin (1977) who identified four principal ways in which play influences child development and lays the foundation for learning in school.

1. Play affects children's motivation, enabling them to develop a more complex hierarchical system of immediate and long-term goals.
2. Play facilitates cognitive decentering as children take on roles in their play and negotiate different perspectives.
3. Play advances the development of mental representations as children begin to separate the meaning of objects from their physical form.
4. Play fosters the development of deliberate behaviors—physical and mental voluntary actions—as children learn to sequence actions, follow rules, and focus their attention.

Elizabeth Jones (2004) has written extensively about the roles teachers assume in supporting children's play as a source of learning. "Teachers support play by providing a variety of things to do, observing what unfolds, and staying nearby to help as needed and to acknowledge children's actions and words . . . We teach young children to play by providing them with space, time, and materials; offering them support in problem solving; presenting new problems for them to solve; paying attention to their spontaneous interests; and valuing their eagerness to learn about the world in which we all live together." Contrary to the prevailing wind, then, we believe children's play is both an essential learning tool for young children, and deeply affected by the quality of the teaching environment in which it takes place. It's worth finding the resources to help teachers learn to do the deep work of preparing for, encouraging, supporting, and building curriculum from children's play.

## •PROBLEM• Child-Directed and Teacher-Directed Approaches Are Presented as Opposed and Mutually Exclusive

For too long, early childhood educators have used "either/or" thinking, juxtaposing child-initiated play against teacher-directed curriculum. Proponents of emergent curriculum have adopted a hands-off approach, mistakenly believing that an emergent approach requires teachers to wait for children to initiate a curriculum idea. Conversely, advocates of the direct instruction approach have overlooked the learning that can emerge in children's play, believing children can't learn unless they are taught by adults. With the passage of the federal No Child Left Behind Act many teachers have brought dittos and drill-and-practice teaching back into early childhood classrooms, believing this is the way to ensure school readiness.

The tension between these two approaches has been heightened by the dynamics of racism, poverty, and privilege. White, middle class children are raised with the expectation that they will self-initiate and tend to do well with this curriculum approach. This is less true for children of color and low-income families who often grow up with a cultural expectation that they will learn what to do from their teachers (Delpit 2006).

We've come to understand that dichotomizing child-directed and teacher-directed curriculum approaches is an over-simplification of the complex process of teaching and learning. Sue Bredekamp and Teresa Rosegrant (1995) describe these as a continuum of teaching behaviors, acknowledging that a curriculum responsive to children, as well as desired learning goals, requires a teacher to move across this spectrum. To determine a helpful teacher behavior at any given juncture, teachers need a relationship with the children and their families, and attention to the details of what is unfolding in the classroom. We propose that teachers master a repertoire of possible actions that can be used as a protocol for guiding children's learning, including both skills in supporting and extending child-initiated activities, and expertise in teacher-directed curriculum. When they are guided to learn this repertoire and supported by a program culture that invests in and trusts them, teachers become effective facilitators of learning.

## •PROBLEM• No Program Infrastructures to Support Teachers' Reflective Practice

The culture of most early childhood programs reflects an insidious mentality of compliance and scarcity. Teachers are viewed as technicians accountable to an ever-growing body of standards and curriculum content. Simultaneously, budgets for teaching staff are carefully limited to meeting ratios with children and adhering to labor laws. Most accredited programs give teachers paid time for weekly planning and annual professional development opportunities. While this is a step in the right direction, it is hardly adequate for teachers to do their job well. Our earlier book *The Visionary Director* offers an extensive set of ideas for creating a program that goes beyond meeting requirements or delivering curriculum to children.

In today's education world, with increasing emphasis on standards and outcomes, a bigger vision can seem like pie in the sky. Sometimes, the force of one person or small team can push a vision forward, but without an infrastructure to support the actual work of living into a vision, sustainability is difficult. Teachers and administrators burn out, become cynical, or give up. Moving a program toward the curriculum approach proposed by this book requires a close examination of your organizational culture and suggests a new approach to your professional development. It isn't appropriate to just require teachers to start adopting some new practices. To support teacher efforts and ongoing professional growth, organizational systems, policies, and distribution of resources will likely need some realignment.

## •PROBLEM• Teachers and Programs Are Required to Adopt Quantifiable "Research-based" Curricula

Teachers have a range of curriculum models to choose from, many of which address current educational thrusts and policies aimed at measurable learning outcomes. Increasingly, programs find mandates requiring them to adopt a quantifiable, scientific, "research-based" curriculum. These mandates should prompt us to ask questions such as these: Who are the researchers? What is their cultural framework? What research methodology and measurement tools were used? Is there any one research methodology that is reliable for all children (NAEYC 2007)?

Thanks to the work of the educators of Reggio Emilia, many early childhood teachers in the United States are being encouraged to see themselves as researchers (Meier and Henderson 2007; Gallas 1994). In light of this possibility, why would anyone adopt a curriculum that gives a script for teachers to follow? In contrast, Deborah Meier and Barbara Henderson (2007) suggest that teacher education involving teacher research holds great promise for improving reflective practices.

We find value in curriculum models that are environmentally based, see children as active learners, offer children choices, encourage teachers to build curriculum from children's interests, and use ongoing observations with a focus on strengths for assessments. We believe curriculum should strengthen children's identities as thinkers and responsible citizens as well as creators of a life-sustaining culture. Curriculum should be developed in conjunction with children's families and communities and be respectful of their culture and home language. Over the years we have gained insights from the curriculum approaches promoted by the British Infant Schools, Bank Street College in New York, and Pacific Oaks College in Pasadena, and our colleagues at the High/Scope Foundation, Teaching Strategies, California Tomorrow, Reggio Emilia, and Aotearoa/New Zealand. The early *Alerta* curriculum (Williams and De Gaetano 1985) and the more recent bilingual, bicultural curriculum approach offered by Sharon Cronin and Carmen Masso (2003) have offered us important insights into culturally relevant programming for young children.

While we understand why a scope-and-sequence curriculum model might appeal to those mandated to adopt a formal curriculum, we encourage you to consider whose interests are served by doing so. We have seen far too many programs where more attention is paid to scripts for outcomes than to what is most significant from the children's and teachers' points of view. It is also worrisome to see training focused on how to deliver a curriculum instead of how to think through the complexities of the teaching and learning process. Again, who benefits and who loses with the promotion of a "teacher-proof" curriculum? Teachers who only focus on carrying out the curriculum and completing their paperwork ultimately lose heart and question whether they want to stay in the field. Defining your work around issues of compliance will lead you to feel like a victim and deaden your spirit. And, such a misguided focus could ultimately undermine your ability to create a vibrant learning community in your early childhood program. There are other, more rewarding choices you could make.

### A Learning Organization

*Consider this story of a Head Start director who told us of the hours and hours she spent researching a curriculum to adopt for her program.*

*Teresa narrowed the curriculum choices down to three, carefully studied all the materials, and met extensively with each of the companies' representatives. Though all of the curriculum packages under consideration were comprehensive in their scope-and-sequence approach, she found pieces in each that were problematic for the approach to curriculum and assessments that she wanted to unfold in her program. Teresa was devoting this part of her early childhood education career to creating what Peter Senge (2000) calls a "learning organization," a Head Start agency that nurtures the thinking abilities of parents, staff, and children. She believed any lock-step, sequenced, "teacher-proof" curriculum would undermine this goal. Teresa agonized over how in good conscience she could justify spending close to a hundred thousand precious taxpayer dollars to adopt this kind of curriculum for her large agency with multiple sites, many human resource needs, and a series of budget cuts coming down the pike. Finally, though anxious about potential misinterpretations and findings by her upcoming federal review, Teresa made the brave choice not to adopt any commercial curriculum. Her decision was guided by her vision for her program and the values she couldn't compromise. And, in the end, her federal review team agreed with her approach.*

You might have a different story. You could be saddled with a curriculum model that has already been adopted for your program, all or some of which seems counter to the approach you would like to take. Perhaps you are a family provider or a teacher in a program with no clear philosophy or curriculum approach guiding your work, independently sorting out how to structure your time with children. Have you been inspired by the stories of the in-depth curriculum work from the schools of Reggio Emilia but can't imagine how to implement such an approach in your setting? As a family child care provider or an infant and toddler caregiver, you might be struggling to understand how to keep your home-like focus while still embracing this notion of curriculum and ensuring that children are learning during their time with you. You could be a preschool teacher diligently trying to integrate the new content-driven curriculum resources addressing standards for math, science, language, and literacy and losing heart trying to juggle it all. Whoever you are, we want to address your concerns, inspire you, and strengthen your ability to live fully and teach well.

## A NEW WAY

Our aim with this text is to put a spotlight on curriculum practices that are meaningful for children, as well as their teachers. We offer you a curriculum framework with a repertoire of possibilities to engage deeper learning. Our goal is to demystify some big theoretical concepts and offer a way to think about the teaching and learning process that is emotionally and intellectually engaging for teachers and children. During a recent seminar, a provider asked us, "Are you talking about a way of teaching or a way of living your life?" We could only smile and answer, "Yes."

With all the demands and ups and downs of working in the early childhood field, how does one approach the job with a lively mind and spirit? What will fuel your passion and your determination not to be confined by a narrow understanding of who children are and what they deserve from us? How can you rise above constraining requirements, limited time, and limited resources to develop more significant experiences for the children and yourself? Whether you are an early childhood student, family child care provider, center-based teacher, administrator, or teacher educator, this book attempts to help you find your own answers to these questions and to strengthen your ability to think through the complex issues of the teaching and learning process.

We want you to see yourself as an inventor who can demonstrate a better way to meet desired learning outcomes and in the process, nourish the heart of your teaching and the vision of what early childhood education could be. Whatever your context, you can use these ideas to deepen your intellectual and emotional engagement in your work. You and the children will find living and learning together a more joyful experience. You will contribute to a revitalized democracy where people have the desire, skills, and opportunity to make contributions, think critically, negotiate conflicts, and invent equitable solutions that respect our planet and all its inhabitants. *Learning Together with Young Children* invites you to take back the joy and meaning of the teaching and learning process. Consider it a call to action.

# A Curriculum Framework for Reflective Teaching

*To enter into a style of teaching which is based on questioning what we're doing and why, on listening to children, on thinking about how theory is translated into practice and how practice informs theory, is to enter into a way of working where professional development takes place day after day in the classroom.*

**SONYA SHOPTAUGH**

When teachers work with curious and questioning minds and see themselves not as disciplinarians or mere transmitters of information but as researchers learning alongside children, then new knowledge is always under construction. As Sonya Shoptaugh suggests, this way of working results in ongoing professional development for teachers as well as meaningful outcomes for children. *Learning Together with Young Children* is a curriculum framework intended to bridge the gap between credible educational theories and research, and the everyday practices of teachers. The process of planning curriculum gives attention to learning domains and standards, but it involves far more than that. We take a comprehensive approach to curriculum development. More than just planning activities or lessons, teachers who follow the tenets of this book will draw on their philosophy, values, and pedagogical theories to create a vibrant classroom culture focused on relationships and inquiry. They will design the physical and social-emotional environment with great care. This initial and ongoing work is the foundation or core of our curriculum framework.

From this hub, a wide-ranging repertoire of teacher actions spirals outward ensuring important learning will take place in daily moments as well as in long-term investigations and projects. As children explore relationships, materials, and activities in this thoughtfully planned environment, teachers move through a continual observation/reflection/action cycle, what Paulo Freire (1970) calls "praxis." They observe and collect descriptive details, photographs, and samples of the knowledge children have been expressing and investigating. Teachers converse with the children, help them see what others are doing, and describe how this is related to other experiences, domain knowledge, and academic standards. They offer additional materials, coach children to acquire useful skills, and continually challenge children to go deeper with their learning. At each juncture, teachers ask themselves the following questions (and others) to critically reflect on what they are seeing and the documentation they are collecting.

- What details stand out that I can make visible for further consideration?
- What in my background and values is influencing my response to this situation and why?
- How might issues of culture, family background, or popular media be influencing this situation?
- Where do I see examples of children's strength and competency?
- How do I understand the children's point of view in this situation?
- How are the environment and materials impacting what's unfolding and what changes could be made?
- How are teacher actions impacting this situation?
- What learning domains are being addressed here and what other learning domains could be addressed?
- What theoretical perspectives and child development principles could inform my understandings and actions?
- What values, philosophy, and goals do I want to influence my response?

Because we believe teachers are creative, competent, and eager to help children learn, our curriculum approach offers a wide berth for their autonomy. Of course, teachers, like children, need others to believe in them, support them, and mentor them into their full potential. For their creativity to flourish and for them to develop professionally, teachers deserve collegial work environments with the time, tools, and technology to support their reflective practice. We know teachers work in a variety of settings, each with its own complex web of concerns to be taken into account in the curriculum-planning process. If your early childhood program has a centralized, top-down set of mandates, standards, and assessment tools, our curriculum framework will guide your thinking as you translate these requirements into specific and meaningful experiences for the children. If your program offers little in the way of philosophical or pedagogical guidance for teachers, our framework helps you clarify your values and beliefs about the teaching and learning process, and offers a structure for planning and responding to children. Our goal is to engage your mind in the dynamic process of teaching and learning, which, in turn, will strengthen your competence and confidence as a reflective teacher. Curriculum for children can't reach its potential for deeper meaning and learning without teachers engaged in their own learning process.

## *LEARNING TOGETHER WITH YOUNG CHILDREN:* THE CURRICULUM FRAMEWORK

Our curriculum framework comprises five critical core practices, each of which has specific principles to guide teachers in adapting that core practice for your setting:

- Create a nourishing classroom culture.
- Enhance the curriculum with materials.
- Bring yourself to the teaching and learning process.
- Coach children to learn about learning.
- Dig deeper to learn with children.

Because two of our earlier books, *Designs for Living and Learning* and *The Art of Awareness,* are respectively focused on designing physical environments and acquiring observation and documentation skills, these core practices are referenced as part of the *Learning Together with Young Children* curriculum framework but not extensively taken up or given their own chapters as a curriculum core practice here.

Neither is the topic of assessment. Tools for assessing children are prolific across the early education field and we don't intend to introduce yet another. The assessment approaches compatible with our curriculum fall under the rubric of "authentic" (Meisels et al. 1994) and are based on documentation data from children's everyday work (Horm-Wingerd 2002). We particularly favor the approach to assessment used in New Zealand with the tool referred to as "learning stories" (Carr 2001) and hope it will become more widely used in the United States. Throughout *Learning Together with Young Children* you will find examples of an observation and documentation process that can easily feed into existing assessment tools and address educational standards.

Planning curriculum that is responsive to children's lives and learning styles requires far more of teachers than choosing a set of lessons or activities to offer. By the same token, it is far more rewarding. Rather than mandating a step-by-step protocol to follow, *Learning Together with Young Children* offers a framework for thinking. When you continually cycle through the set of questions we offer for reflecting on your observations and actions, this reflective thinking process will become second nature to you. As you internalize the principles in each of the core practices of our curriculum, you will find yourself excited about making them your own. Whereas teacher-proof curricula disregard teachers as the most important element in children's learning, our curriculum framework asks you to bring yourself fully into the planning and implementation process.

Trinity Preschool

Tots Corner

## •CORE PRACTICE 1•
## Create a Nourishing Classroom Culture

If you are clear about the ideas and values you want to guide your teaching, the next step is to make sure these values are reflected in the learning environment you create. Our earlier book *Designs for Living and Learning: Transforming Early Childhood Environments* offers many examples of how programs have undertaken this task. If you aren't familiar with this resource, consider reading it as you undertake the ideas about curriculum we offer here. In some ways *Learning Together with Young Children* is a sequel to *Designs for Living and Learning.*

Once you have created an environment that reflects your philosophy and values for children and families, then what? Your next step is to use those same values in creating a classroom culture, a set of expectations, routines, and ways of being together. This requires rethinking some of the standard ways teachers organize time for children; how you spend your time as a teacher; the language and systems you use for communications; and the ways you come together, see each other, and negotiate your ideas, desires, and different points of view. Chapter 2 will launch you into a set of principles to guide your work in creating a classroom culture that demonstrates a high degree of respect for children as capable learners and members of families and communities. You'll also find principles to guide you in forming respectful partnerships with children's families from first encounters through ongoing communications and gatherings. Ideas for bringing democratic ideals into your classroom routines, and for fostering relationships and a sense of belonging and responsibility, are brought to life with specific examples from teachers across the country. You will find inspiring examples of a classroom culture that helps children see themselves as learners and resources to each other. And, finally, there are ideas for creating memory-making rituals and celebrations that go beyond standard birthday parties and graduation ceremonies. Creating a classroom culture involves ongoing thinking about your values, a willingness to experiment and take risks, and constant attention to relationships and the environment. This is the core practice of our curriculum framework—all other teacher actions flow from this foundation.

## •CORE PRACTICE 2•
## Enhance the Curriculum with Materials

When you have an environmentally based curriculum, you pay attention to the environment on both the macro level (the room design and setup) and the micro level (the materials that are available, and how they are presented to children). Again, your values and images of children and the teaching and learning process shape your selection of materials to offer. Our curriculum approach suggests you reconsider many of the typical materials made for children's learning. We encourage you to see yourself as an inventor of new combinations of materials. Draw on your philosophical foundation, your observations of what children enjoy doing, your child development knowledge, and the dispositions, relationships, and learning outcomes you have in mind for children, to create something no one else could come up with. Chapter 3 offers an extensive set of principles for selecting and offering materials to children. As you keep in mind the kinds of play (Piaget 2001) and developmental themes (Curtis and Carter 1996) reflected in children's ongoing play, you can begin to offer combinations of materials that provide for these in open-ended ways. Learning some basic principles for combining and presenting materials as "invitations for learning" will help you entice children's exploration and enhance their ability to focus more clearly. With the children actively engaged, rather than dependent on your instructions for investigation, you will be able to initially stand back, observe, and make deliberate choices about your next actions. When you design open-ended invitations with particular themes or learning domains in mind, you create more possibilities for gathering documentation to reflect the learning, help in planning next steps, and add to your assessment process.

Earlwood Children's Centre

Children First

Earlwood Children's Centre

## •CORE PRACTICE 3• Bring Yourself to the Teaching and Learning Process

A good deal of pre-service teacher education and ongoing professional development is focused on what and how to teach, leaving out of the equation who is doing the teaching. In *The Courage to Teach*, Parker Palmer (1998) reminds us that this constitutes a fundamental deficiency for teachers.

> *The question we most commonly ask is the "what" question—what subjects shall we teach?*
>
> *When the conversation goes a bit deeper, we ask the "how" question—what methods and techniques are required to teach well?*
>
> *Occasionally, when it goes deeper still, we ask the "why" question—for what purposes and to what ends do we teach?*
>
> *But seldom, if ever, do we ask the "who" question—who is the self that teaches? How does the quality of my selfhood form—or deform—the way I relate to my students, my subject, my colleagues, my world?*

Chapter 4 describes an important core practice of our curriculum framework to address this dilemma for teachers. If you don't know yourself well, if you feel powerless in your job, how can you be an effective teacher? Bringing yourself, not just your teaching objectives and techniques, to your days with children requires that you have a heightened awareness of

Clifton School

Martin Luther King Jr. Day Home Center

Burlington Little School

your instinctive reactions to things that unfold with children. What past experiences color who you are as a teacher? What do you value and want to pursue with them? When you reflect on your observations, what do you see as significant and why? Answers to these questions help you more clearly define the possibilities you can offer children.

Even if you are mandated to use a prescribed curriculum—or perhaps we should say, *especially* when you have such a mandate—you can claim your power to make your days meaningful and joyful. Remembering that curriculum is everything that happens in your time with children, your keen eyes and ears must tune in to how to support what is significant to them. In addition to principles for self-awareness, we offer ideas for cultivating a mindset of receptivity and an ability to notice details. You will find principles to help you think through possible actions to take. These include seeking the children's point of view, extending conversations, and bringing awareness to how you are becoming a group of responsible, competent learners.

## •CORE PRACTICE 4• Coach Children to Learn about Learning

Once you develop a classroom culture to foster respectful relationships and an eagerness to explore the provocative materials available, a repertoire of possible teacher actions will heighten your ability to co-create a curriculum that goes beyond the superficial into the exciting process of constructing knowledge. Co-creation is the operative idea here. Until recently, the early childhood education field has juxtaposed two possible approaches to curriculum: teacher-directed or child-initiated. Proponents of one view tend to think negatively about the other. Though our profession's definition of "developmentally appropriate practice" (Bredekamp and Copple 1997) has precluded a drill and recitation approach, it was never intended to convey a passive role for teachers. Teachers may not be up front directing children's recitations, but they are continually playing the role of stage and prop manager (Jones and Reynolds 1992), coach, model, and improvisational artist helping children learn as they play.

Martin Luther King Jr. Day Home Center

There are many things children can only learn with instruction and support from more experienced people. Studying Vygotsky's theories of scaffolding and "the zone of proximal development" (Berk and Winsler 1995) will help you see the vital importance adults can play to enhance children's learning. When young children demonstrate an excitement about the learning process, how do teachers use their skills and knowledge to support them without taking over? The challenge is to help children gain skills and resources in order to understand and take more responsibility for their own learning. Chapter 5 offers specific principles to help you and the children see learning as a process with specific strategies you both can utilize. Teachers use direct coaching when particular skills, tools, or know-how would be useful to the children. You show them how to turn to their friends, reference materials, and stories to be in charge of their own learning.

## •CORE PRACTICE 5• Dig Deeper to Learn with Children

A popular sentiment in the United States is that "more is better" and in early childhood education, this often translates into superficially exposing children to a wide range of curriculum topics. In many ways, this is contrary to young children's nature. They like repetition and immersing themselves in their current passions. Teachers can provide children the experience of disciplining themselves to go deeper, rather than looking for the next entertaining activity.

In trying to use an observation-based, emergent approach to curriculum, teachers often think they

United Way Bright Beginnings

should wait until the children express an interest in something and then plan a unit around this topic. For example, if children's play is repeatedly centered on dinosaurs, then teachers plan a series of lessons related to dinosaurs. How does jumping in with this emergent curriculum "theme" differ significantly from a preplanned version of a dinosaur curriculum project? What might your teaching goals be with such a project? If the curriculum is primarily teacher driven and remains superficially focused on the names and habits of different dinosaurs, the children may acquire some more information, but deeper investigation or significance is limited. A more engaged approach to co-creating curriculum with children's emerging pursuits involves careful observation, analysis, and meaning making. You are guided by an awareness of your values and curiosities. Rather than working with predetermined outcomes, you put your heads together with the children, their families, and your coworkers to study the outcomes your documentation reveals. At times you stand back, while on other occasions you take action, allowing time for joy and meaning to unfold and build. You invent ways of demonstrating how your curriculum meets educational standards, demonstrating courage and a willingness to be different.

Young children have many modes of learning, which Howard Gardner (1999) describes as "multiple intelligences" and the educators of Reggio Emilia (Edwards, Gandini, and Forman 1998) refer to as "the hundred languages." By offering a wide range of materials for children to use in thinking through and expressing their feelings and ideas, providers and teachers can counter the prevailing educational trend to focus only on verbal linguistic modes. This fuller, more complex view of teaching and learning is a reciprocal process where teachers learn as much as the children. Reggio educators liken this to a dance or a game of catch. Everyone has an active role in the teaching and learning process. Children are learning about the world, their own competence, how to work with others, and the contribution they can make. If we are open to it, they teach adults to see the world with fresh eyes. When teachers challenge children to go further with their learning, you learn more about the dynamics of teaching as you support children to invest in the expression of their thoughts, feelings, questions, and discoveries.

As soon as teachers and children become fully engaged in learning, they don't want their time chopped up into little curriculum boxes. Teachers come to recognize that children deserve time for fuller investigations, and you deserve time to reflect on how to support their inquiry. With this understanding, you work to identify particular studies to take up with the children in a more focused and extended way. The question shifts from casting about with "what can I think of to do tomorrow?" to "what focus should I choose from the many possibilities unfolding?" Your choices are guided by your values, your program context, and your desire to integrate meaningful experiences with learning domains and standards.

Chapter 6 focuses on this core practice of our curriculum framework—going deeper into the possibilities for learning. Principles here guide you in using the wide range of children's natural learning inclinations as a springboard for multiple intelligences to work. This includes music, drama, drawing, stories, and big body activities. Central to this process is an understanding that whenever you invite children to use a variety of modes to express particular ideas they are pursuing, they are challenged to consider new perspectives and clarify their thinking. Using your documentation directly with children provides a mirror for further reflection and illumination.

## ADAPT THE CURRICULUM FOR DIFFERENT SETTINGS

As your teaching begins to incorporate the principles for each of the core practices of the *Learning Together with Young Children* curriculum framework, explained fully in chapters 2 through 6, you will find ways to adapt the curriculum for different settings.

Most early childhood programs are operating with limited resources and insufficient working conditions to support the reflective teaching and professional development Sonya Shoptaugh describes in the opening of this chapter. Administrators haven't understood the remarkable advancements their teachers could make if they would reconceptualize their in-service training systems and shift their allocation of dollars accordingly. Carol Brunson Day (2006) describes how this revamping could affect curriculum practices.

> *The economics of paying teachers for five hours of planning time each week seems daunting for Americans, but rather than rejecting this strategy as too costly, it would be instructive to determine what is spent by school systems and Head Start on other forms of in-service training that do not as directly affect classroom practice and do not transform performance. Head Start actually has an ideal staff structure for easily transforming their programs. Education coordinators could become what Reggio educators call pedagogisti. Instead of bureaucrats, they could be teacher educators in-residence. The rich practice we see in Reggio grows out of the continuous exchanges within and among the teaching teams, the analysis and re-analysis of the daily classroom experiences with input from people who have various levels of experience and expertise. The yield is the power to create a personalized, culturally responsive curriculum at the center level.*

Whatever the constraints or strengths of your teaching setting, you can take the curriculum core

José Martí Child Development Center

Denise Louie Head Start

Martin Luther King Jr. Day Home Center

practices we offer and make them your own. To guide you in translating our framework into your context, we offer you numerous examples, each with a principle to inspire your own adaptations. In chapter 7 you will hear how teachers in part-time programs with different groups of children, and teachers with the challenges of sharing a space, use their documentation to create connections among the children. Teachers describe how they are inventing new ways to meet requirements and expand possibilities for prescribed curriculum. There are principles for documenting experiences that meet standards and make assessments relevant and meaningful. If you are working in a program structure with paid time for planning or collaborative reflection on your documentation, our principles for using children's ideas to pursue extended investigations, working with different perspectives, and learning from conflicting ideas will help you make better use of the support your program offers you.

Each time a provider or teacher illuminates a way to put one of our principles into practice, you expand the possibilities for our profession. With our curriculum framework, outcomes for teachers involve lively daily interactions with children; and outcomes for children include the satisfaction of generating their own learning, rather than being the target of someone else's lessons. Contrary to the experience of working with many prescribed curriculums, education with these outcomes offers an experience of living fully now, not only preparing for the future. There are outcomes for the future, to be sure, because teachers and children become hungry learners and knowledge seekers, eager to invest their time in further education.

## CLAIM YOUR RESPONSIBILITY TO LIVE FULLY AND TEACH WELL

As you conscientiously practice the different possibilities for teacher actions outlined in our chapters, you will find a natural rhythm and intuition about which to use when. This curriculum approach is a thinking lens and a methodology for growing yourself as a teacher, along with in-depth curriculum experiences for children. It is important, however, that you not do this work in isolation. Working alone will ultimately leave you frustrated, discouraged, and headed for burnout. Listen to this story about Margie's six-year-old grandson, Coe. When his beloved first grade teacher, Grant, had a car accident and was unable to return to work, Coe and his classmates endured a revolving door of substitute teachers, which caused an increasing amount of unrest among the children and

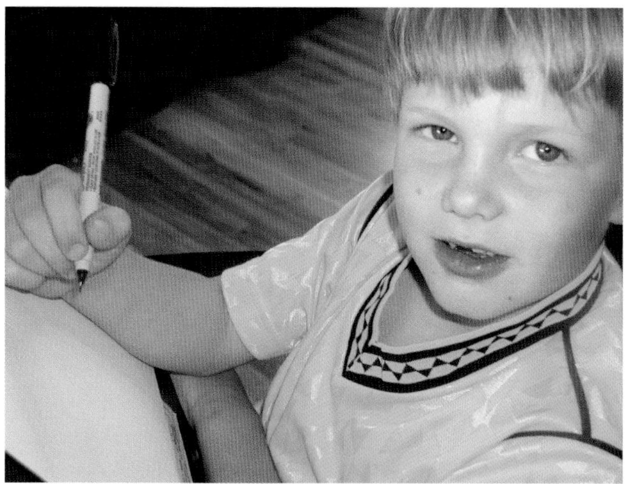
Orca School

United Way Bright Beginnings

their families. By February, Coe's ideas about teachers sounded like this: "These teachers don't know what they are doing and should be fired." "They are just too mean to help us really learn." When April arrived he had some additional ideas: "We need to kill these teachers' techniques by just being nice ourselves so they'll calm down and let us do some fun things." As the school year was coming to a close, Coe's insights deepened: "Teachers need to find someone to talk to. It's really lonely being a teacher."

Finding colleagues to dialogue with, cultivating a "can-do" disposition, inventing ways to get past barriers, and satisfying mandated requirements are essential elements of developing yourself as a reflective teacher. The final chapter of this book brings you stories of early childhood educators stepping outside the doors of their minds, classrooms, and programs to engage with others in creating new possibilities for themselves, their students, and their students' families. The principles offered in chapter 8 remind you to find collaborators, take risks, visit inspiring programs, and continually explore "why" in order to challenge thinking. You will find examples of how to strengthen yourself as a growing leader and change-maker.

Our appendix offers sample planning forms developed by teachers and directors who see themselves as change agents, to bring their organizational paperwork systems more in sync with the *Learning Together with Young Children* curriculum framework. You will also find some calls to action in the appendix, with examples of groups challenging our profession as a whole to imagine a richer set of possibilities for early childhood education.

## UNDERSTANDING THE STRUCTURE OF THIS BOOK

*Learning Together with Young Children* is a curriculum guide, but not an ordinary one. We have not written this book as a prescriptive, scope-and-sequence curriculum. Our curriculum approach is based on a wide, eclectic body of research, particularly from those working to bridge the gap between theory and practice. It draws on academic as well as action research. Most curriculum books are about what you do to and for children instead of illuminating the reality of the teaching and learning process as a dynamic, collaborative experience where the teacher is learning about teaching and learning even as she or he facilitates children's learning. Curriculum books rarely discuss how a teacher's values, ideas, reflections, decisions, and ongoing learning are central to his or her ability to guide children's learning. In this curriculum book, you hear the children's voices and the thinking that influences the teacher's actions. *Learning Together with Young Children* not only promotes a philosophy of praxis—observation, reflection, action—it brings forth the voices of family providers, Head Start and child care teachers, and administrators and teacher educators engaged in this actual practice. Here is the opportunity to learn right along with them and the children.

You will find components of other curriculum books here—materials to use, activities to try, questions to consider—but rather than finding the core practices in lists and directions, they are revealed in principles with stories, photographs, and challenges to you to make them your own. Each chapter begins with a quote, often from outside the early childhood field, but with pertinent wisdom for the curriculum core practice at hand. We recommend you read each quote several times and consider what it means to you before you read further. When you come to the end of each chapter, you might revisit the quote again to see if it provokes more reflections for you.

After the opening quote is an overview of that chapter's core practice of the curriculum framework, followed by a list of **principles** to guide your thinking and practice. The **stories** within each principle offer you a description of how it could look. Teacher stories are a powerful professional development tool (Patterson, Fleet, and Duffie 1995). Most of the time our stories are followed by a section called "Listen to (teacher's name)," which will contain a quote from the provider or teacher offering a window into his or her thinking. Each story concludes with a section entitled "Reflect," which provides more guidelines for uncovering the possible learning this story holds. Sprinkled throughout each chapter are **spotlight vignettes**, which highlight more examples of how providers and teachers have translated our principles into action.

## My Eyes Have Changed

*Family provider Kelly describes her own professional development as she's begun using our curriculum framework:*

*"I am not the same teacher I was when I started this work. The way I think about what I do has changed. I am more comfortable challenging myself to take on different roles with the kids. I have doubled my efforts to strengthen my relationships with my kids so they have that foundation to take risks and to fail and to rebound together. I have made a point of trying new things in front of my kids, so they can see me fumble—authentically fumble and fail—and we can rebound together.*

*My eyes have changed. What I pay attention to has changed. I look for multiplicity now. How many different ways can I understand what I am seeing? I am not so timid about voicing what I see my kids doing; I am getting better at uncovering what they are thinking about as they work. I view multiplicity as a gateway to complexity, whether it is being able to use a craft stick in twelve different ways or revisiting the 'same' idea and uncovering a new way to understand that concept.*

*What I love, though, hasn't changed. The children show up every day expectant of the wonderful things we will create together. It is what drives me to do this work with such thoughtfulness and intention."*

Burlington Little School

Throughout the book we have included two ways to practice the reflective process. We call them **"Your Turn"** and **"Reflection and Action."** Each chapter contains text entitled "Your Turn," which contains specific "assignments" for you to practice an aspect of the curriculum framework. Unless you are reading this book as part of a class, it might be tempting to just read these activities and then skip over the actual task you are asked to do. We strongly recommend you make time to engage with this "invitation" to construct further understandings for yourself. Ideally, you would do these activities with other colleagues.

The second opportunity we regularly offer for you to practice the cycle of observation/reflection/action will appear in the sections marked "Reflection and Action," where one or more of the following questions are highlighted for you to reflect on and consider what actions you might take. The more you practice asking yourself these questions, the more automatic this thinking process becomes in your teaching.

*What details stand out that I can make visible for further consideration?*

*

*What in my background and values is influencing my response to this situation and why?*

*

*How might issues of culture, family background, or popular media be influencing this situation?*

*

*Where do I see examples of children's strength and competency?*

*

*How do I understand the children's point of view in this situation?*

*

*How are the environment and materials impacting what's unfolding and what changes could be made?*

*

*How are teacher actions impacting this situation?*

*

*What learning domains are being addressed here and what other learning domains could be addressed?*

*

*What theoretical perspectives and child development principles could inform my understandings and actions?*

*

*What values, philosophy, and goals do I want to influence my response?*

With this snapshot of what is to come, you are now ready to move through the chapters of *Learning Together with Young Children.* Each chapter builds on the next and depending on where you are in your teaching journey, you will no doubt linger longer with some chapters than others. Returning again to the words of Sonya Shoptaugh, you are embarking on a way of working where professional development takes place day after day in your classroom.

## A KEY TO THIS BOOK'S STRUCTURE

### PRINCIPLES

•PRINCIPLE•

*Presents the concept or practice being addressed in that section.*

### STORIES

*Stories demonstrating the Principles, followed by a commentary (i.e., "Listen to," "Reflect") on what might be learned from the story.*

### SPOTLIGHT VIGNETTE

**Through the Children's Eyes**

*Beyond a formal parent handbook, homemade welcome books for each new family offer a concrete way to introduce your program culture. With the*

*Examples of the concepts introduced from providers and children.*

### "YOUR TURN"

**Your Turn**

To assess how your environment acknowledges understandings of attachment theories and the importance of sustaining children's connections with their families, sketch the floor plan of your room.

*An exercise to help the reader further explore a Principle.*

### "REFLECTION & ACTION"

**Reflection & Action**

*What details stand out that I can make visible for further consideration?*

*

*Where do I see examples of children's strength and competency?*

*Questions to spark new thoughts and behaviors.*

# Create a Nourishing Classroom Culture

*School schedules and teaching strategies need to fit children's natural rhythms rather than trying (and failing) to force them into an artificially adult world which mimics our fast-paced, hard-driving business culture. . . . We need to stop hurrying children. Our school days require time. Time to wonder, time to pause, time to look closely, time to share, time to pay attention to what is most important.*

**CHIP WOOD**

Every classroom has a culture—a set of expectations, language, routines, and ways of being together that shape the group's identity. The culture you develop sets the tone, reflects who you are, and expresses how you want to live and learn with children. If you hold yourself accountable to joyful days, and see yourself as a learner right alongside the children and their families, you'll work with a set of values, not just regulations.

Close your eyes and picture the qualities you want in your time with children and their families. When you consider the rhythm you want for your day, would it be most like a marching song, lullaby, soul, country, or hip-hop? Your policies, the words you use, the pace, the sound, and the feel of your everyday actions and routines shape an identity for the children. Pay attention to how your classroom's culture influences the children's dispositions (and yours!) toward learning and caring for those around them. Teachers and providers typically establish classroom logistics such as rules, space, and schedules with an eye to classroom management and teacher convenience. It's easy to think of logistics as just the framework that allows you to teach, and not the teaching itself. But what opportunities for learning do the rules and routines offer? What are children learning from the space itself? In fact, the logistics have a huge impact on classroom culture and in many ways determine what teaching is possible.

Use quality research to guide your thinking, policies, and practices. For instance, Rima Shore (1997) describes neuro-scientific discoveries of how the brain responds constantly and swiftly to ongoing conditions that promote or inhibit learning. "The impact of the environment is dramatic and specific, not merely influencing the general direction of development, but actually affecting how the intricate circuitry of the brain is wired." You can have extensive curriculum goals, but if children don't develop strong relationships, feel comfortable to make choices, take risks, or try new things, learning outcomes are likely to be limited to behavior compliance and recitation, not the intellectual curiosity and emotional security that sustains lifelong learning and altruistic endeavors.

When early childhood professionals take seriously the implications of valuable research, some traditional routines and policies have to be challenged. For example, many studies show that positive relationships between teachers, children, and families are essential to learning (Shonkoff et al. 2000). Yet many programs continually move children from room to room based on ratios, birthdays, or enrollment openings, disrupting the bonds and friendships that have been forming among the children, teachers, and families. Ask yourself, "What are we doing to honor existing relationships and keep them strong?" If you value the research about relationships, consider ways of keeping the children, teachers, and families together for a two- or three-year period. One possibility is looping, or continuity of care, where a group of children stays with the same teachers as they grow older. (The term "looping" refers to teachers working with the same group of children as they grow older, typically for two to four or even five years. When the children graduate or transition to a new program, the teachers "loop" back to the beginning to work with the youngest children again.) An advantage of looping is that children do not have to start over each year and adjust to a new classroom culture.

Think carefully about each aspect of your policies and practices, in your daily life with children as well as during special rituals and celebrations. The following principles will help you create a classroom culture that supports desirable dispositions and outcomes, as well as vibrant days of living and learning with children.

- Involve children in welcoming families
- Honor each family's uniqueness
- Invest in relationships with the whole family
- Keep children connected to their families
- Gather families for explorations
- Focus on relationships, not rules
- Arrange your space and routines to promote community
- Give children ownership of routines and schedules
- Use children's ideas to pursue investigations
- Help children see themselves as learners
- Coach children to develop negotiation and collaboration skills
- Develop rituals that create memories
- Celebrate real accomplishments

## •PRINCIPLE•
## Involve Children in Welcoming Families

Developing your classroom culture involves thinking through your values and philosophy so that your room setup, use of language, and daily routines create the rhythm for the dance you are all undertaking. And your most important dance partners are, of course, the children's families, who can keep you in step with culturally appropriate and meaningful experiences for their children. To make this partnership work, you need to hear each other's beat and find a common rhythm. This process of tuning in begins with first encounters, and is supported by ongoing communications, systems, and policies that invite multiple opportunities for collaboration in shaping the life of your classroom.

When families first enroll their children in programs, they are usually handed a stack of forms to complete. The provider or director goes over policies, business details, and perhaps a typical menu, curriculum plan, or assessment tool. Teachers may or may not be part of this process. In some programs, teachers do home visits, often with a questionnaire or more paperwork in hand. But if you think of enrollment as the beginning of relationships and participation in a program culture, you might want to refocus these

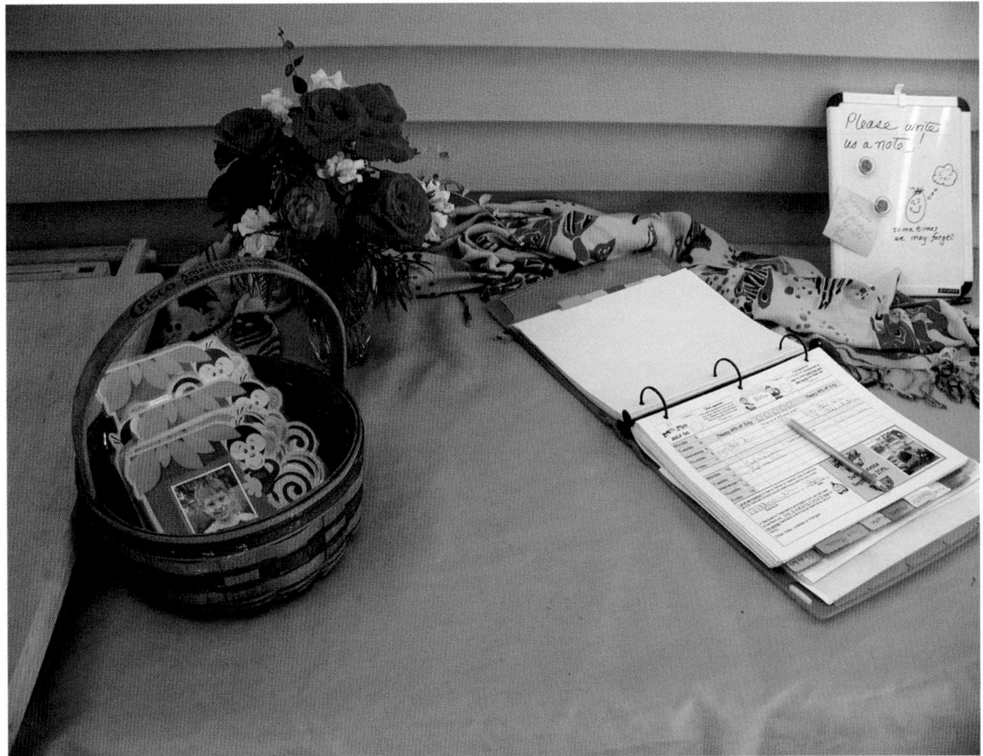


Nancy Gerber Family Child Care (sign-in table)

initial encounters. Rather than treating them as service arrangements or business transactions, consider these first meetings with the care of welcoming someone into your home. There are many stepping stones to consider: how to give a tour to a family, the mutuality you seek during the orientation process, the child's transition into the program, and initial family group meetings. Making sure each of these occasions provides listening ears, sensitive communications, and opportunities for making connections will offer more possibilities for children and their families to feel at home with you. Start with the simple things that are in easy reach to make families feel comfortable and invited into a relationship with you.

- Create meaningful documents that relate to fond memories, not just required information.
- Use photographs to help associate names and faces.
- Host family gatherings that go beyond presentations and help people develop a sense of camaraderie.

## First Encounters

Providers and teachers with relationships at the center of their thinking create an embracing social-emotional climate where people are seen, heard, and acknowledged for who they are. Miss Dee Dee, a lead teacher in a child care program, often gives tours to prospective families. How would you describe the tone she sets during these first encounters? Do you see her efforts to immediately immerse visitors into the culture of her program? How is this similar to or different from what happens in your program?

*When families call to inquire about openings in this center, they are asked to first bring their child for a visit. Miss Dee Dee wants all visitors to her classroom to be warmly greeted by the children and the environment, and she explains this to the children before new faces arrive. She asks them to remember what they felt like when they first started child care and to think of ways*

Martin Luther King Jr. Day Home Center

*to welcome new children. To make adults feel welcome in her room, Miss Dee Dee has used a portion of her precious supply money to purchase a small couch and adult-sized chairs. She hopes this will ease families into this place that is as different from home as it is from a traditional school classroom.*

*As a prospective new family arrives, Miss Dee Dee invites them to sit in the classroom with her briefly and encourages the other children to introduce themselves and invite the visiting child into their play. The visiting child can then stay in the room, or join the adults as they tour the rest of the center. There are relaxed introductions as they move around the center, with children in a room sometimes sharing a story or offering an invitation to join them in play or a snack. She makes a point of introducing the on-site staff, including the cook, janitor, and volunteer helpers. The family typically extends their visit in the child's potential classroom, and then before leaving, Miss Dee Dee escorts them to the office for further conversation with the director. During this time, they receive additional information about the program, answers to any questions, and a registration packet that includes a general center handbook and a welcome letter from the child's prospective teachers.*

### Reflect

Because most of the connections a family will have in a center are with those in their child's classroom, Miss Dee Dee's program launches first encounters there. Hoping the family will feel embraced by the essence of the room, she invites family members to talk about their child, their ideas about becoming part of a child care center, and their hopes for a partnership with a child care program. Miss Dee Dee strives to get a sense of what's important to the family, exploring whether her center will be a good fit for them. She is eager for them to get a sense of the program culture through encounters with the physical environment, the children, and the other staff members. Paperwork, policies, and business matters are the last thing taken up during this first visit because they have the least relevancy to making connections as human beings. ■

## •PRINCIPLE•
## Honor Each Family's Uniqueness

Every family faces emotional and logistical challenges when they put their children in someone else's care, and often financial challenges as well. Schedules must be met, mornings are rushed, traffic can be a problem, and underneath it all, families have a nagging worry about leaving their kids outside their kinship group. "Will these people really know who my child is? Will our family life be respected? Will I be judged if my child misbehaves?" Reassuring words from teachers can help, but remember the idiom, "actions speak louder than words." Find ways to help families see the things they have in common with others in your program. And use concrete objects and symbols to honor each family's uniqueness.

Family home provider Donna plans a series of gradual steps to bring new families into her program. As you read her story, do you see how she simultaneously pays attention to getting families connected to each other while seeking out ways to make the uniqueness of each child visible?

Children First

*Donna and her coworker create thoughtful beginnings with symbols for new families coming to their program. During a spring orientation, she asks some of the current families to be on hand to welcome the new ones. This is the first of several low-key gatherings alternating between her home and theirs, during which Donna seeks insights into the essence of each child. She takes photographs of the child and family members, and gives each family a folder of "homework" to complete over the summer. Each new family is assigned a buddy family who stays in touch with them over the summer. During their last visit before the fall program begins, Donna offers each child a set of possible graphic symbols to choose from, which will be used as a visual element to accompany the child's written name. She creates these symbols from her conversations, home visit, and dialogue with the family, infusing deeper meaning into the High/Scope idea of giving children symbols as an initial literacy device to learn to recognize their own and each other's names.*

### Reflect

Donna makes an enormous investment in a personal relationship with each new family that enrolls in her program, believing this is what they deserve when they entrust their children to her. For Donna, the challenge to design a set of potentially meaningful symbols for each child pushes her to connect intimately with something important about that child and family. She believes that making this visible will make them feel more at home in her early childhood setting. Entry into her program stretches over a few months, so by the time the families come for the first official day in the program, they already have some connections and memories formed with Donna and other families. And they have a clear indication of some specific things to look forward to. ■

## •PRINCIPLE•
## Invest in Relationships with the Whole Family

Whether they are coming to a family home program, preschool, child care environment, or Head Start classroom, each day families have a significant transition to make as they entrust their children into a care and educational setting outside their control. This transition can be eased when providers and teachers create conditions that invite a mutually respectful and trusting relationship. Relationships are two-way streets. How can you extend yourself so that the children and their families get to know you personally? What gestures will encourage them to share their lives with you?

### Crossing the Threshold

*When Kristin, a Head Start teacher, initially visits the home of an incoming family, she uses the time to play with the child and share information about herself—her family, her favorite activities, and her approach to teaching. Often working with an interpreter, she asks the family members what they would like her to know about them, and how she can support them as they send their child to her classroom. She explores ways the family can become involved in the classroom activities. Then, during the school year, Kristin waits at the gate as the Head Start bus pulls into the parking lot of her building. Children spill out and rush to her with hugs and exuberance. Other children arrive by car with family members and Kristin stays on the playground to meet them as well. She exchanges greetings with the families, often lingering for informal conversation, stories, and updates on things in their lives.*

Denise Louie Head Start

### *Reflect*

Kristin is thoughtful about starting her relationships with children and families, initially in home visits, and then each day of the week. She recognizes that learning doesn't just start with her planned activities for the children, but instead, at home with the children's families. The foundation of her curriculum must be built on solid relationships with the children's families, demonstrating cultural sensitivity and attention to the dynamics of power and privilege. There are certainly forms to be filled out, but these aren't the centerpiece of how Kristin approaches these relationships. She knows that for trust to be built, she can't appear to be an interrogator or home inspector, but rather, someone respectful and forthcoming. In sharing stories about herself, she invites a relationship with the family's stories. Then, throughout the year, whatever the weather, Kristin starts the day outside. She's noticed that her immigrant and English language learning families are more willing to stick around for a while when they enter through the playground area, rather than immediately having to cross the threshold of the classroom door. Kristin's strategy of starting the day on the playground with the children stems from her child development knowledge as well. She recognizes that to get to the program, children have either been sitting on a bus or in a car for a while and they need some big body time. ■

## Through the Children's Eyes

*Beyond a formal parent handbook, homemade welcome books for each new family offer a concrete way to introduce your program culture. With the children's ideas on what kids need to know to become part of the group, you are clearly demonstrating that this is a place where children's ideas are valued. Family provider Donna and center-based teacher Ann guide children in making pages for the welcoming book with questions and suggestions like these:*

- *How can new children and families learn what we do here?*
- *Can you make a map of our space with ideas about what you can do in the different areas?*
- *What suggestions do you have about how to negotiate with others about taking turns or sharing?*
- *What can you tell new kids about the kinds of things you might learn when you're in the program?*
- *Can you give ideas on how to be responsible and contribute to the group?*
- *What should kids do if they have a problem?*
- *What special activities can new families look forward to?*

*The following pages are extracted from a welcome book at Donna's program, Children First.*

*(sample page from Children First welcoming book)*

# Helping

Kids have many important jobs at Children First, jobs that help keep our school tidy and make it a comfortable place to work and play.

## Clean-Up Time

Every day before meeting, kids work together to clean up the classroom and playground. Cleaning up is hard work, but when you tackle a big job and get it done, you will feel very proud of yourself!

Gigi drew "the mess in the blocks" and "the clean up," counting carefully to make sure every block in "the mess" was put on the shelf in the cleaned up picture. Gigi said,"This is Emi if she cleans up the blocks, she's got two blocks. These are the shelves, you clean the blocks to put on the shelves."

Aimee, Zora and Gigi clean up the big blocks outside.

Audrey: You can't stop clean up-ping you have to clean up until it's clean. And the people who are helping you with the job has to stay until you're done.

Gigi: They can clean up the blocks or the kaplas if someone needs help, someone can help somebody. Like a kid or a teacher can help someone.

*(sample page from Children First welcoming book)*

**Taking Care of Messes**

When kids are working and playing, sometimes they spill or make messes by accident. Making mistakes is always OK. What's important is doing what you can to fix your mistakes – like sweeping up rice that spills out of the rice table, or mopping up water you spill. Sometimes you can help with messes you don't make, too – like the way Gigi is helping the teachers sweep leaves off the deck. And sometimes you tidy up just because it's fun – Annabelle is sorting the rice table toys by color.

*(sample page from Children First welcoming book)*

## Helping Your Friends

There are many important ways kids help each other, like Gigi is helping Ian with opening his lunch, and Lee is helping Susanna steady her pile of climbing-up pillows, and Ayla is helping Audrey with her shoes. Friends help each other with their work and with their play and especially with their feelings.

**Here's what the Children Firsters want you to know about helping other children:**

Emi: Kids help each other when one kid like gets hurt then the other kids says, "I'll go get a teacher."

Gigi: That they can help any people, any people can help the other people to know how to write or draw if they don't know how to write "Annabelle" or "Zora" or "Ayla" or "Lee" or "Micah" or "Joseph" or "Susanna" – that's the lot of kids.

Ayla: Well, once Lee couldn't reach the calendar so I helped her.

Micah: You have to help them if you want to. You hold your hand and pick them up with your hand.

## •PRINCIPLE•
## Keep Children Connected to Their Families

Early childhood lore suggests our goal is to help children separate from their families when they come to our programs. This contradicts the substantial body of research and literature emphasizing the importance of attachment between a child and his or her mother or primary caregiver and the experience of loss when they are separated (Shore 1997). Yes, we want children to feel at home and form strong relationships in our programs, but we must simultaneously do all we can to keep children connected to their families when they are with us. Likewise, teachers should be empathetic when children miss their families, but also alert to routines that make them feel powerful, not victims of circumstances. Do your routines encourage children to see themselves as emotionally strong and capable of problem solving? Do you notice how children are a resource to each other, offering comfort and encouragement?

Martin Luther King Jr. Day Home Center

### Carrying My Mama Around

In a classroom culture that honors and encourages strong connections, even very young children will demonstrate their abilities to empathize and negotiate relationships. For instance, when Deb began working with toddlers, she created routines to smooth the transition between home and child care. The children began to draw on these routines to comfort each other. Does the following story challenge you to rethink any prevailing theories about children's egocentrism?

*Throughout Deb's toddler room, images of the children's families add to the homelike atmosphere she seeks to provide. Hanging on the cupboard doors are large framed photos of the children and their family members. The photos are accompanied by a short narration of things about their family life. On any given day you will find children excitedly pointing to pictures*

Martin Luther King Jr. Day Home Center

*behind the frames, acknowledging who they recognize in their own family or that of their playmates. Sometimes they kiss the image behind the Plexiglas, or use a sponge to wipe their mommy or daddy's face. The children often carry around other smaller frames of family photos, at times putting them in the doll bed or on a table where they are playing. During initial times of morning drop-off and separation, Deb prompts children to find their family's photo. The children become accustomed to this routine and, during the day, might take a framed photo to a child who is in need of comfort. They do this as well with the homemade books featuring photo stories of the children reuniting with a parent. Each of these gestures offers reassurance and supports the children's connections with their families and each other.*

### *Reflect*

Deb's story highlights the role of concrete objects in making values and early childhood research come alive in your classroom. Deb has created an environment where familiar family faces provide comfort and ease feelings of loss during the long hours children are away from their families. Noticing how happy both the children and their families are when they reunite at the end of each day, she photographs these moments and creates little homemade storybooks to help the children remember that this joyful time will come again at the end of each day. When you watch them closely, you see how observant children are to everything around them. We wonder how Piaget (2001) overlooked some easy-to-see empathetic gestures, and concluded that toddlers are egocentric! ■

## A Family Altar

*When Mia and her family went to China to adopt their second child, Mia's teacher Myrna suggested they bring back something to represent their trip and expanded family. Myrna wanted to acknowledge this big change in Mia's life and provide ways for her to play out any of her feelings, be they excitement, pride, fear, or insecurity. Mia returned with a little tea set for the classroom and Myrna used it to create a little invitation for Mia to share her story with her classmates.*

Hilltop Children's Center

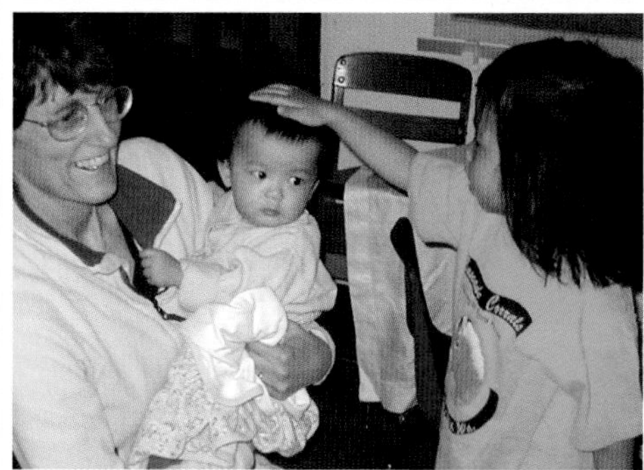

Hilltop Children's Center

**Your Turn**

To assess how your environment acknowledges understandings of attachment theories and the importance of sustaining children's connections with their families, sketch the floor plan of your room. Then go through each of the following possibilities, coding your floor plan with the numeral indicated.

Put a 1 in all the places where children's family life and culture are reflected and nourished.

Put a 2 in all the places where children can find comfort when they miss being with their families.

Put a 3 in all the places that remind children that they will be reunited with their families.

Put a 4 in all the places where the children's family members can feel at home, relaxed, and respected in the room.

Put a 5 in all the places where the children and their families can get to know more about and bond with you.

How do you see each of these ideas as supporting children's need to have secure bonds with their families and caregivers?

If you find you don't have any clear examples of one of the above items, make a plan for something you can add. Then move on to assessing your daily routines and policies to see if there are any changes you want to make. For each idea you have, make an action plan with a timeline for yourself.

## •PRINCIPLE•
## Gather Families for Explorations

Most programs hold some kind of a fall meeting for families, sometimes including the children and in other cases, just adults. When you plan these initial and then ongoing family gatherings, how can they reflect your values and goals for mutual relationships? Such meetings will have a very different feel than ones where the teacher or director occupies a one-way street giving out information, expectations, or expertise. To support the classroom culture you are trying to develop, think in terms of family gatherings instead of business or information meetings. Food and music are always helpful components, as are easy ways for people to mingle, converse, and get a sense of each other and your program. When you do take up business, or devote time to communications about your philosophy, routines, and pedagogy, do so in a way that parallels what you do with the children. Providing experiences, not just information, builds solid partnerships and reframes the notion of parent education.

### Exchanging Ideas and Gifts

Ann and her coworkers have developed key elements for their family gatherings that involve different explorations from year to year. As you read this story ask yourself how sharing the children's ideas might inform the collective understandings of their families. What's the purpose of the gift exchanges they do?

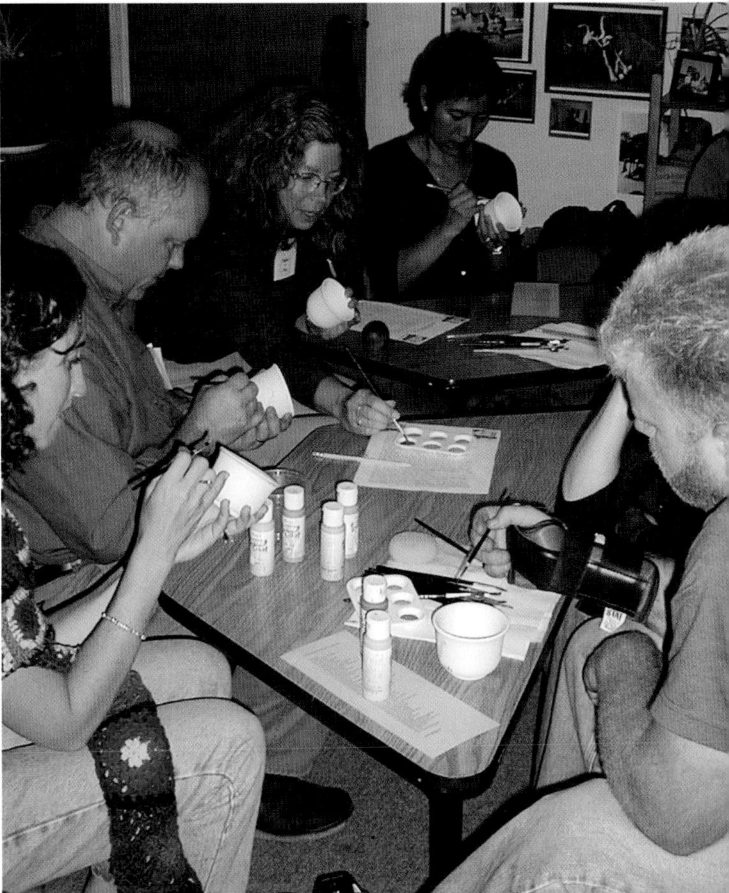

Hilltop Children's Center

*In planning their fall gathering, Ann and her fellow teachers choose a big question or idea to explore first with the children in the classroom, and then with the families during their meeting. For instance, one year Ann chose to pursue the question, "What's the same or different between home and school?" and another year she and her team focused on, "How do very young children understand friendship, and how is that the same or different from how adults understand friendship?" As the families discuss their ideas, teachers offer documentation of the children's thinking on the questions, which typically provokes a deeper discussion about the topic and the ways in which children can inform our understandings. Teachers also offer parallel hands-on experiences for the children and parents, asking them to leave surprise gifts for each other. Examples of these gifts include painted dishes, personalized nap pillows, or treasure boxes. One year, Kendra and Brad, Ann's after-school teaching colleagues, created an activity around the idea of bedtime rituals. The children created a representation of their bedtime rituals, leaving their names off their pages so that the family members had to guess which page belonged to which child. This was not only a sweet gift for the families, but provided a way for them to explore the similarities and differences among their families as they read and looked at the children's work. As their return gift, the children's family members each created a page about their childhood bedtime rituals, which were then bound together into a book with the children's pages.*

### Reflect

Rather than repeating the same activity during each fall family gathering, these teachers draw on the same elements and pedagogy, but have a different set of questions. This keeps both the teachers and families looking forward to the tradition and the creativity that will emerge. Exploring the same question with the children and the families broadens perspectives and deepens insights. When the families hear the collective voices of their children, they move beyond a concern about whether their individual child "measures up" and marvel together at how children's thinking can enhance their own. Making surprise gifts brings excitement and shared anticipation. These experiences raise awareness of the value of making memories rather than buying things. They provide opportunities for each group (families and children) to think about the others' perspectives and what might bring collective joy to people they love. ■

## Expressing Wishes

*Working in a large child care service in Canada, Bev uses her September meeting as a two-way street, not only answering the parents' questions, but asking them to consider hers. She provides paper and drawing tools and asks, "What kind of adult would you wish your child to be? Please write or draw your thoughts." Though some parents are hesitant at first, Bev offers encouragement, humor, and thoughtful questions to get their creative juices flowing. As the evening comes to a close, a lively discussion and heartfelt, original creations emerge. These pages with parent wishes are posted for a few weeks in the hallway, and then preserved in a book, which is kept in the classroom.*

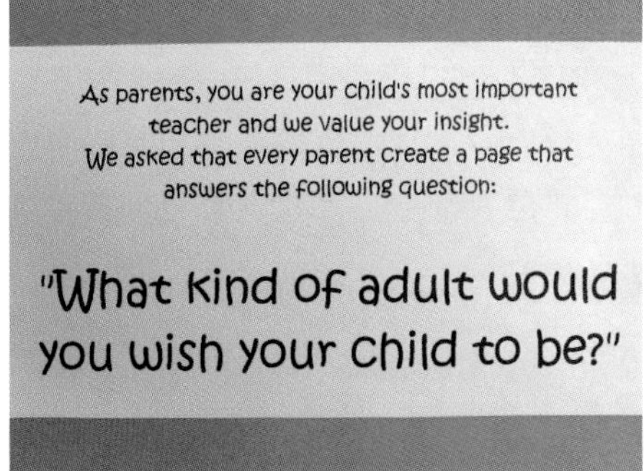


Discovery Children's Centre

Discovery Children's Centre

**Your Turn**

Practice planning a welcoming routine or family gathering that reflects the values that you want to be part of your classroom culture. Use these questions to guide your planning process.

- What elements do you want to be part of the welcoming of new families into your classroom?
- How can these be translated into specific practices?
- For an initial classroom family gathering, what could you focus on to create an activity for the families that offers an enjoyable way for them to connect to each other, while also making connections with experiences or ideas their children are exploring?

## •PRINCIPLE•
## Focus on Relationships, Not Rules

Every group needs a set of norms to work with, and in most early childhood programs this typically consists of a list of classroom rules on the wall and the teacher's voice continually reminding the children of how to behave. However, a classroom culture focused on relationships and shared excitement in learning sets a different tone for behavior management. Teachers plan for and respond to children's curiosities with shared inquisitiveness. They encourage children to learn about each other and the world around them, and the teachers recognize that this will reflect what Howard Gardner (1999) calls "multiple intelligences," not conformity to a standard way of acquiring knowledge. Classrooms focused on relationships are lively, not quiet and orderly. They are living laboratories for learning to negotiate individual desires while participating as citizens in a democracy and caring for our planet.

## Talking Chicks

As you read the following description of Jacky's classroom and look at the photos, ask yourself, "What could she be thinking?"

*Located in an old elementary school building, Jacky's room has many of the features found in a typical early childhood environment, including limitations such as built-in counters and inadequate storage space. Around the room are learning centers with child-sized furniture and a variety of materials at children's eye level. The room includes a number of plants and Jacky brings in unusual animal visitors, like the chicks and duckling in the photos, and helps children care for them. Noticing the children's repeated efforts to be close to the chicks, she puts one of the chicks on top of the incubator to suggest the idea that the chick, too, might desire a "talking" relationship with the eggs still hatching. She approaches an intrigued child who has dragged a chair to boost himself up on the counter. "What do you think the little chick is trying to tell the eggs inside?" she asks. Children move about the room in a relaxed, easy way, enjoying the materials and each other's company. When Jacky spots a child who has climbed on a table for a better look at his castle drama, she joins him with an invitation to converse about his idea. As she gathers the children together on the rug for group times, Jacky invites them to choose a seat, join in the singing, sharing, and story time, or just be an observer.*

Kensington Site, Montgomery Child Care Association

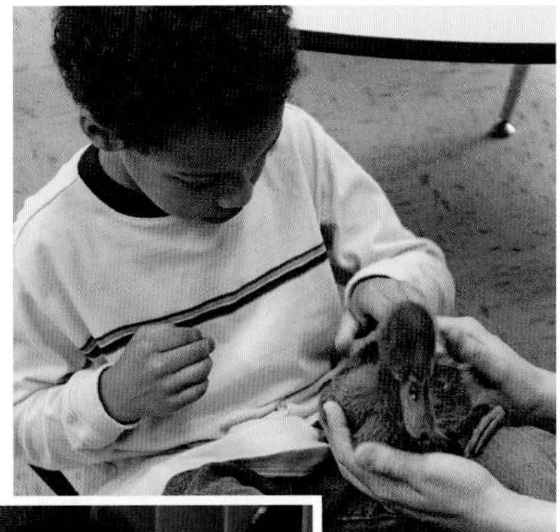

Kensington Site, Montgomery Child Care Association

### *Reflect*

Creating a community of active, joyful learners is central to Jacky's thinking. She wants children to feel connected to and care for each other and the natural world, so she brings the natural world into her classroom. Jacky believes children are capable of making responsible choices, so she respects where they want to sit and the ways they choose to participate during group times. Jacky's classroom culture focuses on caring, curiosity, and inventiveness, not children's compliance with rules; rather than scolding or invoking a keep-your-feet-on-the-floor rule, she recognizes and supports children's interests and their unusual solutions to the barriers that face them. ■

## •PRINCIPLE• Arrange Your Space and Routines to Promote Community

As you set up your room environment and put routines in place, think in terms of community, more than classroom. Young children feel more relaxed in a homelike environment than in an institutional school setting. In fact, Jim Greenman (2006) suggests early childhood programs set aside the term "classroom" in favor of "home bases" in assigning children to rooms. Our earlier book *Designs for Living and Learning* offers an array of examples for arranging your space to create a welcoming, cozy environment. This process requires ongoing reflection and incorporating new considerations depending on your specific group of children and the values influencing your thinking.

Likewise, as you develop routines for the children and their families, focus on nurturing a sense of belonging to a community, rather than putting children in an institution.

## Worms and Hot Wheels

Notice in the following story how Myrna and John have designed their space and routines for their group of three-year-olds in their full-day child care program. Look closely at how they spend time at the start and end of each day. What is the role of their table-top invitations in their routines to welcome children and families?

*To begin each day, Myrna puts a few things on tables, including breakfast food and interesting materials to pique the interest of those entering the room. As they arrive, the children hang up their coats and immediately go exploring, sometimes with a parent in hand. Myrna moves between greeting new arrivals, replenishing food at one table, and sitting with the children at another, conversing about what they are discovering. Today she*

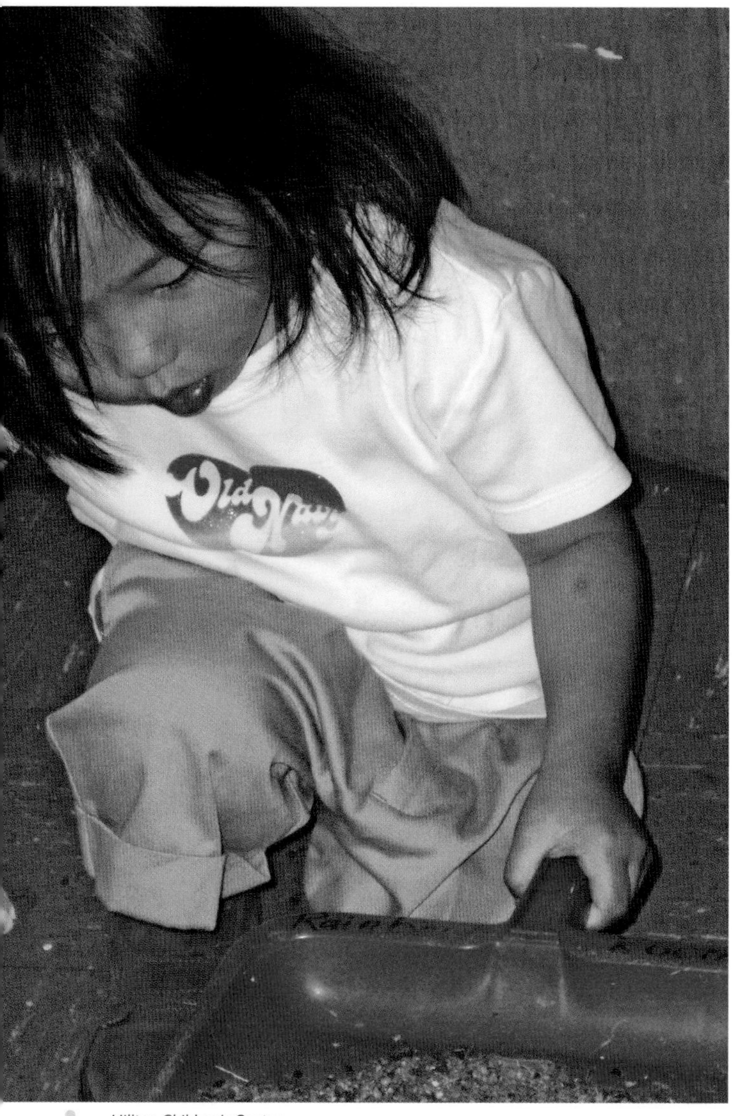

Hilltop Children's Center

*has put out a tray of dirt with worms and magnifying glasses. She takes a few minutes to jot down observations and take pictures. When most of the children have arrived, Myrna gives a reminder about breakfast and how much time remains before they will gather for circle time. She collects some tools for cleanup and eases children into the transition to their group time with requests such as, "Who would like to learn how to use this dustpan? There are sponges and a bucket for our table cleaners."*

*John works a later shift in this same room and the way he ends the day mirrors how Myrna starts the day: he puts out snacks and some interesting materials on a*

Hilltop Children's Center

*table with an eye on welcoming families to relax a bit after their busy day. He finds things from his own childhood, such as his Hot Wheels car collection, inviting parents to linger and reminisce before rushing home.*

### Reflect

Myrna and John believe children and families need time to transition between home and child care. They use routines that feel more like home than school, with relaxed eating and conversations. Their rhythms and pace allow them to make connections with individual families and accommodate different preferences and schedules. Both of these teachers create invitations related to their own passions; Myrna is an avid gardener and John is a Hot Wheels collector. Instead of flashing lights or ringing bells for transitions, John and Myrna use their relationships with the children to engage them in cleanup. They know the children love to use adult tools and see themselves as able to make a contribution to the smooth functioning of the room. Routines in this room create a welcoming, relaxed atmosphere, giving both children and parents a feeling of belonging. ■

## Don't Get Stumped

Shaping your environment with your philosophy and values doesn't mean things always stay the same. As children use the space, continually consider whether it is working to support your objectives. The following story describes a teacher engaged in this ongoing reflective process. As you read, notice how Deb uses her observations of the children to make adjustments and include their families in the classroom culture she desires.

Burlington Little School

Burlington Little School

*Deb holds group meetings with the children in the large block area of her small, cottage-like classroom. For a while, an exceptionally large wooden stump served as a focal point in the area, reminiscent of a space where people could gather around a campfire to sing and tell stories. During their playtime children often used the stump as a setting for little dramas. Ultimately, the stump proved too small for displaying the variety of objects children brought to group meetings. As a result, Deb invited the children's parents to a party to construct a new platform to replace the stump in the center of the block area. The work party itself had the feel of the children's building and construction activities, with lively stories, laughter, and different ideas about the best design approach for building the platform. The children now use the new platform for some of their building and construction. When they gather together for meetings, they put samples of their work or objects from home on the platform. Sometimes Deb spotlights a new material in the center of the platform, discussing possible ideas for its use.*

### Reflect

Growing relationships is central to how Deb thinks about growing curriculum. She wants the children to experience themselves as part of a community and sees group gatherings as an important expression of that. However, Deb recognizes that her disposition doesn't lend itself to easy group management and she doesn't want to take on the role of the preschool police. She wants group meetings to have the excitement of gathering around a campfire or dining room table, instead of the aggravation of constant reminders to sit quietly on a designated space or carpet square. The tree stump offered this spirit, so when it proved too small, Deb sought to replace it with something that created the same sense of a gathering place. Instead of simply finding or building something herself, she invited parents to build the platform together for their children, hoping to create the same lively community experience she provides for the children. ■

### Go Out Singing

*Taking a step beyond individual classroom singing, Ted and his colleagues have developed a Friday afternoon community singing ritual to end their week together. Ted moves from room to room with his guitar, inviting all the children to gather. Teachers, office staff, and often the children's family members attend the sing-along as well, sometimes bringing a new tune to share. Over time, the children have learned a wide repertoire of songs, which have been put into songbooks that travel between the children's homes and school.*

Burlington Little School

**•PRINCIPLE•**

## Give Children Ownership of Routines and Schedules

Most teachers follow a common set of established routines and techniques for managing children's time. On paper these get formatted into a daily schedule, which moves children through little blocks of time to "cover" their curriculum, including full group experiences, typically referred to as circle time; small group time, usually led by the teacher with a particular lesson in mind; snacktime; free choice or learning center time; and time to play outside. But, if you want your classroom to feel more like a nurturing learning community than a factory production line with flashing lights and ringing bells, you'll shape the structure of the day around the natural rhythms of breathing in and breathing out (cycles of robust activity, eating, resting). If you follow the ideas of Lev Vygotsky (1978) and social constructivism, your goal will be to set up routines and rules that encourage children to actively work together to contribute to each other's knowledge, instead of emphasizing individual achievements. You will be looking for ways to have the environment and routines, as well as your interactions with children, help scaffold the children's ability to focus and collaborate.

When Kristin first began working as a teacher in Head Start, she inherited all the familiar routines of a typical early childhood classroom. But the more she began to consider her philosophy and values, the more dissatisfied she became with these standard practices. She steadily began making changes and her classroom now has a very different feel. As you read her story, how would you describe Kristin's image of children? Is this similar to or different from how you view children and your goals for their time with you?

Denise Louie Head Start

Denise Louie Head Start

Denise Louie Head Start

Denise Louie Head Start

*At the beginning of her third year of teaching, Kristin's room no longer has a job chart posted on the wall. Instead, you see children moving around the room with tremendous confidence that they know what has to be done each afternoon they are together. To give children ownership of the room, Kristin uses small group times during the first weeks of school to demonstrate how to tidy up different parts of the room, organize snacktime, welcome visitors, and even tend to each other's bumps and scratches. Now when Kristin approaches what in the past would have been a rigid cleanup time on the schedule, she goes around to small groups of children at play, asking what they are working on and if they need more time or if they are ready to have snack or go outside. If the children have different ideas about this, they negotiate about when and how to move on to the next activity. Having taught each other how to count to ten in their home languages, they vote on which language to use for a countdown and they begin restoring the room for their play the next day. Kristin rarely uses general announcements for the whole group unless it's about something exciting she wants them all to pay attention to at that moment.*

### Reflect

As we see in Kristin's story, creating classroom norms can look and sound very different when you are consciously working with a set of values that go beyond group management goals. Kristin has set up an environment with materials accessible at the children's level and ownership of the schedule and routines in their hands. Her classroom culture is very child-centered, where the teacher is a facilitator, not a director; a demonstrator, not a disciplinarian. Kristin decided things like job charts didn't fit with her goal of creating a community where all the children care for each other and the room. She doesn't want to dictate or limit who will be a "helper" each day, but, instead, supports and nurtures the children's natural sense of empathy for each other and their desire to be helpful. Cross-cultural appreciation is woven into the fabric of living together as they learn words in each other's home languages, and negotiate different paces and senses of time. ■

### Your Turn

Aligning your daily routines with your philosophy and values is an ongoing process. To assess where you are in this work, spend some time analyzing your daily schedule. Jot down the daily schedule you imagine working best for you and the children, from the beginning to the end of their time with you, with approximate timeframes indicated. Then assign one of three colors for each of the following categories and use them to color-code your schedule:

**1st color:** Teacher chooses and directs what happens

**2nd color:** Children and teachers negotiate the focus of what happens

**3rd color:** Children choose and engage in self-directed activities

Now, looking at your color-coded schedule, add up the number of minutes devoted to each color and kind of time planned for the children.

- Is the schedule balanced or is it dominated by one kind of time far more than the others?
- Count up the amount of time children spend in planned transitions on your schedule. What portion of the whole schedule do transition times consume?
- What chores and tasks in your room could children be invited to take more ownership over?
- What ideas do you have for routines to introduce so that your daily life with children is compatible with your values?

## •PRINCIPLE• Use Children's Ideas to Pursue Investigations

As teachers begin to work with the curriculum framework discussed in this book, they find many new, exciting opportunities for extending children's learning. Your choice of the many possibilities to pursue will be guided by your values, your program context, and your desire to integrate meaningful experiences with learning domains and standards. Consider experiences that children regularly encounter as holding potential for deeper learning and empowering them to take some action based on their investigation. For instance, if the children seem fascinated by the arrival of the garbage truck each week, this could become the focus of study to undertake. The challenge with this kind of project work is to keep uncovering the children's interests and questions, rather than rushing in to teach them a bunch of information about garbage workers. Commit yourself to developing curriculum that uncovers more and more about the children's ideas, rather than shaping it around your own knowledge and ideas. This not only demonstrates respect, but also helps children see themselves as thinkers, inventors, and theory makers.

### We Have Stumps

As you read teacher Lynn's story, notice how her work to involve children in designing their new playground gives children ownership and a sense that their ideas are important and are taken seriously.

*Lynn works in a large full-day child care program with a new Reggio-inspired building. As funds became available for new playground construction, the teachers began seeking a way to involve the children in its design. The initial formation of a work team or project group sprang from Lynn's reflections on a parent's passing comment: "Rachel has some ideas about materials for the room." Lynn was aware that Rachel had sophisticated conversation skills, yet was hesitant to become involved in group endeavors. Would challenging Rachel to also think about materials for the playground strengthen her confidence to be actively vocal in group work? The next day, Lynn informally asked Rachel to find some friends on the playground to come up with some ideas for the new design. Rachel approached two nearby girls and sure enough, her conversation and facilitation skills were evident in Lynn's documentation.*

*Rachel: "Do you have ideas for the new playground?"*

*Natalia: "Stairs?"*

*Rachel: "Stairs to go up? You have ideas for the climber. What do you want, Sarah?"*

*Sarah: "Stumps."*

*Rachel: "We have stumps."*

*Natalia: "Other stumps."*

*Rachel: "To go up the climber? What else? We're talking about the new playground. What do you want to add to the new playground?"*

*As the children came inside, Rachel announced she wanted to tell Amy, the director, about the group's ideas, and after hearing her confident report, Lynn and Amy concurred that it was time to launch a formal project group to uncover the children's playground ideas.*

*Over a period of months, Lynn met with the project group, documented their ideas, and had the group report to the whole class. She met regularly with Amy, as well, seeking threads of meaning and finding questions to guide her next steps. Lynn provided drawing opportunities for the children to represent their ideas and introduced them to the blueprints the landscape architect had developed. She and Amy decided that the children needed to understand that a bike track was already a feature of the architect's design. As the children's drawings of their playground ideas proliferated, Lynn and Amy carefully studied them. They noticed that ideas were randomly drawn on their papers. To coach the children to better grasp the spatial relations involved, Lynn gave them each a piece of paper with a circle on it, representing the bike track, and told them the climbing structure they wanted would have to be built with the path in mind. The next time they met she challenged them to move from individual drawings to one group drawing so they would have to make some compromises together.*

*Lynn projected an enlarged copy of the blueprints on the wall, asking the children to first trace the bike track. Those who had previous experience in tracing projected images taught the others how to do the drawing process.*

*Rachel: "You have to stand on the side so the shadow doesn't cover it."*

*Ellie: "We want to see what it looks like, not the people's shadows."*

*They traced a few other features of the architect's ideas and then put the paper on the floor to consider where to place the climbing structures they had in mind. Lynn decided it was time to go outside and walk the actual space.*

*Ellie: "I don't think there's enough room for all of our plans."*

*Rachel (walking around): "We can use that tunnel for the castle. It's going to be too small, but over there should be fine."*

*Many times the children would hold their arms apart when Lynn asked how big something would be. She asked them to think about where and how children would enter and exit the climber. With their ideas continuing to expand, Lynn told them they needed to choose some priorities. They decided that along with the castle, one stump cluster should go between the bike track and the classroom wall. The children's ideas were brought to the architect for inclusion in the final design.*

*With a construction schedule breathing down their necks, Amy and Lynn wondered whether it was time to bring the project to a close. Would the children take up the challenge to now think about how their ideas could be built? Could they speculate about what John, their carpenter, would need to do to bring this design to life? Would this question launch a new phase of the project, uncover possible theories about the construction process, and begin a potential investigation of the tools and equipment that would be needed? They would have to come up with a new provocation to test out these possibilities.*

Clifton School

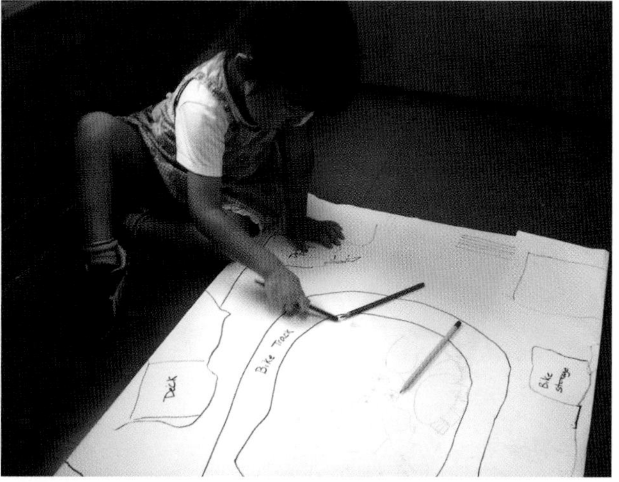


Clifton School

Clifton School

Clifton School

## Reflection & Action

***What details stand out that I can make visible for further consideration?***

*

***Where do I see examples of children's strength and competency?***

*

***How do I understand the children's point of view in this situation?***

*

***What learning domains are being addressed here and what other learning domains could be addressed?***

### *Listen to Lynn*

"Each decision I made was guided by the goal of having some of the children's ideas come to fruition. I wanted them to realize that whatever structures they wanted would have to be either inside the bike track or have to go over it. Once I recognized they didn't have a clear sense of the spatial relations, I invented the circles for them to work with. Then I wondered, 'Would they be able to work with a formal blueprint? How might this challenge their ideas?' After we moved from individual to group drawings, I thought they needed to actually start putting their bodies in the space itself. They were extremely supportive of each other's ideas, but only Ellie seemed to realize not everything would fit. I'm afraid I introduced the idea of prioritizing what they wanted most, instead of gradually letting them reach that conclusion or coming up with another solution on their own. A good lesson in slowing down and also seeking out more conversation with Amy or my coworkers. It's challenging to stay with the children's pacing of things."

### *Reflect*

Lynn's ability to see Rachel's strengths and challenges was significant in forming the project group. At each step of the way, she reminded herself to take the children's ideas seriously, not dismiss them because they didn't understand the spatial relationships between the bike path and their desire for a climber and stumps that resembled a castle. Lynn actively used her documentation, not just for display, but to collaboratively uncover the children's ideas with her director. She realized she needed another set of eyes, ears, and perspectives on what ideas were worth pursuing.

Lynn's introduction of the papers with circles, her challenge to create a group drawing, the projection of the blueprints on the wall, and the opportunity for the children to explore the space with their bodies were all strategies for scaffolding the children's learning—attempts to boost their grasp of the spatial relation of the design and the social relations in their group. Finally, because she took time to reflect on her own actions, Lynn found some fine lessons for herself.

This story illuminates some important "layers of value" for teachers questioning what projects to pursue:

- Will the work empower the children?
- How will we demonstrate that we respect their ideas?
- What are the possibilities here for our learning as teachers? ■

**•PRINCIPLE•**

## Help Children See Themselves as Learners

Which of your routines shape children's dispositions to see themselves as members of a vibrant learning community? Which ones primarily serve the teachers' convenience and undermine an eagerness to continue to investigate and experiment? Lilian Katz (1993) suggests that dispositions, or habits of mind, are critical goals for children's learning. What changes are needed in your classroom practices if you value dispositional learning alongside the acquisition of knowledge and skills? For instance, if you want children to have what Katz calls "a robust disposition to be curious, to investigate, hypothesize, and experiment," you will need to make your own such dispositions visible to the children and highlight to the children your observations of their desirable dispositions. Katz believes one of our primary educational goals should be to develop in children the disposition to go on learning. She says, "Any educational approach that undermines that disposition is miseducation."

## Engineers and Architects

As a preschool teacher, Adrienne uses daily routines that focus the children on what they are doing and learning together. After reading her story, ask yourself, "What are the goals this teacher has for the children's identity development?" Notice how she infuses her values and goals into the daily routine prescribed by the curriculum model her program uses.

*Around Adrienne's preschool classroom you can see growing evidence of the classroom culture—little books with stories and photos of what the children do, say, and think in each area of the room. These homemade books grow out of her ongoing observations and conversations throughout the day. For instance, if you were to move in closely, you would hear a comment such as this from Adrienne as she approaches the block area where four boys are having a heated debate about the structure they are trying to build: "Oh, I see you guys are doing just what architects do, challenging each other's ideas about how to keep that building from falling. You might need to think like an engineer too. Engineers and architects work together to make sure that building structures are safe and won't fall down in earthquakes. They need to figure out how much weight the bottom supports can handle and how to balance the weight so things don't tip over. Architects try to find interesting shapes for their buildings so they look beautiful from the inside and from the outside. What engineering or architectural ideas are you trying to figure out?"*

*Throughout the day, Adrienne calls attention to what different children are doing. "Oh, look everyone, Marcella created this amazing shade of purple on her painting." When she calls an end-of-the-day meeting, the children bring something they have been working on or thinking about to share with each other. A smile of recognition crosses the children's faces as they hear a familiar tune with new lyrics: "Good-bye all you painters, good-bye scientists too, good-bye you architects, we hate to see you go."*

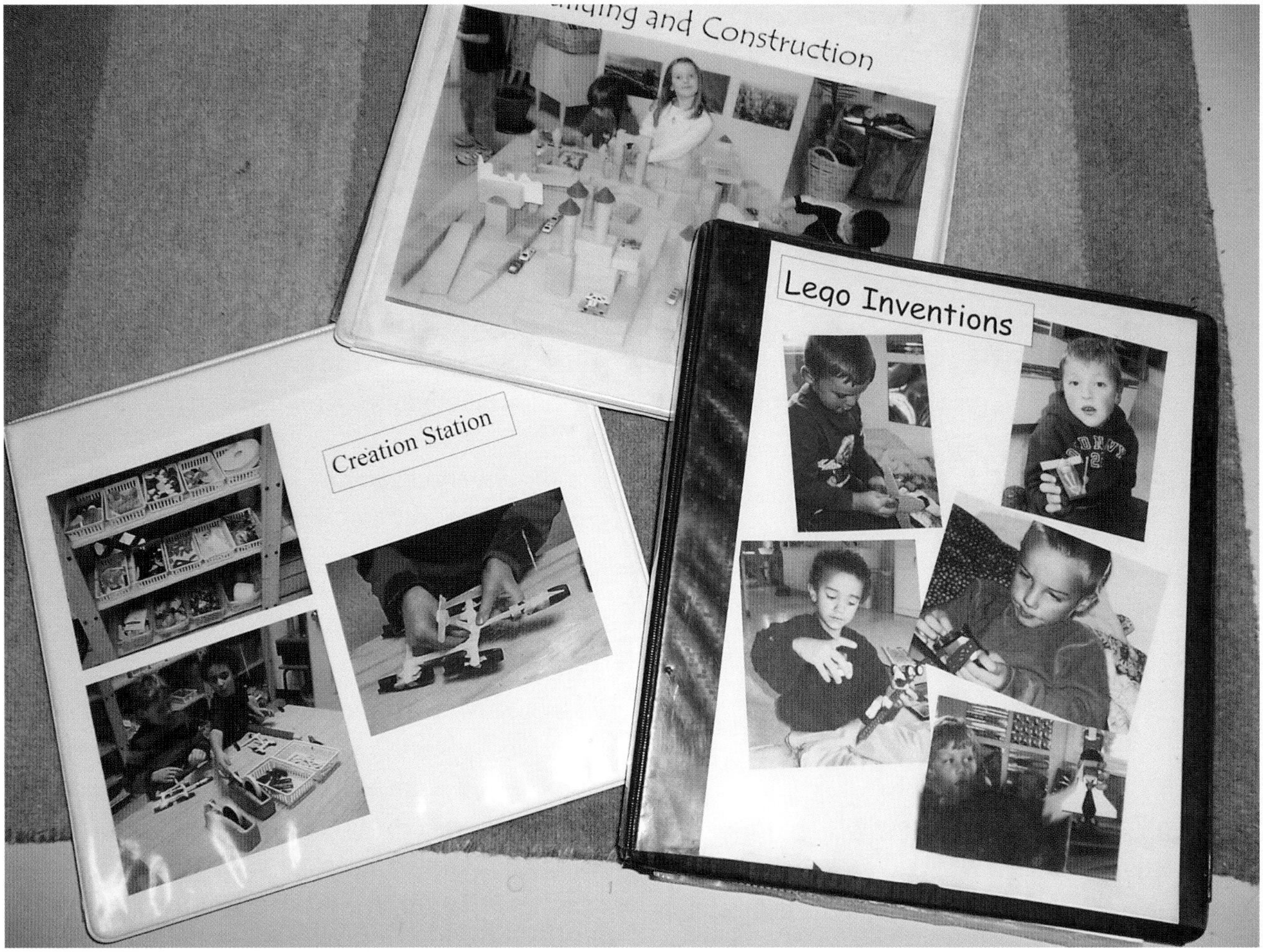

Burlington Little School

Bold Park Community School

### *Reflect*

Drawing on the High/Scope Foundation's research (Hohmann, Banet, and Weikart 1979) of how children learn through play, Adrienne takes the High/Scope notion of "plan/do/review" to a new level with her daily routines of continual acknowledgment, revisiting, storytelling, and singing about what the group members have been doing. Her goals go beyond just giving recognition to individuals. Adrienne wants her teacher talk and stories to help the children see themselves as thinkers, collaborators, inventors, friends, responsible community citizens, and contributors. As she integrates her values into addressing learning domains, Adrienne uses vocabulary with the children that strengthens their understandings of possible academic pursuits for themselves. She creates documentation displays and homemade books to grow their sense of history and identity as learners. These classroom documents include examples from previous years so that children recognize they are part of a larger group of investigators and inventors learning in her child care program. ■

## •PRINCIPLE•
## Coach Children to Develop Negotiation and Collaboration Skills

Many teachers strive for conflict-free classrooms with rules about how many children can play in an area and a timer to enforce sharing of toys. But when your goals for children include developing skills for living in community and as citizens in a democracy (Johnston 2006), you will provide opportunities for negotiating conflicts, working with different perspectives, and taking responsibility for group decisions.

Teachers can find any number of resources on behavior management, but do these offer children ongoing ways to see themselves as problem solvers and competent negotiators? Children benefit greatly from routines that support them to work through conflicts in ways that reinforce values of mutual respect, empathy, and generosity. What routines give children experiences to nurture these dispositions and acquire problem-solving skills?

### Spicy Work

Teachers at Hilltop Children's Center have built into their classroom culture a small group routine they call "Spicy Work," adapted from the book *Tribes: A New Way of Learning and Being Together* (Gibbs 2000). Notice how the teachers demonstrate that they trust the children while scaffolding their negotiation skills.

*During the fall months of each school year, Ann, Sandra, and Megan talk with each other about how the children's relationships are developing and when they might benefit from introducing their Spicy Work routine. Spicy Work groups provide children with a structured opportunity to learn and practice skills in communication, collaboration, and negotiated decision making. When they feel the time is right, the teachers call their whole group together to introduce the Spicy Work idea as a new game to learn. The teachers put together teams of three children and give them the task of making a plan together for how to spend their time. Ann, Megan, and Sandra craft Spicy Work teams with an eye on sparking new friendships. Sometimes they group three strong leaders together, hoping they'll challenge each other in useful ways; or they put together three children who are typically quiet and tend to cede their voice and power so they can experience the safety needed to take risks; or they may bring kids together across a broad age range to spark understandings across differences.*

*There are three rules to the Spicy Work game. The first rule is that you stick with your team; you might want to play on your own, but during Spicy Work, you stay with your group the whole time. The second rule is that all the kids on the work team make a plan together for what to do; you have to keep taking turns telling ideas until you make a plan everyone agrees to. The third rule is that a whole team decides together when they're done. Teachers demonstrate possible options when kids can't agree on a plan. You can change your idea: "Let's build a spaceship instead of a house or a boat." You can put your ideas together: "Let's build a house that's also a boat." You can take turns with your ideas: "Let's build a house first; then we'll build a boat second." During the first stages of learning Spicy Work, teachers initially coach children in how to take turns stating their ideas until they come to consensus. After each Spicy Work game, teachers bring all the children together to go over what happened and how they got through any disagreements around conflicting ideas. Using the Spicy Work routine every week or two through the winter and spring deepens relationships and enhances the children's social and communication skills.*

Hilltop Children's Center

## Reflection & Action

***Where do I see examples of children's strength and competency?***

*

***What learning domains are being addressed here and what other learning domains could be addressed?***

*

***What values, philosophy, and goals do I want to influence my response?***

### Reflect

This Spicy Work routine is a challenge for the children and teachers alike. Teachers have to trust in the process just as they trust children's efforts to learn to walk, speak, or ride a tricycle. This doesn't mean teachers abandon children and leave the process to chance. Instead, they carefully scaffold this learning with demonstrations and the language of negotiations. The language and structure of the Spicy Work routine gives each child the power to veto or to agree, to venture an idea or modify an idea. Teachers must remember that when things get "real spicy" between the children, their job is to model how to negotiate, rather than jump in with a solution. A demonstration, as opposed to a rescue or adult takeover, gives children respect and an example to use in the future. Teachers can also share their own personal stories of learning to do something hard, the benefits of practice, and the rewards of making new friends.

Ann, Sandra, and Megan believe in children's abilities to get through difficulties. They honor their passionate negotiations, acknowledge the children's careful thinking, and celebrate the affectionate, warm relationships children develop as a result of this routine. Once the children learn the Spicy Work negotiating routines, they readily bring these skills to other play experiences throughout the day. ■

## •PRINCIPLE•
## Develop Rituals That Create Memories

Planning for children's learning is no easy task. It is a complex process that requires careful attention to the many details of translating your values, philosophy, and research-based child development knowledge into a concrete pedagogy. Nonetheless, we recommend you undertake this serious work with the spirit of planning a party to celebrate the lives of your favorite friends. After all, working in early care and education, you have the opportunity to form relationships with our most precious citizens and their families. They bring you their hopes and dreams, sometimes undefined, nestled deep in their hearts. You have the opportunity to meet up with their longings, to be known, to learn, and to live fully in the world. Planning a party suggests a lively way of being together, rather than maintaining an institution with a culture of compliance. Parties are by nature very social. Sometimes they include a celebration of a special accomplishment, life transition, or event, and at other times they are designed just to bring people together to enjoy each other's company.

The human family thrives on rituals and celebrations. Rituals are different from habitual routines. Rituals may be simple or elaborate and consciously or not, they are created with a longing to honor or create a memory, often employing symbolic gestures or objects. Children quickly come to understand the notion of a party, but the symbolic importance of a ritual may not be uncovered until they explore this memory later in their lives.

## Dabs of Flour

In her family child care program Billie doesn't use the formal "plan/do/review" process of the High/Scope curriculum, but she does have a reflection time at the close of each day. As you read her story, ask yourself what children who leave your program might say many years later when they remember their time with you. What special memories are you trying to offer?

*A big sign posted on Billie's refrigerator says "You Never Know When You're Making a Memory." You can see Billie's instinctive understanding of this motto in her daily routines. At the end of each day, before the first children begin to leave her home, Billie gathers the group together and asks, "What do you remember about this day?" Their answers often include not just big events, but little details that reveal the importance of their relationships. For instance, one child described "watermelon juice dripping down Baby Keagan's chin and how his face looked when it hit his bare tummy." Another child remembered her friend helping with an ice pack when she fell and scraped her knee. Sometimes the children mention something particular about Billie, "You put flour on our noses." And gleeful laughter tumbles from everyone when a child recalls, "You looked funny doing the chicken dance!" As parents arrive for pickup, some of these memories are shared again, offering a chance for questions and more smiles.*

Heart and Home Family Child Care

*Billie gained a more powerful understanding of the important memories she created for the children she cares for when she went to the college graduation of Claire, the very first child Billie cared for in her home twenty years earlier. Billie asked Claire what she remembered most about the time spent in Billie's family child care home, and without hesitation Claire said, "You putting a dab of flour on our noses to make the recipe turn out whenever we baked cookies together." Billie was surprised because she had never thought of this as a big deal and it certainly never appeared on any of her curriculum plans.*

### Reflect

Billie's story illuminates the importance of viewing everyday moments as the foundation of your curriculum as well as the value of simple rituals for providing fond memories of childhood. It's tempting to view planned activities as your curriculum for children's learning, but if you think in terms of memory making, you recognize that everything that happens is part of the curriculum and has the potential to symbolize a ritual—every interaction, song, phrase, ice pack, or dab on the nose. Grown-up Claire's words have helped Billie pay attention to how rituals become part of who we are. Billie still gently dabs a smidge of flour on the noses of the children she cares for in her home. It is a ritual of love that the children remind her to do if she forgets, so she knows it is important to them. ■

### Planting Seeds

*For fifteen years, the kindergarten children in Bev's class have been planting seeds from their lunch-time apples and oranges. Jeffrey, a kindergarten student, took great care in planting and tending his orange seed and sure enough, it grew quite well and became a significant feature in the classroom where it remained, even when Jeffrey moved on. Each time the plant was repotted, the story of Jeffrey's endeavor was told. Two of his younger sisters and his brother moved through the room, with special attention to keeping this legacy growing. Jeffrey is nineteen now and occasionally returns to Bev's room to see how the tree is growing, liking that this part of himself has remained to help shape the room's identity.*

Discovery Children's Centre

## •PRINCIPLE• Celebrate Real Accomplishments

As you work to create long stretches of open time for children to play, negotiate relationships, and engage deeply with each other, supplement these daily experiences with specific activities and rituals that foster a group identity and sense of history for the children and their families. Remember to stop periodically and acknowledge and celebrate the joys of living and learning together in ways that connect children to each other, their families, their culture, and their wider community. Most early childhood programs dedicate some time to recognizing birthdays, first steps, lost teeth, and special events such as an addition to or loss in the family, a travel excursion, or a holiday celebration. This gives recognition to individual children, acknowledging that their community cares and honors important events in their lives. Once again, clarify the values you want to influence your choice of special rituals and celebrations. Plan events that will sustain your classroom group culture as well as appropriately acknowledge individuals.

Ann, along with numerous other teachers, uses homemade books to mark important occasions in her classroom. What social, academic, and classroom culture goals does this activity meet?

*Ann routinely has the children in her class, as well as the children's family members, create pages for homemade books, which are then used in the classroom or sometimes sent home as gifts for families. These books have words and images from the children as well as photographs, drawings, or symbolic collages, and they sometimes include the same components from families. A book might be focused on birthdays, how families celebrate winter holidays, Dia de los Muertos (Day*

A Goodbye Book

For our friend

Natalie

From the kids and teachers

In the Garden Group

Hilltop Children's Center
April 2002

Raven: "I'll miss you, and I hope that this book that we're making you will help you remember us. I like the way you smile."

Liam: "I miss you. I like how you draw."

Drew: "Natalie, goodbye. I will miss you. Could you come visit our school sometime? I wish you have a happy time at your new school and your parents have a happy time at their work and that you have happy stay-home days. I don't like it when you go. I like being at Hilltop with you. And I love you. I hope you have happy days with your dad and mom. I like playing with you."

Marc: "Bye, Natalie."

*of the Dead), or heroes and sheroes such as Rosa Parks, Martin Luther King Jr., and Cesar Chavez who inspire the children to stand up for fairness. When a child leaves her group, Ann and her colleagues work with the other children to make a good-bye book (like the pages reproduced here from Natalie's good-bye book) with drawings, photos, and reflections on their friendships and memories. They unveil the book by inviting the departing child's family to a special good-bye celebration, usually with a snack at the end of the day.*

### *Reflect*

Rather than following the cultural trend to commercialize all occasions, Ann creates personalized ways to acknowledge significant experiences in the children's lives or their community. She also invites the children to commemorate people who are important to them. These homemade creations make the children's ideas visible and they serve as memory books for future years. They demonstrate to children how ideas can be written down and read back and explored more fully through drawings, photographs, and collages. This is an important literacy outcome for young children. ■

## Crossing the Bridge

Graduation ceremonies are educational traditions, but are they developmentally appropriate for young children? Notice how Deb creates for the children a meaningful understanding of leaving preschool.

*Deb has created a ritual to symbolize the transition from preschool to kindergarten by escorting each child across a garden bridge purchased from a landscaping store. During the weeks leading up to the ritual she and her coworkers have conversations with the children to explain the meaning of this change in their lives, and how it touches the hearts of their teachers and their families. The teachers describe how the bridge symbolizes this impending change. Some children are excited about becoming "big kids," while others are hesitant about leaving what is familiar. Each of these emotions is explored in conversation and with props. The children's collective sentiments are incorporated into the ritual, creating a unique celebration. For instance, one year, the children wanted to cross the bridge alone. The ritual was changed so that instead of the teachers holding the children's hands while they walked over the entire bridge, the teachers held the children's hands only until they reached the center of the bridge. At that point the teachers dramatically threw their hands in the air with a celebratory cheer and the children finished crossing the bridge alone.*

Burlington Little School

### Reflect

Deb and her colleagues recognize that the end of a child's preschool years is significant for both the adults and the child. Some families are filled with pride and a sense of collective accomplishment because this is the first graduation for their kinfolk. Others are reluctant to see their babies grow up. Teachers, too, have these same emotions. They have invested themselves fully in these relationships and now the children will be leaving. When teachers are sensitive to the range of everyone's feelings and perspectives, they can translate the prevailing sentiments into a ceremony with authenticity instead of a meaningless school tradition. ■

## Making Diplomas

*During the weeks leading up to the last day of preschool, family provider Donna King and Parent Co-op teacher Erin use the children's playtime to unobtrusively move around the room and ask the children what they have observed each of the other children learning during the year. Family members are invited to add their ideas as well. The observations are recorded for each child on chart paper, rolled up as large diplomas, and read at the graduation ceremony with family members, friends, and classmates standing to cheer.*

Lakewood Co-op Preschool

Children First

Creating a classroom culture with routines, rituals, and celebrations that communicate your values and intent for your time with children is like choreographing a dance to be performed over and over again, each rendition a bit different because of the ever-changing cast and the particulars of that time and place. When you invest the time to help everyone learn the dance and find their parts, you set the stage for great things to unfold.

### Your Turn

Practice planning a ritual or celebration for a meaningful season or event with children and families in your program. As you plan, ask yourself these questions:

- What values should guide this experience?
- How can we make this ritual/celebration as inclusive as possible?
- What symbols can we include to represent the meaning of this event?
- How can we acknowledge our relationships in this ritual/celebration?

# Enhance the Curriculum with Materials

*The materials have their own inner life and their own story to tell. Yet they can be transformed only through their encounter with people. When we leave room in construction with materials, leave silence or pause or breathing room, that helps the materials themselves to express what they can express.*

**ELENA GIACOPINI**

Materials in early childhood programs are the bones of the curriculum and the foundation of the teaching and learning process. They support what the program values, and frame the possibilities and actions for living and learning with children. Collections, offerings, and arrangements of materials reflect your values, what you believe children deserve and are capable of, and how you see your role. What guides your current thinking about materials and how the children use them? Do you look forward to discovering interesting treasures to give to children? Do you eagerly anticipate what children might do with the materials you give to them? If you compare collecting materials for children to the pleasure of finding a gift for a dear friend, you will likely transform the way you view your teaching job (Brosterman 1997).

When you want to give a gift to someone, you happily search for something you think she will love. You carefully select the gift and present it in a beautiful way, with colorful wrappings, ribbons, and fond words. You eagerly anticipate the surprise and delight your gift will inspire, and you trust she will love it because it came from knowing her so well. In child care or teaching, the gift of materials comes from your relationship with the children. The materials represent a bit of you and who you are, as well as the tender way in which you know the children. The children accept these gifts with appreciation, bringing their own ideas and passions to them, which in turn is a gift to you from them.

To enhance children's use of the materials toward more complex learning, you must challenge yourself to become mindful and deliberate with what you provide and how you provide it. In this chapter, we offer a set of principles to help you examine the elements and possibilities inherent in the materials you collect. These principles will enable you to see the "inner life" that materials can express during encounters with people, as Reggio educator Elena Giacopini suggests above. The last half of the chapter presents an additional set of principles describing guidelines for how to organize and set up materials as invitations for focus and intention. If you carefully study the photos, examples, and stories given in this chapter and take the time to try the activities mentioned here, you are certain to grow your skills, knowledge, and understandings, and experience the enhanced joy and richness materials can bring to your daily work with children.

**Principles for Examining the Elements and Possibilities in Materials**

- Select materials using an enhanced view of children
- Invent new possibilities for familiar materials
- Draw on the aesthetic qualities of materials
- Choose materials that can be transformed
- Provide real tools and quality materials
- Supply materials to extend children's interests
- Layer materials to offer complexity

**Principles for Arranging Materials as Invitations for Focus and Intention**

- Create orderly, beautiful arrangements
- Provide a background for the materials
- Store diverse items in matching containers
- Group together similar materials with different attributes
- Give attention to size, scale, and levels
- Arrange materials to suggest how they might be used
- Reposition materials to spark a new interest
- Display books and other visual representations with the materials
- Offer collections of materials to highlight a learning domain

## EXAMINING THE ELEMENTS AND POSSIBILITIES IN MATERIALS

Children constantly use materials to learn about the world, explore their questions, and represent their thinking. Their initial work is to examine the properties and functions of materials. As children manipulate materials and learn their properties, they begin to notice something in the material that reminds them of something they already know. With this connection to something familiar, they begin to use the materials to symbolically stand for that idea or experience. As children get more familiar with how objects can represent ideas and concepts, they begin to intentionally use materials for this purpose. Our colleague Joan Newcomb calls this "thinking in things." Teachers can plan for and enhance this process by reflecting on your own ideas and experiences with materials and seeking to know as much as you can about the materials you offer. The following principles and examples can serve as a useful lens for examining and selecting materials to heighten your curriculum.

### Sandbox Gifts

*Examine the collection of materials offered in the sandbox in the photo on the following page. The staff of this program took the time to collect and present materials in this way because they believe children deserve experiences that invite their fascination and sense of adventure. They also believe the children in their group will be capable of learning to use the materials with skill and care. As a result of these beliefs, the teachers make a commitment to find multifaceted materials, carefully arrange them, and then guide the children in their explorations.*

Earlwood Children's Centre

•PRINCIPLE•

## Select Materials Using an Enhanced View of Children

The educators from the schools of Reggio Emilia have advanced the professional discourse about how teachers' image of children dramatically affects the kinds of materials you offer and how you expect children to use them. Your image of children limits or enhances their experiences and abilities. Consider the typical materials available for infants and toddlers. Most of them are made with bright, primary-colored, hard plastic surfaces and commercial cartoonlike figures designed to beckon children's attention. They usually have a cause and effect component for the child to stumble upon or be shown—a button or knob that rings a bell, whistles, beeps, or lights up when you push it. Once the child figures out the simple ways for using the toy, there is little else to engage with. What do these materials say about the image of these young children? Inherent in these toys is the view that babies have limited capabilities or inner resources so they require attention-grabbing, over-stimulating, external experiences in order to stay interested in something. These materials have a narrow focus on health and safety, and a mistaken view that these children "can't do much." Such materials do little to engage a child's lively mind or extraordinary ability for sensory exploration of textures, temperatures, motion, and sound. They don't tap into children's deep desire to learn and hone their skills and aptitudes, nor do they cultivate sustained attention to their explorations.

If you were to examine what children are offered across different cultures, you'd learn that children acquire whatever the adults value and believe the children are capable of, need to know, and deserve (Small 1999). This is a powerful reminder as you examine your own view of children when providing and using materials with them. Reflect on your own attitudes and approaches as you study the following examples of teachers offering materials from the standpoint of an enhanced view of children.

Martin Luther King Jr. Day Home Center

▲ *The children in this room regularly climb on the chairs, tables, and anything else they can find to get up higher. The program budget is on hold and the teacher has been told she'll need to wait to buy a piece of equipment for indoor large motor play. In the meantime, she wants to offer the children a challenging but safe opportunity for climbing. She used some sturdy block shelves as the base for this Plexiglas mirror bridge. Sitting close to the children as they climb, she sees the determination and feeling of competence they gain as they make their way across the bridge. The teacher looks forward to helping the children negotiate the new challenge that emerges as they head toward each other in the middle of the bridge.*

Burlington Little School

▲ *The variety of glass containers these boys are using offers them rich experiences for their sensory investigation, including exploring volume through the height, width, and transparency of the containers. The fact that the containers are glass instills a greater sense of responsibility as they play.*

**Your Turn**

What is your reaction to the two previous photos? How do your values and your view of children contribute to your response?

Now, consider how your view of children is influencing the materials you offer. Make a list of five materials that you regularly provide to children. What values and images of children do these materials suggest?

## •PRINCIPLE•
## Invent New Possibilities for Familiar Materials

Do you see yourself as an inventor and explorer side by side with the children as you plan and interact with them around materials? If not, you might start by looking at the typical materials associated with good early childhood programs—blocks, sensory tables, puzzles, painting easels, and clothes and accessories used for dress up.

Early childhood educators are indebted to the pioneering work of researchers and practitioners such as Friedrich Froebel, Rudolf Steiner, Maria Montessori, Caroline Pratt, and the educators from the schools of Reggio Emilia. Based on their deep interest in and observations of children and their fascination with theories about children's development and learning, they invented learning materials that today are often taken for granted and used without much thought. When you take the time to examine more closely why these materials are used throughout early childhood programs, you discover the obvious: young children are drawn to these materials because they offer multiple possibilities for pursuing different learning domains in an active, open-ended way. As you reconsider these familiar materials and study the vigorous thinking of the above-named inventors and researchers, you might discover for yourself the deeper fascination and insight that informed their work. As you look more closely at the possibilities, you will be able to highlight the attributes of familiar materials by offering them in different combinations or within a special setting. You can closely observe the children's use of these materials and work to expand the potential they hold for deeper meaning, joy, and complexity. Study the following examples for using typical materials in new ways.

Burlington Little School

▲ *A thoughtful teacher carefully chooses puzzles with more than one way to use them. This particular puzzle can be put together in its frame, or used to create a design using the elements of color and shape. How might further study occur as a result of using the puzzle with the mirrors on the shelf and wall?*

Burlington Little School

▲ *These popular building toys are placed on a mirror in front of a sunny window, taking advantage of the interplay of light, reflection, and the colors of the translucent blocks. The addition of books related to color and other objects for investigating colors extends the possibilities for further study and deeper understandings.*

▶ *Block building in this room has many layers of complexity and, literally, multiple levels for investigation. Notice the different surfaces, heights, and sizes of platforms for building. The clothesline, pulley system, and spotlights invite creative endeavors in engineering and design. How have these typical building blocks been enhanced by this teacher's invention?*

Evergreen Community School

▶ *Observe the out-of-the-ordinary materials offered in this dramatic play area. Along with some traditional materials for dress up and tea parties, there are also keys, stones, and various other loose parts. What guesses do you have about how children will use these props in their dramatic play?*

Hilltop Children's Center

Clifton School

◀ ▲ *The infants in this program will be surrounded by sounds, textures, and softness as they make their way into this unique structure designed for their exploration and learning. How did the inventor of this musical landscape take into account the children's abilities and interests in order to expand their exploration of sound?*

### Your Turn

- Choose a typical material in your room and observe how the children use it.
- Draw on the children's use of the material to brainstorm a list of ideas of other ways this material might be used or added to.
- Try something from your list, observing what happens with the children as a result.

### Wondrous Water

*This water fountain is in the entry area of a child care program where children and families wash their hands upon arrival. The glimmering, golden basin is irresistible to the children as it is just their height and the children can easily turn the water on and off all by themselves. If you look closely at the water on the child's hand and on the basin, you can see the beauty and wonder of this magical substance called "water" as it drips, splashes, and reflects the light and color around it. The expression on the child's face signifying his passion for this experience is infectious.*

Martin Luther King Jr. Day Home Center

## •PRINCIPLE•
## Draw on the Aesthetic Qualities of Materials

*All of us collect fortunes when we are children—a fortune of colors, of light and darkness, of movements, of tensions. Some of us have the fantastic chance to go back to our fortune when we grow up. Most of us don't have that chance—that is the tragedy.* —Ingmar Bergman

Human beings, and children in particular, are drawn to the sensory and aesthetic properties of materials. Ingmar Bergman, the Swedish film director known for rich and unusual visual imagery in his films, reminds us in the quotation above that aesthetic elements are fortunes that heighten our pleasure and interest in the world. Young children continually notice these elements and offer you the "fantastic chance" to revisit with them in your daily work lives.

*Aesthetic* is from the Greek word meaning "a perceiver" or "sensitive" and is a branch of philosophy dealing with the nature of beauty. The word *aesthetic* can be used as a noun meaning "that which appeals to the senses." The early childhood profession has a long history of providing sand, water, fingerpaint, and other materials that attract children because they excite and soothe the senses. Yet the notion of aesthetics can go far beyond these typical approaches. Cultivating an aesthetic sense enhances the ability to see, explore, appreciate, and find joy in the beauty of the world. Aesthetic beauty can be found in the shapes, forms, lines, patterns, textures, light, colors, shadows, and reflective aspects of the things around you. It is part of the natural world and also visible in most human endeavors including art, architecture, many areas of design, and even cooking. Experiences within the aesthetic realm can evoke feelings of wonder, curiosity, surprise, humor, awe, inspiration, and a sense of peace and tranquility.

Rather than just relying on naturally occurring aesthetic experiences, imagine how you could enhance children's instinctive inclination to notice aesthetic elements with more attention to them in your program. You can add liveliness, calm, complexity, and beauty to your curriculum by planning for these materials as an integral aspect of your days together. You can respond to children's innate awareness of this aspect of the world by carefully selecting and arranging materials to highlight the rich aesthetic elements surrounding you. Study the following examples of teachers bringing beauty and wonder to children's learning with attention to aesthetics.

Burlington Little School

▲ *The teachers in this room have given extra attention to adding materials to enhance aesthetic development beyond typical materials for sensory play. The shiny metal tubs that range in size from small to large and the matching metal containers and scoops invite children to notice further aesthetic details and concepts beyond their sensory investigation. The sparkly sand pellets (found in the cat litter section of pet stores) and the plastic swans and snowflakes evoke treasure hunts, dramas, and a sense of wonder.*

Earlwood Children's Centre

▲ ▶ *The caregiver in this infant program has planned this offering of materials with attention to many aesthetic elements. Notice the variety of textures in the fabrics, feathers, pillows, and play things. The sheer fabric hung above the area takes advantage of the outdoors, creating dappled light and shadows. Study how the use of color invites attention as well as unites and creates a soothing feeling. The children are drawn to the objects, which are hung where the children can reach them, as they shimmer and move in response to the breeze as well as the children's actions. What else do you think will attract the babies as they spend time in this space with these materials? How would you feel as a caregiver in this environment?*

Earlwood Children's Centre

Martin Luther King Jr. Day Home Center

▲ *The rich color, smooth textures, and interesting shapes of the wooden fruit and trays collected from a thrift store make an aesthetically appealing invitation for the children in this program. They are drawn to the way the items look and feel, and love holding them, banging them together, carrying them around, and placing them in the divided sections of the tray. Contrast the aesthetic elements of these materials with the primary-colored, plastic toys that are usually offered to toddlers.*

Sunflower School

Alhambra Head Start

◀ ▲ *Look closely at each of these photos and notice their sensory and aesthetic qualities. What do you notice about the textures, shapes, patterns, lines, light, and colors? What feelings do these collections of materials evoke?*

Burlington Little School

Evergreen Community School

**Your Turn**

Gather your own collection of materials that draw you to their aesthetic qualities. Explore these materials side by side with a small group of children. Observe closely what you see the children notice and also what you notice about the textures, colors, and shapes of the materials. After you have completed this experience, make a list of the words and phrases that describe the aesthetic elements you experienced, both the concrete aspects and the feelings. Keep this list as a reference for planning and conversations with the children.

Burlington Little School

▲ *This invitation includes stuffed and toy animals, a collection of animal-patterned fabric pieces and furs, baskets of napkin rings, bones, and brushes.*

## •PRINCIPLE•
## Choose Materials That Can Be Transformed

Materials that are open-ended and can be transformed have the power to call on children's internal resources, experiences, and imagination in multiple ways for multiple purposes. Children have great energy and enthusiasm for materials with interesting properties that can be used for design or construction, or made into props for a drama or pieces for a game. Recycled materials, special collections of unusual items or unknown treasures, and things from nature all encourage divergent thinking as children use them for meaningful learning. These items also promote the value of recycling and reusing, rather than consuming and discarding. Materials with familiar shapes or forms can be gathered to suggest the possibilities for their use. Children are likely to incorporate these into a variety of play activities. They may be used in combinations with other materials for inventions or representations of ideas they are exploring.

Study this collection of open-ended materials that adults gathered for children to discover. The following photos show the different ways toddlers, preschoolers, and schoolage children used these materials.

▼ *The toddlers immerse themselves in the piles of fur, drawn to the sensory and aesthetic qualities of the materials, including the soft yet very different textures, and the interesting colors, shapes, and patterns. Notice how the children are examining specific aspects of the materials, looking closely at their attributes and then trying out ideas. The children discover that the basket can be a hat. Looking through the basket, they can see a different view of the world and they also can use the basket for holding other materials. Can you see how you might think of their behavior as asking and answering questions, or a way to try out their theories? "What does this look like, feel like, move like?" "How is this like something I already know?" "What can this be?" "What can I do with this?"*

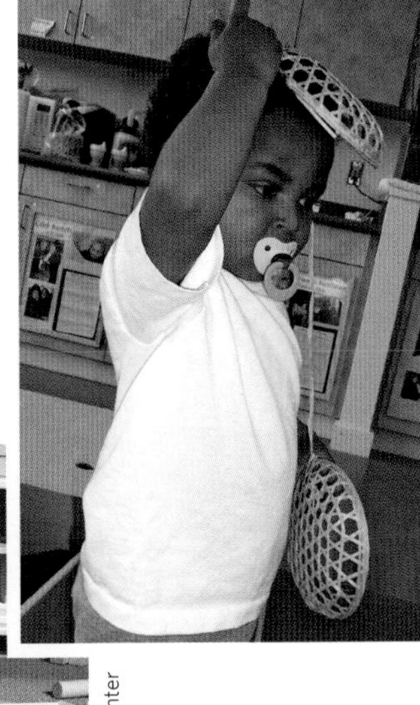

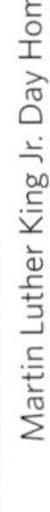

Martin Luther King Jr. Day Home Center

Burlington Little School

Burlington Little School

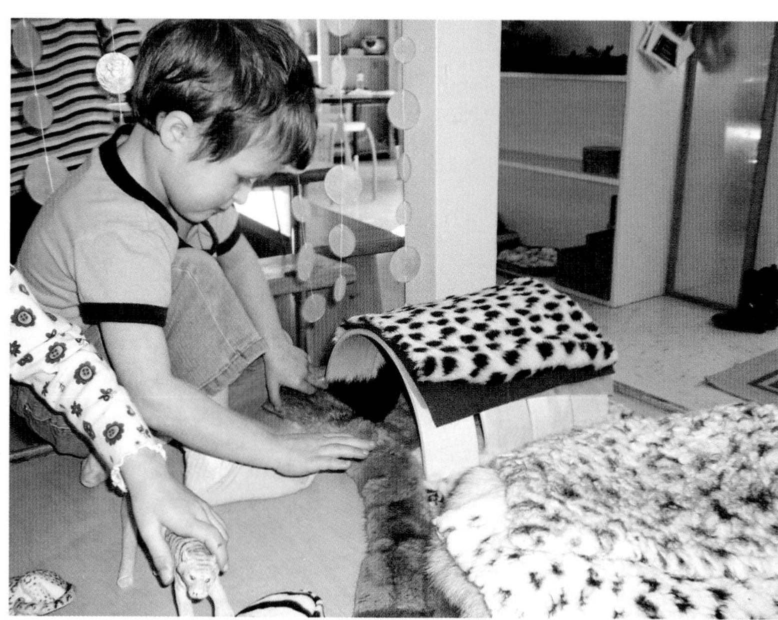
Burlington Little School

▲ *The preschool children are also drawn to the sensory and aesthetic aspects of the materials. They explore these aspects and quickly move to using them for symbolic representations. The napkin rings become the casts for the animals' broken limbs. This idea prompts a group decision to make a hospital for the sick animals. Each of the children creates a cozy habitat decorated with the luscious fur where their animals hide from the "spies" that are coming after them. This drama continues for a period of time. Each day more elaborate stories unfold as the children find new ways to transform the materials.*

Bloom Family Home

Bloom Family Home

Bloom Family Home

## Reflection & Action

***Where do I see examples of children's strength and competency?***

*

***How do I understand the children's point of view in this situation?***

*

***How are the environment and materials impacting what's unfolding and what changes could be made?***

▲ *The abundant fur pieces evoke tenderness in these school-age children as they wrap the animals in softness, creating comforting, cozy beds. Their designs and constructions grow, and the materials become a vacation resort complete with swimming pools and a roller coaster. The architecture of the roller coaster is a serious endeavor as the children find a way to connect the fur pieces together, keeping at it until they are successful at getting the basket of bears to zoom down and around the fur track.*

*Examine these photos for examples of interesting open-ended materials. What details do you notice about the materials? What do the materials remind you of? What predictions would you make about how different-aged children might use the materials?*

▲ *Lining up carpet squares* Burlington Little School

▲ *Building with spools and cove molding* Burlington Little School

▲ *Designing with triangle quilt rulers* Burlington Little School

▲ *Stacking hat boxes* Burlington Little School

### Your Turn

Now gather your own collection of open-ended materials and interact with them yourself, using these questions to guide your exploration:

- What do the materials look, feel, sound, and smell like?
- How do they move?
- What do they remind you of?
- How could you use them to build or construct something?
- How could they become a prop in a drama?
- How could you use them to play a game?

Next, offer these same materials to a group of children and observe closely how they use them. Notice the similar and different ways the children use the materials.

Burlington Little School

## •PRINCIPLE•
## Provide Real Tools and Quality Materials

Many of us were lucky to have relationships during our childhood with people who had passions and skills that they were willing to share with us. Perhaps it was an auntie who taught us to use her sewing machine, or the next-door neighbor who was an ace car mechanic, willing to coach us in using the shiny tools hanging in the garage. We likely have fond memories of these experiences because someone respected our capabilities and believed we could learn to use real objects from the grown-up world. When children are provided opportunities to use "real" tools and materials of high quality, they feel respected and taken seriously. When they are trusted and shown how to use and care for these tools and materials, children live up to the responsibility of using them and as a result bring more focus and intention to their work. Additionally, real tools and high-quality materials allow children to produce more meaningful and beautiful work. The following examples show how powerful these materials can be for children's self-esteem and learning.

Burlington Little School

▲ *In these photos, four-year-old Priya is offered a collection of real artist tools, including a variety of brushes, ink pens, colored ink, and high quality art paper. Notice her attention to detail, and the purpose she brings to her work. As she explores the tools and the ways she can use them for different effects, the result is a series of gorgeous paintings.*

*Contrast this to the typical painting materials usually offered to preschool children—thick paints, thick brushes, and paper that causes the paint to run or drip—materials that don't lend themselves to the careful work Priya is engaged in.*

Burlington Little School

Burlington Little School

*Children in this group earnestly took up the challenge of learning to use hot glue guns for their recycled sculpture project. The teacher took advantage of the children's strong desire to use this real, somewhat risky tool by inviting them to think through their work more carefully. She began the project by instructing the children how to use the tool to avoid burning themselves. She suggested they look through the materials and think about how they might use them in their sculptures. When they had gathered the materials, she challenged the children to draw a picture of what they wanted to build and then use the drawing as their plan for building the sculpture. The children eagerly took up her suggestions, and increased their skills and competence with these challenging tasks.*

Burlington Little School

*The children approached the work involved with these air pumps seriously because these tools required skill and knowledge to get them to work successfully. The children shared strategies they discovered for using the air pumps to fill the balloons with as much air as possible.*

## Reflection & Action

***What in my background and values is influencing my response to this situation and why?***

*

***Where do I see examples of children's strength and competency?***

*

***What values, philosophy, and goals do I want to influence my response?***

Hilltop Children's Center

▲ *The children and teachers in this full-day child care program bring their lunches from home. Teacher Liane naturally includes chopsticks with her lunch so she can eat her food as she does at home. Rather than dismissing the children's interest in this eating utensil, she takes the time to demonstrate how chopsticks are used and makes a mental note to bring more of them to the table for future instruction.*

Burlington Little School

▲ *The children's eagerness to use real tools inspired this teacher to offer a basket of wrenches and bolts in the drama area of the room. She then drilled holes into the bottom part of the loft so that the children could use the wrenches to screw the nuts and bolts in and out of the holes. This is a challenging task for the children, one they return to again and again. Sometimes the work with the wrenches becomes part of a drama around building something, but more often the satisfaction of this "real" work with "real" tools is the focus.*

### Your Turn

Reflect on the tools and materials that you offer children, including art, drawing, and writing materials; paints, paintbrushes, pens, pencils, and paper; and tools for clean up and maintenance.

- How many of these tools and materials are made specifically for children?
- How many are real tools made of high quality materials?
- What changes can you make to offer children tools and materials that will enhance their work?

## •PRINCIPLE•
## Supply Materials to Extend Children's Interests

Your observations of children's interests, developmental themes, family life, and culture can guide your selection of materials. When seeking new, engaging materials for children, it is useful to remember what you know about individuals in your group as well as their collective interests and developmental themes. As adults, our familiarity with common materials may limit the possibilities we see in them. Young children, on the other hand, are new to this world and still see its magic and wonder everywhere around them. They approach experiences with an open mind, unencumbered by frameworks and labels. Because they are in the process of exploring and constructing an understanding of their world, they notice the details and try out a variety of operations and interactions with everything they encounter. If you take their point of view while looking for collections to offer, your planning and the children's exploration and learning will be more joyful. Study the following examples for ideas on how to offer materials to extend children's interests.

Burlington Little School

▲ *Helena and Amelie have been playing side by side, pretending to care for the baby dolls in the drama area. These three-year-old girls have a shared experience of new baby brothers being born into their families. To honor and respond to this major life change and to help them see the connection they share, their teacher asked their families to bring photos of the girls with their new baby brothers. The teacher then framed the photos and put them in the drama area. She also made sure to have plenty of baby care props in the drama area that invite the girls to play together around this new experience. The teacher's invitation is accepted as the girls spend every day together learning to be caring big sisters and deepening their relationship as they play.*

Martin Luther King Jr. Day Home Center

▲ *Noticing that her toddlers love to take the lids off of their food containers at snacktime, dump out the food, and then spend a long time putting the lids back on, this teacher's thrift store excursion uncovered a number of coaster sets of different shapes and sizes in matching boxes with lids. She arranged them as an invitation to challenge the children to match the coasters to their boxes and fit the lids on top. The variety of beautiful textures, colors, and shapes added to their investigation and enjoyment.*

▶ *The children in this program enthusiastically explore the vibrant colors, varying weights, and different sizes of pumpkins and other small gourds they see growing all around the farm valley where they live. They cart the pumpkins around and use them in their dramatic play. Then they cut them open to explore the gushy insides, roast and eat the seeds, and use the meat for cooking and baking projects. With the remaining pumpkins, the teacher gives the children opportunities for developing skills and competence with hammers and nails, preparing them for later woodworking projects. The cycle is complete as they save some seeds and put the remaining pumpkin parts into the compost bin. Months of work with the pumpkins offers multiple opportunities to be a part of the larger meaning of the farming in their community.*

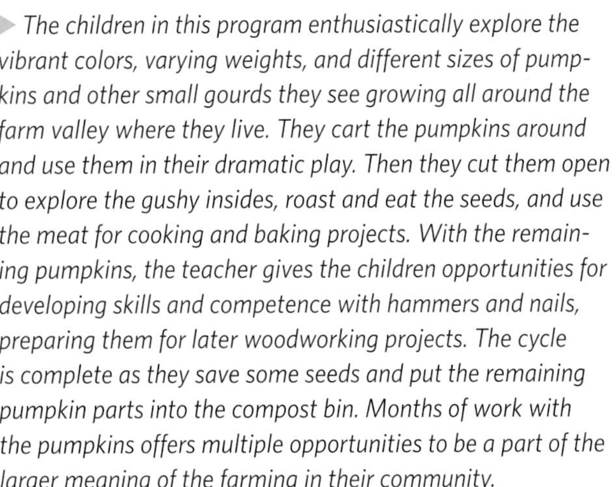

Burlington Little School

### Your Turn

Observe a child or group of children using materials in your room. As you notice the details of what they say and do, can you see connections to what you know about them, their family life, and their stage of development? Decide what other materials you might offer them to extend an interest. Observe what they do with what you offer.

### Fairy Dramas

*Sage came to school with a book about fairies that included illustrations of the fairies' beautiful homes in the natural world. Her teacher, observing that many children gathered with Sage during the week to look at the book, decided to offer some materials to extend their interest. The children eagerly took up the invitation to work with the appealing materials, using the craft sticks, beads, and artificial flowers to design and create their own fairy people, and a reference book to inspire their work. As the children completed the characters and their habitat, their work expanded as they began a drama using their inventions as props in the story. At the end of the afternoon, when they seemed to be done with their building and drama, their teacher encouraged the children to draw pictures and make a book about their fairy story so they could remember it when they came back the next day.*

Burlington Little School

Burlington Little School

Burlington Little School

## •PRINCIPLE•
## Layer Materials to Offer Complexity

To build on children's learning with materials, it is useful to offer combinations of materials that lend themselves to many uses and extended investigation. When children are interested in an idea or concept, providing different materials to extend their exploration helps them make further connections and build on their ideas. Not only do they use the materials to represent their current thinking, but they increase their skills and go deeper in exploring new ideas through the multiple activities they bring to the work.

Jean Piaget named the different kinds of play he observed children use as a part of their learning (Mooney 2000). Drawing on his observations, you can offer combinations of materials for sensory exploration, functional play, construction, drama, and games. Providing a sensory base such as sand or playdough, and gradually adding materials related to the different kinds of play extends the amount of time and complexity of children's play. Sensory materials keep children reinvesting in the invitation, which allows them to see more possibilities for the other objects available to build or design something, create a drama, or make up a game. Below is a series of examples of how family providers and teachers created an initial invitation using playdough as a sensory base and then added layers of possibilities over time. What ideas does this give you for using materials to expand the complexity of work with playdough and other favorite materials?

Mother's Quality Family Child Care

▲ *This family provider created an invitation with new materials for playdough to give children an opportunity to explore impressions with household and natural items. She offered out-of-the-ordinary items as well as items that children were familiar with to see how they would explore them. She observed without interfering with their explorations, giving them the opportunity to find out for themselves how they could use these items. The children used the beautiful materials with the playdough to make designs, invent dramas, and sort and classify shapes and sizes of their dough creations.*

A Place for You Family Child Care

A Place for You Family Child Care

▲▶ *Four-year-old Beia eagerly accepted teacher Kelly's invitation to use new and interesting materials with the playdough. She started out with shells, pressing them in the playdough to make indentations and then creating a gorgeous shell sculpture. When she noticed the screws, she had a new plan. "I am making your birthday cake," she told Kelly.*

*There weren't quite enough screws on the tray for Beia to finish going all around the "cake," so Kelly asked her how many more screws she thought she would need. Carefully, Beia touched several points around the remaining dough, counting.*

*"Five," she estimated.*

*So Kelly found some more screws, and to their surprise, five wasn't enough.*

*"Three more," was Beia's next guess, after eyeing the remaining space. Three did the job! After a moment or two, Beia removed the "candles" and put them back on the tray. Then, she carefully covered up the holes that the screws had made.*

A Place for You Family Child Care

Burlington Little School

## ARRANGING MATERIALS AS INVITATIONS FOR FOCUS AND INTENTION

If our intention is to invite children to pursue their exuberant interests in the world and express their unique ideas, then just like thoughtful gift giving, we must pay careful attention to not only what we offer, but how we offer the materials. What's the curricular equivalent of beautifully wrapping a present for a friend? Children are very observant and alert to the context in which materials are available to them. They look for cues from the adults and the environment to guide their actions in how to use things and how to care for them. If materials are carefully chosen and beautifully presented, children are more likely to respond by using them thoughtfully and caring for them.

Burlington Little School

▲ *This teacher has a science area located near the playdough table and she noticed that the children often brought the small plastic snakes and lizards from the science area to incorporate into their playdough work. The animals always sparked some very interesting dramatic play. The children built playdough habitats and set up playdough communities for the creatures to live in. Since observing this play, the teacher now sets out thoughtful combinations of materials for building and designing as well as a variety of animals and people to extend their dramas with playdough.*

### "I'm Getting This Ready."

*Teacher Janelle strives to artfully and creatively arrange and present materials, with the hope of inspiring further creativity from the children. Seeing materials arranged purposefully encourages the children to care for them in a more respectful manner. Emily, one of the oldest children in this mixed-age class, was inspired to start organizing invitations of her own. One morning, she spread a large scarf on the small table in the dramatic play area and arranged an assortment of crayons and markers in a beautiful basket. She then laid out a piece of paper by each chair at the table. When Janelle asked Emily what she was working on, she responded, "I'm getting this ready for the other children to use."*

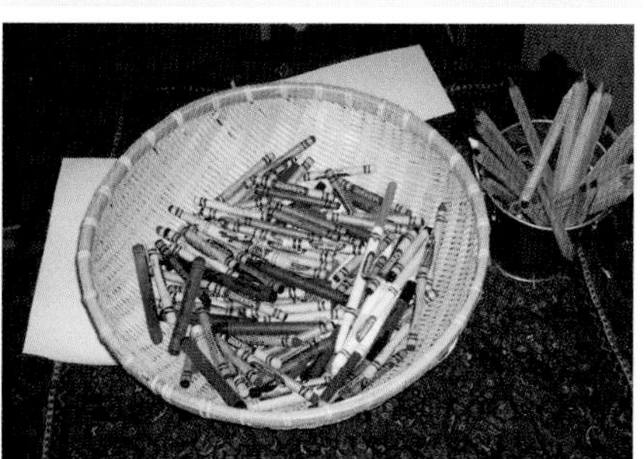

St. Charles Child Development Center

The collections of materials you put together suggest possibilities. Where you place materials and how you arrange them communicates in a powerful way the values and intentions you have in mind. For example, offering materials with broken and missing pieces on crowded, cluttered shelves doesn't show respect for children's abilities nor invite them to focus on the potential for exploration and learning. This type of presentation also speaks loudly to children about the lack of care and attention to the things in the room. In contrast, thoughtfully collecting materials for their possibilities for investigation and action, and beautifully arranging them to draw attention to their attributes and relationships invites children to focus on what is available and to dive into engaging work. Drawing on ideas of other thinkers who have developed approaches to offering materials in these thoughtful ways (see Mooney 2000 for examples), here are some principles and examples to consider when collecting, arranging, and offering materials.

Earlwood Children's Centre

▲ *This gorgeous presentation of materials beckons children with the magic and wonder it holds. The calming shades of blue and the careful arrangement of the larger items on a large mirror and the smaller stones on the smaller mirrors draws the children in, helping them to focus and inspiring their exploration and creativity.*

## •PRINCIPLE•
## Create Orderly, Beautiful Arrangements

Picture a farmer's market or grocery store produce section with a stunning arrangement of produce for your perusal. The fruits and vegetables are probably organized by variety, texture, and color. The grocer or farmer has purposefully fashioned different heights and levels for each of the items to create a sense of balance, order, and beauty so you are drawn to and can clearly see what is available. These same elements can enhance children's attention to and use of materials. Like adults, children are drawn to orderly, beautiful arrangements of materials. The thought teachers give to the arrangement of materials communicates respect for the children and the importance you place in the activities you offer. Children can see more clearly the aspects of the materials and the possibilities for their use. They also take extra care as they play, believing these must be special offerings because of the striking way they have been displayed. Study the following examples to inspire your own arrangements of materials.

Earlwood Children's Centre

▲ *This invitation uses natural-colored mats and wooden bowls to contrast with the beauty of the greenery that the children are using for this work. The lovely wooden bowls highlight the color and shape of the materials, encouraging closer investigation. The orderly display of the materials also encourages children's attention to the task at hand.*

## •PRINCIPLE•
## Provide a Background for the Materials

Including a background of a tray, cloth, or frame provides a figure-ground focus and a clear palette for children's use of materials. A background both draws your eye to focus on what materials are available and creates a container for the exploration process.

Burlington Little School

Burlington Little School

▲ *The individual black mixing trays communicate that each child has a space for working alone to mix the colored water and cornstarch. The large white tray defines the space for the messy work of the whole group working together. Do you see how each background offers a clear but different focus for the task at hand?*

Burlington Little School

▲ *This collection of materials is an invitation to explore herbs and spices. Look closely at how each tray, plate, and basket defines the work area and highlights the work to be done. This presentation sends a message to the children that the herbs and spices share common elements, and also have individual aspects to notice and ways they can be explored.*

## •PRINCIPLE•
## Store Diverse Items in Matching Containers

When you want to have a wide array of materials available for children, you are faced with the challenge of avoiding clutter and helping the children focus on what's available. When diverse materials are offered in matching containers or baskets, you can clearly see the individual items and their unique attributes. Compare this to a jumble of items in one basket, or many different kinds of containers with many different items in them. Beyond the orderly, attractive appearance, an arrangement of diverse materials in similar containers allows the children to see what is available for their use and communicates respect for the materials used in the room.

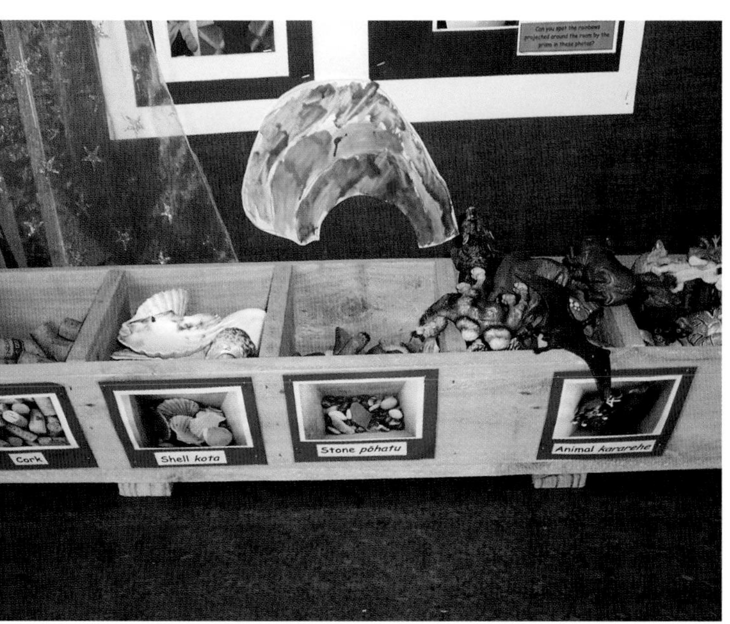


Tots Corner

▲ *Although this wooden planter box holds a number of different materials, each collection is easy to identify. The container itself, as well as the photos labeling the contents, creates a framework for seeing what's inside.*

Burlington Little School

▲ *With diverse items in each of these baskets, the shelf does not look cluttered because the baskets are the same color and size. The matching baskets create a context for each item and a clear view of the contents. Think of how this display would look if the materials were stored in containers made of different materials, colors, and sizes.*

## •PRINCIPLE• Group Together Similar Materials with Different Attributes

Offering a collection of materials with similar aspects (such as their color or what they are made of) but also different attributes (such as their size or texture) helps children notice and explore the differences more thoroughly than if they are offered a jumble of materials with nothing in common. Study the following examples to see this in action.

Burlington Little School

▲ *This collection of similarly colored containers in the sensory table is inviting and offers a deeper learning experience because all the items have a similar transparent blue color and a common function as containers for dumping and filling the lavender-scented rice. But the materials also give children the opportunity to explore their different sizes, shapes, and textures. Compare this to the more typical disarray and overstimulation of a sensory table overflowing with an untidy heap of mismatched containers and other objects hiding the substance inside.*

Martin Luther King Jr. Day Home Center

Martin Luther King Jr. Day Home Center

▲ *This observant teacher knows the babies in her room are drawn to the things that feel substantial to touch and have varying elements to explore with their eyes, ears, hands, and bodies. When she discovered a collection of wooden massage tools at a thrift store, she knew she had found treasures for her babies. These materials all have common elements, such as the lovely natural wood color and texture to explore, but they each have different shapes, sizes, bumps, and grooves. The babies find this collection intriguing to look at, touch, and manipulate, in the process comparing how the objects are the same and different. They find them interesting to hold, carry, drop, and make sounds with. The wheels and other moving parts fascinate the children as they turn and spin them.*

## •PRINCIPLE• Give Attention to Size, Scale, and Levels

When you change the scale of similar materials and offer them on different surfaces with different levels, children have more opportunities to use the materials in new ways. Providing materials that range in size from small to large, or offering them on a platform, the floor, or the top of a shelf, gives children new perspectives where they are confronted with different challenges. Notice the possibilities in the following examples.

Burlington Little School

▲ *These children spent a week exploring color mixing and pouring water with measuring cups and scoops (seen in the first photo). The teacher wanted to extend their investigations by offering a larger scale for mixing, dumping, and filling, so she provided these larger tubs (seen in the second photo). The children can now draw on their previous experiences with the small materials and take their exploration to another level.*

Burlington Little School

Burlington Little School

Burlington Little School

▲ *The teachers in this room offer multiple opportunities for building and construction on different platforms at various levels. The children can work directly on the floor, on the raised platform, or on the large trunk. Do you see how working on these different surfaces and heights might change and expand their play?*

## •PRINCIPLE• Arrange Materials to Suggest How They Might Be Used

When teachers carefully select materials, they have ideas about how the children might engage with them. To help children see the possibilities you see in the materials, create a suggestion as a part of the setup. This helps children create initial ideas about how to get started with the materials and may also encourage them to do something they might not have considered. It's gratifying when children do what you imagined with materials. At the same time, be sure to stay open to the surprises they come up with that you never dreamed of.

Earlwood Children's Centre

▲ *These items have been thoughtfully placed in the sandbox; their placement suggests the exciting possibilities for their use, a suggestion that will inspire the children's play. Examine this photo from a child's point of view. What does the setup suggest the children do?*

▶ *Look closely at the collection of materials in this photo. The combination of materials and the way they are arranged suggest several different ways to explore these materials. The children are invited to look closely with the magnifying glass or to pick up the grapes with the tweezers and transfer them into the small bowls. What other guesses do you have about what children might do with this activity? What other suggestions could you offer through the arrangement of these materials?*

Hilltop Children's Center

Hilltop Children's Center

▲ *In the first photo, the teacher has assembled a beginning construction on the tray to attract the children's focus and attention. In the second photo, the teacher has hinted at a way to use the pattern blocks. These small suggestions spark the children's thinking and communicate that it's okay to dive in and get started.*

Burlington Little School

## •PRINCIPLE• Reposition Materials to Spark a New Interest

Moving materials to a different location in the room can stimulate a new interest and a new way to use them. Materials that have been on a shelf for a long time have new appeal when moved to a tray, a table, or the floor. Putting materials next to items they have never been used with helps children combine them in different ways. The following examples show this at work.

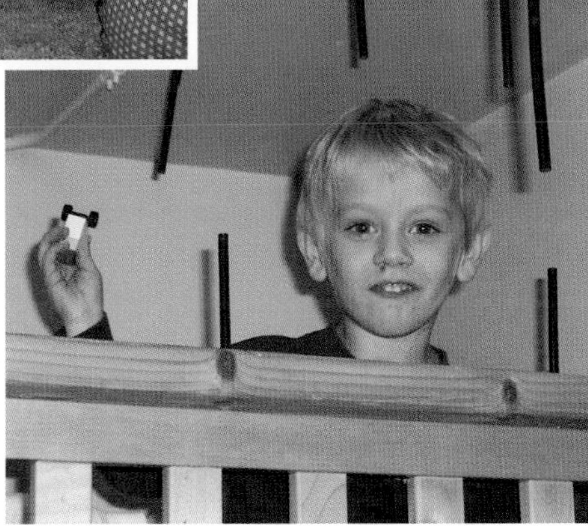

Burlington Little School

▲ *This teacher knew that magnets would stick to the metal pipes of the classroom loft so she put a basket of magnetic tubes and balls up there for the children to discover. As you can see in the photos, the children found many new and interesting ways to explore these materials.*

Earlwood Children's Centre

Earlwood Children's Centre

▲ *Inviting children to use materials outdoors evokes different uses for the materials and extends outdoor learning. The teachers from the program represented in these photos use the outdoor learning spaces in the same way they use the indoor space, planning for small and large group areas and manipulative and dramatic play. What difference do you think this will make in how the children use these materials?*

## •PRINCIPLE• Display Books and Other Visual Representations with the Materials

Adding visual and symbolic representations to an invitation of materials gives children another resource for investigation and learning as they make connections between the real objects and the photos, drawings, or stories about them.

Burlington Little School

▲ *This teacher was inspired by the work of artist Andy Goldsworthy so she provided rocks and ice and an art book with his photos. Notice how the children used the book as a resource to create their own ice and rock sculptures.*

Hilltop Children's Center

◀ *Along with magnifying glasses and real worms in petri dishes, this teacher provided books containing information about worms and their bodies. As you can see by the photo, the images in the book were very pertinent for the children's exploration with the other materials.*

## •PRINCIPLE• Offer Collections of Materials to Highlight a Learning Domain

Although learning is embedded in all the collections of materials described here, when you want to highlight a particular learning domain or concept, you can create invitations with that focus. As with materials provided for open-ended exploration, children often discover attributes, principles, and concepts, or practice skills that are part of your desired learning outcomes.

Earlwood Children's Centre

▲ *The teachers in this program put forward special invitations throughout the environment for children to explore academic skills through self-directed lessons. This photo shows one they provided around letter recognition and use. Can you think of other ideas for self-directed materials for academic skills?*

Earlwood Children's Centre

Earlwood Children's Centre

▲ *These teachers wanted to provide more science learning for the children in their group and believed the children would be intrigued by studying frogs. They designed and offered this invitation and then got out their pens and clipboards to record what the children did with the invitation and said about frogs. This gave them insight into where to go next with their explorations around science.*

## Your Turn

Each of the photos here reflects one or more of the principles for creating invitations for focus and intention. Review the principles below and study the photos to see if you can see the principles at work.

- Create orderly, beautiful arrangements
- Provide a background for the materials
- Store diverse items in matching containers
- Group together similar materials with different attributes
- Give attention to size, scale, and levels
- Arrange materials to suggest how they might be used
- Reposition materials to spark a new interest
- Display books and other visual representations with the materials
- Offer collections of materials to highlight a learning domain

Earlwood Children's Centre

*Your Turn continued*

Burlington Little School

East L.A. Community College Child Development Center

Burlington Little School

St. Charles Child Development Center

*Your Turn continued*

Earlwood Children's Centre

Once you have studied these principles, practice offering invitations with playdough and props for four to five children.

Provide a good quantity of freshly made play-dough. The playdough should be white or a deep color. Supply an attractive, solid color mat or tray for each child to work on. Display a small collection of materials from each of the following sets of materials in attractive baskets, trays, or bowls.

**Tools for Making Imprints**

- Shells with textures
- Massage tools that move
- Other interesting objects with designs for imprinting using different sizes, shapes, or textures

**Materials for Designing**

- Shells of different sizes, similar and different kinds
- Small stones and rocks of different sizes, similar and different kinds
- Small tiles of different and similar colors and shapes (free samples are often available at tile departments of home improvement stores or specialty home decor stores)
- Small beads and/or beach glass

*Your Turn continued*

- Incense sticks and herbs to add fragrance (lavender, rosemary, mint)

**Materials for Construction**

- Craft sticks
- Sample paint chips (free samples are often available at paint departments of home improvement stores or specialty home decor stores)
- Cubes (from early childhood catalogs)
- Sushi mats cut into smaller pieces

**Props for Dramas**

- Small plastic animals
- Herbs and flowers, real and artificial
- Small tea sets, dishes
- Wheeled vehicles

Set up the invitation on a table in an attractive way, arranging the trays or mats in front of each chair, with a large piece of playdough at each place. Put the baskets or trays with tools or props in the center of the table where everyone can reach them.

Offer the invitation each day, for at least a few weeks, adding props over time, responding to the children's interests.

Document what the children do with the materials by taking photos and writing down descriptions. Put these observations in a binder and add this to the table alongside the invitation. Use the following questions to reflect on what you are observing:

- What did you see? Be as specific as you can. What do the children seem drawn to or curious about? Are they interested in the materials? In the way you displayed and offered the materials?

*Your Turn continued*

- What are you curious about? Are the children doing what you expected or is something else happening? (Why might it be the same or different from what you expected?)
- Are there any assumptions, themes, or theories that the players seem to be centering their exploration around?

As you reflect on your experiences with this activity, consider how it might impact your ongoing offering of materials to children, not only with playdough, but other invitations that might incorporate the principles discussed in this chapter. Materials that are "layered" with multiple possibilities allow you to stand back, observe, and have more to bring to your conversations with the children's families and your coworkers, as well as more insight into what next steps you might want to plan. As you build your curriculum around engaging materials, you will then be ready to explore other actions to expand your teaching repertoire, which is the focus of the remaining chapters.

# Bring Yourself to the Teaching and Learning Process

*If we are not fully ourselves, truly in the present moment, we miss everything. When a child presents himself to you with his smile, if you are not really there—thinking about the future or the past, or preoccupied with other problems—then the child is not really there for you. The technique of being alive is to go back to yourself in order for the child to appear like a marvelous reality. Then you can see him smile and you can embrace him in your arms.*

**THICH NHAT HANH**

When early childhood educators design a learning environment with values in mind and offer engaging materials to explore, you set the stage for meaningful experiences to unfold. You have ongoing roles to play to deepen children's interests and knowledge, and further your own passion for teaching. Your teacher behaviors must go beyond herding children through typical activities and outcomes associated with early childhood curriculum. Then, as Thich Nhat Hanh suggests above, you can let go of preoccupations and go back to yourself to really see children and the deep joy of this work.

But how can you do this when every year there are more guidelines to follow, more curriculum content to include, and more standards to adhere to? If you look honestly, it's not the curriculum or requirements, but your behavior and responses to children that are the biggest factors in what occurs in your room. When you heighten your awareness, you realize the power and possibilities you have to enhance experiences for the children and yourself. As you take up the challenge and responsibility for this dynamic process of teaching and learning, careful observation is required, along with ongoing self-reflection and the courage to think and act outside the boxes on your curriculum form. The following principles will help you take charge of your role to build relationships and lively learning experiences with children.

- Claim your power
- Think through your actions
  - Know your teacher scripts
  - Know your professional influences
  - Know your theoretical influences

- Cultivate a mindset of receptivity
- Seek the child's point of view
- Notice the details to discover more possibilities
- Share conversations following the children's lead
- Support children's connections with each other
- Take action on behalf of children's strengths

## •PRINCIPLE• Claim Your Power

You use power daily in your work with children, often inadvertently, without paying attention to your purpose, and without examining the effects of your actions. If you fail to think in terms of purpose and effect, you might easily ignore, stifle, or overwhelm children's innate desire to learn. In today's educational climate, you might feel obliged to use your power on behalf of curriculum mandates or outcomes. Yet policy makers, curriculum designers, Italian educators, or even your immediate supervisors are not often in the room with you when you are with the children. You may bring their influence and feel the pressure for accountability to outcomes, but you are the one who has the power in the moment-to-moment decisions and responses you make to children. You decide what to pay attention to, what to stop, and what to emphasize and help grow. When you stay mindful and act with your values and goals in mind, you become a powerful mediator of children's learning. Rather than abandoning your ideals or philosophy on behalf of mandated standards, you can take charge of the role you play in furthering meaningful experiences for children.

### Kristin Sees the Light

As you read the following story about Kristin and the children in her Head Start class, can you see how she is claiming her power to provide a meaningful approach to meeting outcomes?

*Weeks of constant rain have kept Kristin and her group indoors where she has been busy observing and filling out required paperwork for the children's individual assessments. Late one afternoon, at the end of week three, the rain finally stops and a small sliver of blue sky and sunlight appears through the clouds. The children alert Kristin to the light peeking through the windows and she agrees it is time they all head outside. The children eagerly put their materials away and joyously spill onto the playground they haven't seen in days. Kristin takes her clipboard and camera with her and begins to document the numerous play themes that spread out over the yard.*

Denise Louie Head Start

Denise Louie Head Start

*One group of girls is making sand birthday cakes with woodchip candles. Proudly counting their work, they declare, "We have eight cakes!" They invent an elaborate, collaborative system of sending buckets down the slide where a girl fills the bucket with sand to make a cake, then hands it off to another child to deliver to those waiting at the top of the slide. There the cake receives a candle and is placed on the birthday display. On the other side of the yard more counting is the focus as children are collecting worms. "Six worms!" a boy with limited English exclaims excitedly. One child mentions she has recently seen a snake, and a lively discussion ensues about snakes. "They stick their tongues out." "No, they go 'sssssssssss.'" "No, they wiggle back and forth!" The children teach each other English, Chinese, and Spanish as they share the words for "snake" and "worm" from their home languages. By the doorway to the building, in a trench dug to ease the flooding, more children are digging out water with shovels and pouring it into bowls. One of the children names the muddy water "chocolate." Now the game takes a different turn as the children scoop up chocolate ice cream. The play grows again as bowls of ice cream are offered for sale to friends in other parts of the playground. Much imaginary money changes hands as the eager children form a line to buy the pretend ice cream.*

### Listen to Kristin

"These past few weeks of constant rain and our agency's emphasis on performance standards and paperwork have really dampened my enthusiasm for this work. But something happened for me today when we were finally able to go outside to play. At first I couldn't stop my worries about all the standards, the learning domains, the checklists, the assessments, the curriculum forms, and the administration looking at me with stern eyebrows wanting an explanation of how I will accomplish all of this. Right in front of my eyes, as I watched the children, I could see every area of learning represented on that playground today. It reminded me of my faith and beliefs that say these children are a precious gift. I am not here for the administration, for the government, or for the politicians. I am here to experience the joy of these children, and to provide a place where they are allowed to be who they are. These are wonderful people who couldn't care less about muddy pants or raindrops on their noses, who aren't for a second thinking about 'school readiness.' They are simply being, and I am reminded I need to stop at times to simply be. Sure, I will take pictures and share them with the children. We will pore over them and decipher ways to build upon their interests and learning. But today I reminded myself that these experiences are valuable for what they are: spontaneous moments of wonder, discovery, and delight. They are an opportunity for me to really see."

### Reflect

You can see in the details of Kristin's story any number of possible learning outcomes imbedded in the children's play. As Kristin says, "right in front of my eyes" the children were counting, learning language from each other, exploring scientific concepts, solving problems, and inventing new ideas and actions. By closely observing the details of the children's play, Kristin had opportunities to assess and plan for math, language, science, multicultural education, and social skills. But an equally important aspect of this story is Kristin's reflection on her own attitudes and feelings. Rather than succumbing to discouragement, she sees her power to follow the children's interests and reframe the requirements to include the joy and complexity of these unfolding activities. Kristin is bringing herself, her beliefs, values, and passions to her work, which fortifies her to claim her power and take responsibility on behalf of more meaningful experiences for the children and herself. ■

## •PRINCIPLE•
## Think Through Your Actions

Young children spend almost every waking moment working to make sense of the world around them. Endeavors like the ones in Kristin's group happen all the time. But too often teachers are distracted, focused on requirements, problems, or the schedule, and thus miss the incredible opportunities germinating around them. To take advantage of these openings for deeper joy and learning, you must stop to examine influences on your thinking and consider possibilities for the actions you might take. The daily work of early childhood teachers is complex with ever-changing dynamics related to program parameters and the group of children and families, as well as your own views and background. Within this context you move about your day reacting and responding to what is unfolding around you. Responsive curriculum requires slowing down, making conscious decisions, and staying alert to what unfolds. To be purposeful, you must be aware of the various influences on your actions.

## Know Your Teacher Scripts

In her book *Developmentally Appropriate Practice in "Real Life,"* Carol Anne Wien (1995) suggests that it is "teacher scripts," learned from your own experiences with teachers, that determine your actions with children. Because you are making multiple decisions, thinking on your feet all day long, you often respond from these "scripts" or unexamined views of what teachers do. The following is a list of typical teacher scripts:

- Make sure children follow the rules and routines and adhere to the time schedule.
- Intercede when children are in conflicts or are displaying risky behaviors.
- Plan learning activities to keep children busy and meet standards.
- Help children stay on task and complete a project.

Certainly, most of these behaviors are a necessary part of working with children, particularly a group of children. There are rules, requirements, routines, and activities to complete. Yet limiting yourself to the role of "preschool police," which many of these behaviors suggest, is unpleasant for both teachers and children. Lilian Katz (1998) analyzes teacher behaviors in her comparison of the schools of Reggio Emilia with those in the United States:

> *The content of the relationships between our [U.S.] teachers and their pupils tends to be dominated by information about the child's conduct and level of performance. Thus, it seems that the content of relationships between teachers and children in our early childhood settings, when not focused on mundane routines, is about the children themselves. In contrast, my impression of Reggio Emilia practices is that to a large extent the content of teacher-child relationships is focused on the work itself, rather than mainly on routines or the children's performances on academic tasks. . . . Adults' and children's minds meet on matters of interest to both of them.*
>
> *A program has intellectual vitality if the teacher's individual and group interactions are mainly about what the children are learning, planning, and thinking about, plus their interest in each other, and only minimally about the rules and routines*

This seemingly simple observation from Katz has many challenges for considering your role as a teacher. Rather than emphasizing curriculum activities and routines, your actions could be guided by your own curiosity and an eagerness to meet up with the children's hearts and minds. You could acknowledge what you are seeing and offer ongoing ways to explore their interests and likely connections with other children. When you see your role as learning alongside the children, your actions are very different than when you're thinking of yourself as a conveyer of information, mediator of conflicts, or driver of standards. You draw upon responses that include the behaviors of a stage manager, a coach, and a news analyst and broadcaster.

## Know Your Professional Influences

Many commercial early childhood resources reinforce a limited teacher script approach to teaching. Workshops may offer techniques and catchy acronyms, but these don't help teachers examine the dynamic process of teaching and learning with children. Catalogs promise their packaged activities will help teachers efficiently reach desired outcomes. However, using them with children reveals fleeting satisfaction when they lack context and involve no real investment on the part of the children or teacher. Clearly, professional resources are important to your work, and new ideas and activities keep you fresh and growing; but you should be diligent in choosing resources that challenge you to fully examine the complexities of your work.

### Know Your Theoretical Influences

In addition to teacher scripts and commercial materials influencing your work, your images of children, conscious or unconscious, control the actions you take. This reminder is one of the greatest contributions from the educators of Reggio Emilia (Gandini and Edwards 2001). Read the words of Carlina Rinaldi:

> *Each of us has his or her own image of the child which is reflected in the expectation that we have when we look at a child. Some focus on what children are, what they have, and what they can do, while others, unfortunately, focus on what children are not, do not have, and what they are not able to do. Some focus more on their needs than on their power and capacity. As a result you have positive or negative expectations, and construct a context that values or limits the qualities and potential that you attribute to children.*

Before exposure to the educators of Reggio, other European child development theorists strongly shaped definitions of best practices in the United States. Perhaps their ideas influence your thinking as well. Drawing on the theories of Jean Piaget and Maria Montessori, our professional organization, the National Association for the Education of Young Children (NAEYC), initially imbued the definition of developmentally appropriate practice with a belief that young children learn best through self-initiated play and discovery, and teachers should foster independence. Wanting to protect children from authoritarian teaching and push-down academics, many teachers have embraced these beliefs and interpreted them to mean that teachers should take a "hands-off" approach. Ironically, these same teachers readily intervene and take action to guide children's behavior, with the value of protecting individual rights and learning to take turns. Unfortunately, this protective stance and emphasis on individualism is not only culturally biased, but obscures the actual competencies that children have. In the name of developmentally appropriate curriculum, teachers could easily be "dumbing children down" (Gatto 2002).

Teachers may think they are protecting children, but perhaps they are working with a diminished view of children's capabilities. In addition, they may well be marginalizing other cultural perspectives that value interdependence over independence and learning in groups over individual efforts and achievements. Many communities of color in the United States have experienced this as another form of racism. Current experts have urged teachers to re-examine the central role of the social context for children's learning, and the important role of adults in scaffolding that process. In fact, this discussion typically draws on the writing of Lev Vygotsky (a white man from Russia) instead of referring to research by U.S. educators of color such as Lisa Delpit, Gloria Ladson-Billings, Lily Wong Fillmore, or Cecilia Alvarado. As you examine the possible theories that guide your work with children, take care to recognize the historical and cultural context from which they sprang.

#### Chew on This

*Jonathan started working in the toddler room while taking early childhood classes at the community college. After seeing the lead teacher, Miss Aurora, feeding one of the children, he felt concerned and decided to talk with her during naptime. "Miss Aurora, why were you feeding Ming Gong? He's too young to be using a fork and spoon. He would be much more independent if you just let him eat with his fingers. I couldn't understand what you were saying to him, but I hope you weren't being critical and lowering his self-esteem." Miss Aurora took a deep breath and patiently tried to explain. "Ming Gong's parents want him to learn to be careful with food and not waste anything. I was showing him a good way to eat and talking him through it in his home language. Independence is not the focus for Ming Gong's parents. Being careful with food and eating the American way is what they're concerned about. What I'm concerned about is demonstrating that I understand and respect their wishes."*

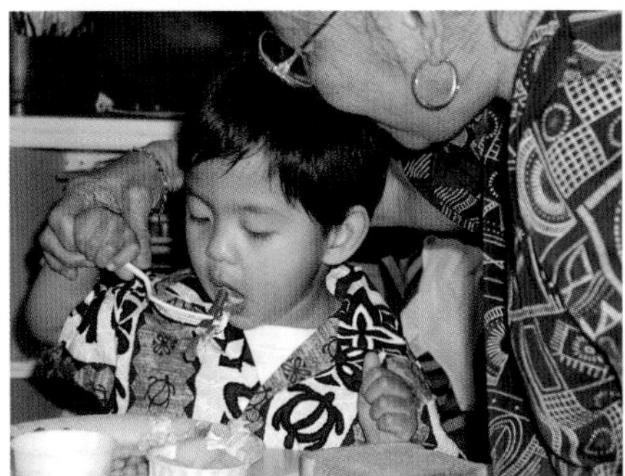

Martin Luther King Jr. Day Home Center

Though they may differ in their definitions of best practices, most child development experts agree that children benefit from a structure and adult actions to support their learning. Sometimes these actions are obvious, and at other times less apparent. For instance, when teachers see the documentation stories of the remarkable in-depth investigations of children in programs inspired by the Reggio approach, they are often left wondering how a teacher or activity got from one point to the other. What did she see, say, or do to make this happen? It's not clear what role the teachers played to bring out these ideas in children and enabled them to focus and work together so productively. It's tempting to think, "my kids could never do that," or "I would never be able to pull that off with all the other things I have to get done," because these stories omit many details of the invisible structure and implied teacher actions that make their work so significant. It is often hard to translate how this work could support and deepen learning related to standards. This is one of the primary purposes of *Learning Together with Young Children* and the curriculum framework, to help you think through your actions to support deeper learning experiences, especially when you have others prescribing what your curriculum should be.

## Helping Hands

Here's a description of an ordinary moment in a toddler room and three teacher responses to it. Read the story and then notice how each teacher has a different disposition to what is unfolding.

*Sixteen-month-old Savannah is playing at the sensory table when her child care teacher begins moving around the room cleaning up the toys and singing, "Clean up, clean up, it's time to get ready for outside." The teacher has twelve kids to get ready for her group's turn on the playground. She approaches the sensory table where Savannah is diligently working to lift the lid to close up the table. Savannah is having difficulty because her body is in the way. Another child, Kyle, is standing close by watching Savannah's efforts. As you read each teacher's story, consider what influences might be shaping the teacher's response.*

Mountain School

### *Maya's Response*

Teacher Maya doesn't acknowledge Savannah's attempt to help with cleanup. She's worried about how much time it will take to get the rest of the group ready and she wants to make sure they get enough time outdoors. She takes Savannah's hand and leads her away, closing the sensory table herself. Maya says to Savannah, "It's time to go outside, let's get you ready. You too, Kyle, I'll help you put sunscreen on."

### *Listen to Maya*

"It always takes so long to get the kids ready for the next activity. Today we almost missed our scheduled outdoor time because the children wanted to keep playing and they dawdle so much during our transitions."

### *Reflect*

Maya seems to be influenced by the clock and schedule in this moment, rather than considering Savannah's point of view and the learning possibilities inherent in this situation. Maya may be working from an unexamined teacher script of helping children follow the routines and get to the next planned activity. Playing outdoors is an enjoyable and important activity for the children, and Maya may have wanted to make sure the children had enough time for that. Teachers regularly have to make choices about how to use their time. But Maya could have verbally acknowledged Savannah's work, even while making a conscious decision to move her along in order to keep to the schedule. She might have said something like, "Wow, you're working so hard to close that table. Thank you. Now let's act ready to go out." If Maya verbally recognized Savannah's attempt to close the table and made a mental note to involve her in lending a hand in the future, their relationship would be strengthened, and Savannah's hard work would be acknowledged and supported.

### *Tanya's Response*

Tanya thinks to herself, "How cute, Savannah wants to help with cleanup, but she really doesn't know how to close the lid." She moves closer to help. "Here Savannah, let me do that for you." She lifts the lid herself as Savannah and Kyle watch.

### *Listen to Tanya*

"I got such a kick out of Savannah trying to close the sensory table today. She is such a cute little thing. I was worried as I watched her struggle with that lid and I thought she might pinch her fingers. I made sure I helped her before she got mad and frustrated or, even worse, hurt if the lid fell on her."

### *Reflect*

Tanya finds Savannah's attempts endearing, but doesn't seem to take her seriously, perhaps because she is influenced by her view of the limitations of Savannah's age and lack of spatial awareness. Rather than seeing Savannah as competent and able to do this task, she worries about Savannah getting hurt or frustrated and feeling bad about herself. Yet, if Tanya observed more closely, she would understand that Savannah sees herself as capable; this is why she attempts the task and keeps at it. If Tanya brought this more competent image of children to this moment, she might act differently. She would see how Savannah would continue to see herself as capable if her efforts were encouraged, and come to see herself as a contributing member of this community.

### *Phillip's Response*

Phillip closely watches as Savannah uses great focus and determination to get the lid on the table. He gives her a few minutes to work on her own and then decides she might benefit from some coaching. Phillip moves to her side and says, "Savannah, you are working hard to lift the lid of the table so you can close it. May I show you what I know about how to make this job easier?" Noticing that Kyle has been watching all along, Phillip invites him to learn too. "Kyle, you might be interested in this too. See? I stand at the side so my body doesn't get in the way. Then I use my strong muscles to lift up the lid and it turns over as I close it." Phillip demonstrates as he describes his actions. He invites Savannah to try, and because the lid is a little heavy for Savannah, he suggests they all work together. "Kyle, you stand over on that side with Savannah and I'll stand on this side. Here we go!" They lift the lid together and the job is done.

### *Listen to Phillip*

"I was so impressed with Savannah's determination to help with cleanup today. I see this all the time with my group. They know about our room and routine and they want to help. I try to take their efforts seriously and use every opportunity I can to teach them to do things. It may take a while, but eventually they really do learn. I want to encourage their strong desire to be contributing members of this group. Most people would never believe how amazing these very young children can be."

### *Reflect*

What could be influencing Phillip's decision to stop and take time for this moment with Savannah and Kyle? Phillip has identified the role he wants to play in children's learning—he looks beyond the schedule and planned curriculum activities to the value of this moment. He knows the demands of the group and the need to have a consistent routine, but also believes that moments like this are also part of the curriculum, holding possibility for meaningful learning. Because he sees these children as competent, he takes the time to coach them and, in turn, helps them live into their competence.

Obviously, teachers cannot always take advantage of every possible learning moment with each child. You must balance what individuals deserve with the needs of the group as a whole and the value of consistent routines. However, even when there isn't time to engage as fully as Phillip did in the example above, you can avoid responding from unexamined teacher scripts and interacting with children primarily about rules and routines. You can notice and acknowledge their efforts and interests, and you can see them as competent and inquisitive. As you make choices about how to use your time, you can think through the influences on your actions and decide to make more purposeful decisions. Acknowledging the unfolding moments in your group invariably creates more possibilities. These instances are not events in between your teaching, but rather, central to furthering your relationships with children and the teaching and learning process. Once you begin to approach your work this way, you will see the abundant opportunities for strengthening relationships and learning all around you. The challenge then becomes choosing what interests to follow and expanding your repertoire so that unfolding moments grow into meaningful curriculum. ■

### Your Turn

Choose a morning to keep track of what unfolds as you work with the children. If possible, do this with a coworker. Notice the flow of the day, what the children were involved with in general, and some specific times when you interacted with individuals or directed the group. At the end of the morning, write down an account of what occurred in enough detail to jog your memory as you reflect on the following questions.

- What impact did your curriculum activities and daily schedule have on your actions and decisions?
- When might you have followed the children's ideas and interests, but didn't?
- How did your image of children and their capabilities influence your actions?
- What other factors (environment; family/culture/community; media; biases; mandates/policies) might be influencing you and this situation?
- When did you claim your power on behalf of more meaningful experiences for you and the children?

## •PRINCIPLE• Cultivate a Mindset of Receptivity

*As teachers, we need to create a climate of receptivity, which does not mean merely the willingness to listen carefully or patiently. It has to do with quieting your state of mind as you prepare to listen. It means not pressing on too fast to get to something that you think you "need to get" as the "purpose" or "objective" of the conversation. There's something about silence and not being in a hurry that seem to give a message about receptivity. Children need some reason to believe that what they say will not be heard too clinically, or journalistically, or put to use too rapidly, and that the gift they give us will be taken into hands that will not seize too fast upon their confidence, or grasp too firmly, or attempt to push an idea to completion when it needs to be left open, incomplete, and tentative a while.* —Jonathan Kozol

As Jonathan Kozol suggests, the place to start in our work with children is to stop! Teachers must slow down in order to take in the moment, see what is afoot, and give the situation time to unfold. On the surface, stopping and waiting doesn't look like action, but it is the primary place to begin when supporting in-depth work with children. The first action we take is within ourselves. We make it our practice to observe closely for the details of what is happening. Silence and not being in a hurry tell children that we are open to being changed by their ideas. This is the basis of true conversation and learning. As we stop to look and listen, we are absorbed in our own learning process to understand the children, as well as reflect on our interpretations of the situation. When we stop and wait, we communicate respect to the children and honor the possibilities inherent in ordinary moments. Paying closer attention to these moments enhances our delight in the children as we gain a profound respect for their insights and abilities. We come to trust them as partners in the teaching and learning process and love the work we are doing. Working in this way requires cultivating a very different mindset. You come to see yourself as a researcher, intellectually engaged in what is emerging. You are able to live with uncertainty and put your head together with the children, trusting that your shared pursuits will be meaningful and useful.

### Ramp It Up

As you read the next story, notice the details of teacher Cindy's receptivity to the big noise and action of the children in the block area, and what unfolds as a result.

*A group of children in Cindy's child care room have been passionate about building ramps with blocks. When the construction is complete, the children zoom small cars down the ramps, causing them to fly all over the room. Their work is loud and boisterous and involves big body action as they try to get the cars to fly as fast as they can. The flying cars crash against the walls, windows, and sometimes get very close to other children. Cindy redirects the children's actions, warning them of the dangers of the flying cars. "Keep the cars on the ramps to get them to go fast. It's too dangerous to throw them like that." Rather than taking the cars away and stopping the play, Cindy responds to their quest for speed and brings them some golf balls. "I have a new idea. These golf balls can go really fast. I'll let you use them, if you roll them. If you throw them, they will be really unsafe and I'll have to put them away." The children eagerly begin to build ramps and live up to Cindy's guidelines about rolling them. And indeed, the children are able to get the golf balls to race down the ramps at exciting speeds, without throwing them.*

Burlington Little School

Burlington Little School

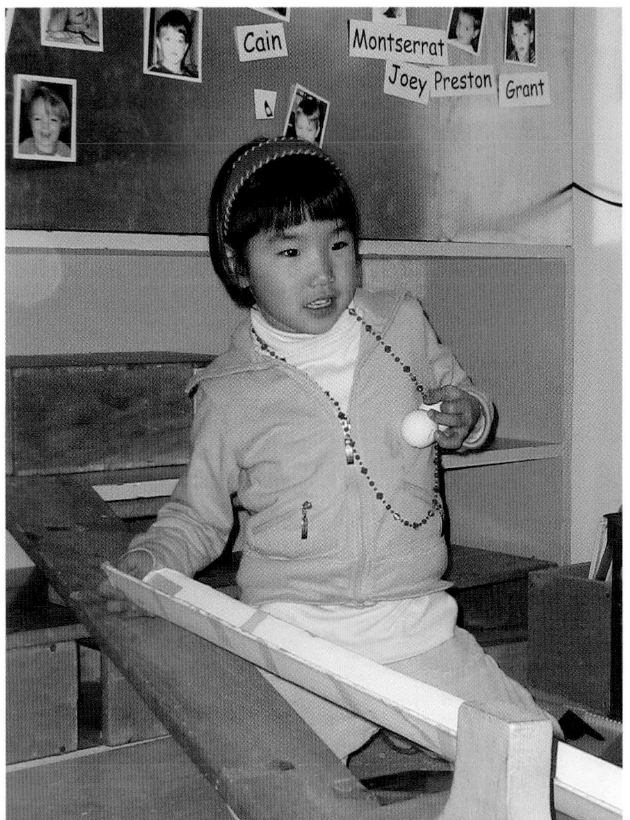


## Reflection & Action

***What in my background and values is influencing my response to this situation and why?***

*

***How are the environment and materials impacting what's unfolding and what changes could be made?***

*

***How are teacher actions impacting this situation?***

### *Listen to Cindy*

"As I observed and listened to the children, I kept asking myself these questions: 'What are they trying to accomplish here? What is so thrilling?' I realized that they weren't just being loud and crazy, but instead trying to get the cars to go as fast as they could. I think I was brave to decide to offer them golf balls to help them accomplish their speedy goals. I thought it would motivate them to pay more attention and use some control as they worked. I was thrilled that the children took this work seriously and followed the guidelines I set out. It was exciting to watch them learn about the physics of speed. I'm so glad I followed my hunch that speed was their real interest, not random, wild play."

### *Reflect*

Many teachers would jump right in and stop the noise and the potential danger of this play. But Cindy's mindset of receptivity enabled her to wait before jumping in with her adult agenda. She allowed the children's interest to unfold and grow and then used their passion to enable them to go deeper with their learning. Rather than inadvertently learning about the physics of gravity and speed through their random play, or stopping it altogether, the children's exploration became more purposeful with Cindy's challenge. ■

### No Ordinary Moment

*No child was meant to be ordinary and you can see it in them and they know it too. But then the times get to them and they wear out their brains learning what folks expect and then spend their strength trying to rise over those same folks. —Annie Dillard*

*Study the look on Hannah's face and how it symbolizes this quote by Annie Dillard. Hannah sees herself and this moment in her life as extraordinary. Her own image reflected back to her in the mirror brings her absolute pleasure. When was the last time you looked at yourself in the mirror this way? Can you remember why you stopped? If we still looked at ourselves and experienced life in this way, we might see others similarly, and that could transform how we live together on the earth. We can choose to notice and learn from young children's point of view, or sadly, as Dillard suggests, be one of "those folks" that children must "rise over."*

Martin Luther King Jr. Day Home Center

## •PRINCIPLE•
## Seek the Child's Point of View

When you watch young children closely you will notice their intense focus and determination, curiosity and delight. Whether happy or sad, angry or tired, young children bring to every encounter an instinctive optimism and an eagerness for experience. Their natural drive ensures that during the early childhood years, their brains will develop faster than at any other time. The estimated number of brain connections that develop is a staggering 250,000 per minute. During this time there are no ordinary moments!

The child's perspective can inform your decisions and actions and is critical to understand if you are to engage children in a deeper teaching and learning process, and at the same time, enhance your own experience. It takes practice to look and listen attentively. You must suspend for a moment any agenda you might have for what the children should be doing. Instead, put yourself in their shoes to understand the experience from their point of view. Spiritual masters around the world know that the practice of being present in the moment can bring peace and joy to people's lives as well as anchor it with profound meaning.

### Fabrics Galore

*When Carline, an infant caregiver, saw a beautiful pile of colorful fabric, she immediately knew her group of seven- to eighteen-month-old children would love it. She decided to play with the fabric herself to learn about it, and think about what the children might do with it. She wrapped herself in the fluffy cloth and waved it in the air. She thought about how the children would love to dance with the fabric, and play hide and seek. She tried to imagine what her little ones might experience and think about. "If I cover my head, will I be able to see you? Can I find you? Will you be able to see me? When I wrap myself in the fabric, I'll feel safe and comfy." She knew the children would be drawn by a sense of wonder as they explored the textures of the fabric. "Is it soft or hard? How does it smell? Can I eat it?" With these thoughts in mind, Carline couldn't wait to see what her group of children would do with the giant rainbow of colors.*

Burlington Little School

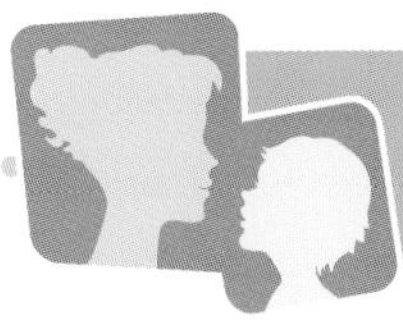

## A Bounty of Bracelets

In the following story, discover with Deb how attentive her one-year-old children are when she stops to consider their point of view.

*Deb offered a collection of colorful, sparkly bracelets packed in clear plastic containers with lids. The children examined the bracelets closely, noticing how they sparkled in the light. They were fully engaged in putting the bracelet rings back into the cups and fitting the lids on. Oscar immediately knew what the rings were for, so he spent a very long time putting every bracelet he could get ahold of onto his arm. When Deb pointed this out, the other children seemed to understand the importance of this work for him and let him have more bracelets so he could complete the task. At one point, Kiran began purposefully throwing the rings onto the ground in front of him and watching them as they spun around and around like a top until they slowly lost momentum and wobbled to a stop. When Deb noticed what Kiran was doing, she called the other children's attention to his idea. This captured their interest, and along with Deb, the children all began playing this new game of throwing bracelets and watching them spin.*

Martin Luther King Jr. Day Home Center

Martin Luther King Jr. Day Home Center

Martin Luther King Jr. Day Home Center

### Listen to Deb

"I immediately knew from my previous observations of the children that they would love the plastic, sparkly bracelets I found at the Dollar Store. As I observed them with these materials, they were absorbed in using them just as I predicted. They focused intently on putting the plastic rings back into the cups and carefully putting the lids on. I'm always so intrigued by how seriously toddlers take this kind of work. When

I saw Kiran deliberately throwing the bracelets, my initial reaction was to jump in and stop this behavior. One of my ongoing goals is to help the children see how to care for our materials. Fortunately, before I jumped in, I stopped to look at the situation from his perspective. What I realized is that Kiran had discovered that if he threw the rings just the right way, they would spin around and around like a top and then slow down and stop. I was thrilled to learn this new way to explore the bracelets, and called the other children's attention to Kiran's idea. I'm so glad I stopped to see Kiran's point of view. I was just amazed that he figured this out; he's only fourteen months old! His discovery is now a part of the learning games we play with the bracelets, and the children are getting quite good at controlling this small aspect of the science of physics."

### Reflect

Deb stops to observe the details and conscientiously works to consider Kiran's point of view. Her analysis of the situation allows her to respond in a way that furthers his study of the spinning bracelets. She sees the possibilities for collaboration, as she invites the children to learn from Kiran. As you reflect more on this story, we invite you to get curious about other details you've read. How do these very young children come to respect and learn from each other when verbal language is so limited? Why do toddlers find exploring containers with lids so fascinating? Do they feel the satisfaction of conquering the challenge of a tricky puzzle when they are successful in putting on the lid? Perhaps they are soothed by the security of knowing that some things in the universe can be put together just right. Getting curious about the children's point of view will keep you intellectually engaged in your work. ■

## Taste Tests

How often do you jump to conclusions about what is happening with your group? In the following story, notice how Neda realizes her initial impressions of a child's communication were missing the child's point of view.

*Neda offered her toddlers an array of fresh fruits and plastic knives for cutting. For each fruit they cut open, Neda pointed out what was inside, sharing in the children's delight and surprise of each unique fruit. Along with discovering the fruits' internal beauty, the children eagerly began taste testing. As Anna tasted the lime slice, her face puckered and she called out a disgruntled sound. Neda acknowledged, "Yes, limes have a sour taste, don't they?" Anna wasn't satisfied with this response. She kept pointing to the lime with an animated face of concern. "You don't have to taste that one," Neda offered. Still dissatisfied with the response, Anna went to the sink, climbed the step stool, turned on the water, and proceeded to wash off the lime. As Neda observed these actions she exclaimed with surprise, "Oh Anna, now I think I understand. Are you trying to wash that sour taste off the lime? Try tasting it again. Did washing work?"*

Urban Village Two, Neighborhood House Head Start

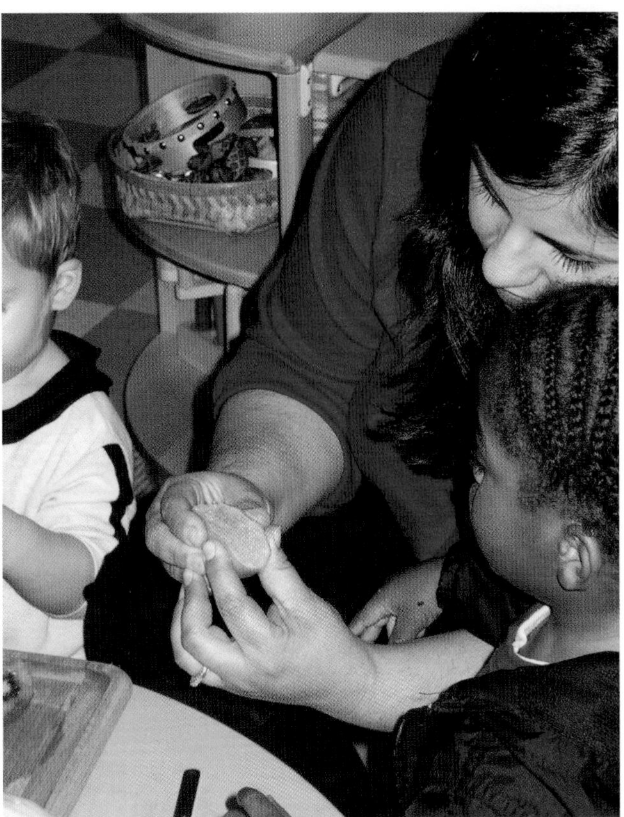

Urban Village Two, Neighborhood House Head Start

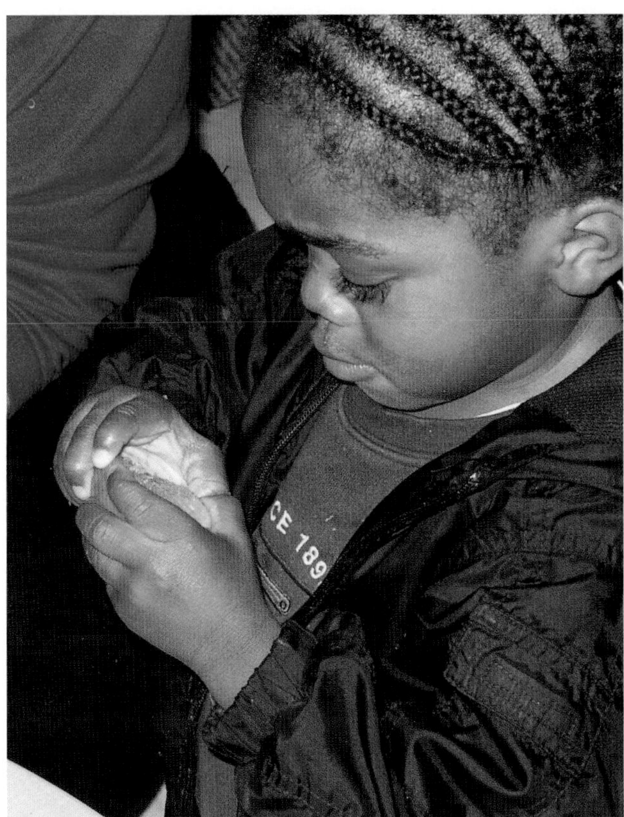


Urban Village Two, Neighborhood House Head Start

### *Listen to Neda*

"I love to plan activities for my toddlers that offer them new experiences. Watching their amazement at what they found inside each fruit helped me to see the fruit in a new way. Through their eyes I noticed the interesting shapes and textures and the gorgeous array of colors. The children showed me how to immerse myself in the fragrance and savor every bite. I had a delightful surprise when Anna came across the taste of the lime. She kept making faces and I tried to tell her she didn't need to eat it. When she went on a mission to wash off the lime I finally saw her idea. It was a shock to her that I would give her something that tasted so nasty and a revelation to me that such a young child could be such an independent, competent thinker."

### *Reflect*

Because Neda's approach to this activity was to observe for the children's perspectives, she was looking for the details that showed their thinking. This mindset allowed her to consider Anna's theory: that her teacher wouldn't have given her something that tasted bad, so the lime must have something on it that needed to be washed off. Rather than trying to "teach" her about the fruit, Neda invites further investigation of Anna's theory when she offered her the logical next step, to test out her theory by tasting the lime again. This story is a powerful reminder that even very young children are theorymakers, working to understand and communicate their ideas. Neda's thoughts and actions are a good model of how to look beyond our adult viewpoints to really seek those of the children. ■

**Your Turn**

When you seek the child's perspective before responding, rather than just focusing on behavior, you choose an action that will expand the learning experience. To get an insight into what the children might find interesting in a material, try exploring materials before offering them. Choose a material you think the children will find engaging. Think about your group and make some guesses about what they might be drawn to and what they might notice. Play with the materials yourself and notice your own discoveries. These explorations will alert you to language you can offer the children as they use the material. As you prepare yourself with these explorations, you get ideas about possibilities that might unfold, but you stay open to surprises that you didn't anticipate. Offer the materials to the children and then use the reflection and action questions list on page 21 to observe, make meaning, and respond to their points of view.

### •PRINCIPLE•
## Notice the Details to Discover More Possibilities

Teachers can uncover the children's point of view by noticing the many small things that are occurring within the group. Children look closely at details adults take for granted. Adults are quick to assign a meaning and a label to what they see. When you just summarize or make generalities from your observations, you don't have much information to use for making meaning. To capture the specific details of what you hear and see, a clipboard and pen, a sketch, a tape recorder, or a camera are tools to help you. Your role is to highlight the details of the unfolding moments, not only for yourself, but for the children.

## Sand Scientists

As you read the following story, ask yourself what might have emerged if the teacher had noticed the details of what the children were doing. What guesses do you have about children's theories and understanding based on the details in the story?

*In a program designed for children identified with special needs, two four-year-old boys played near each other in the sand. Hector seemed to be on a mission to fill a plastic plate with sand. Over and over again, he piled the sand on top of the plate and then used the back of his shovel to slap the sand and make it flat and even with the rim of the plate. He used significant force as he pounded the sand with the shovel. At one point, he moved near Sam who was playing in the sand. Hector watched Sam for a few minutes, noticing that he was also working to flatten the sand. However, instead of using a shovel, Sam used a plate and in a single motion, flattened his sand mound. Hector waited until Sam put the plate down, picked it up, and, with obvious satisfaction, copied Sam's method. Sam began to whine and complain, saying, "He took my plate." Teacher Julia moved in quickly and made Hector give the plate back to Sam, suggesting that he wait his turn. The conflict was settled and Hector was redirected to another area to play.*

**Reflection & Action**

***What details stand out that I can make visible for further consideration?***

*

***What in my background and values is influencing my response to this situation and why?***

*

***What theoretical perspectives and child development principles could inform my understandings and actions?***

Desert School

Desert School

Desert School

### *Listen to Julia*

"Sam and Hector got into it again in the sandbox today. I'm glad I was nearby to help them figure it out so their disagreement didn't get out of hand like it often does."

### *Reflect*

Julia didn't see any of the details that could have led her to respond differently. Let's take a closer look at the details and the missed opportunities in this situation. Can you see Hector's purposeful efforts as he explored the properties of the sand and invented tools to accomplish his ideas? He learned from his observation of Sam, and successfully applied this new learning for his own purpose. Seeing these details could enhance the image of Hector as a competent learner, rather than only viewing him as a child with special needs. The teacher also missed an opportunity to point out Sam's good idea and how Hector learned from him. Rather than reinforcing Sam's complaining, she might have suggested he practice being a coach, to show and describe his ideas to Hector. Imagine how encouraged the boys' parents would be if the teacher shared the details of their skillful ideas and actions in this situation. Instead, these opportunities were lost as the teacher moved in to resolve the conflict. ■

Obviously, the work of a teacher is complex and you don't often have time to sit back and look for all the details. But this story is a reminder that you need to plan for regular opportunities to capture details. Doing this will help you see that each situation has multiple perspectives and possibilities for interpretation and help you to mediate your responses and actions with this in mind.

## •PRINCIPLE•
## Share Conversations Following the Children's Lead

Fortified with the children's perspectives and careful observations of their work, teachers are ready to share conversations with children. Children are "doers" who don't often reflect on their activities. Talking about what you see points children's attention to the properties and characteristics of materials, people, and actions that they may not have noticed, or do not yet have the words to describe. Describing to the children what you see unfolding offers the possibility that they will go further with their investigation and encourage their thinking to move to a new level. These are not just casual conversations; instead they require teachers to practice using the details and children's viewpoint in conversation. The difference between these kinds of interactions and those that interrupt children's pursuits is that the focus stays with the child's current actions or interests, extending rather than shifting. As you follow the children's lead, you can help them connect their interests to the larger world, extend their vocabulary and their receptive and expressive language skills. You can remind them how what they are now doing connects with something they have done previously with you or with their family. You can also advance the learning process if you authentically engage with children around your own life experience, sharing your ideas and viewpoints on their interests.

Authentic conversations that follow the children's lead look very different than teaching techniques lacking a reciprocal process. You might view it as the dance of teaching and learning with children. It is a complex set of rhythms and turns, requiring sustained attention and sturdy shoes, but the added significance and pleasure in your work is well worth the effort.

## Dough Dances

As you study the following simple conversation between Janie and Tomas, picture the warm body language between them and the ease with which Janie gives value to his work. Her words are limited, but one action builds on another, and the connections Janie is making are layered with meaning for both of them.

Sedro Woolley Head Start

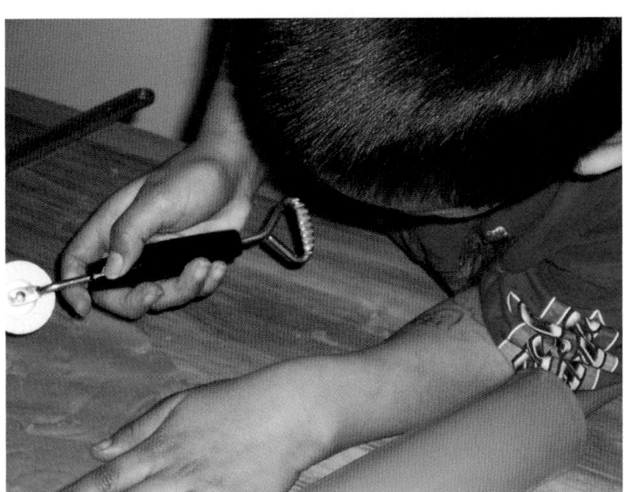

Sedro Woolley Head Start

*Janie is sitting at the playdough table next to four-year-old Tomas in her Head Start classroom. The other children have gone off to play elsewhere, while Tomas diligently continues using a crimping tool along the edge of his playdough hearts.*

*Tomas: "After I do all of these cookies, I'm going to bake them."*

*Janie lights up as she looks at his work: "You have done a lot of work here. I see marks all around the edges of each heart."*

*Tomas too lights up: "I'm going to show you how to do it."*

*Janie: "Okay, show me."*

*Tomas demonstrates how to carefully make marks around the edge of the dough with the crimping tool. He seems to relish the role of teaching as he points to the hearts and says: "You do the small ones and I'll do the big ones. You have to follow the lines all around."*

*Janie leans in, showing she takes his instructions seriously. "Okay, I followed the lines. Now what do I do with them?"*

*His interest seems piqued and Tomas decides what to offer next. "I have to take the side off." He cuts an edge off one of the hearts and leans in to examine what he has done. "I made a medium size."*

*Janie looks curious about his repeated reference to size and adds an additional thought. She asks, "How do I know which are the medium? Do we have to measure?"*

*Tomas: "You do it this way." He takes his crimping tool and makes a line from edge to edge—bottom to the top, and side to side. This divides the dough into quarters.*

*Janie, imitating what he did: "You mean like this?"*

*Tomas: "You have to make it bigger."*

*Janie watches him closely and imitates his actions again.*

*Janie: "I see what you are doing, you made it smoother."*

*Tomas: "Here, let's do this."*

*He works on his own design with the tool. Janie follows his lead and shows him the design she's made on her dough.*

*Tomas: "It looks like a boat."*

*Janie: "Where do you see a boat?"*

*Tomas, pointing: "There is the bottom and those are the sails."*

*Janie: "Oh, I see it now. I didn't have that in mind, but it did come out looking like a boat."*

*Tomas keeps working. He shows his new design. "Look, I made a star."*

*Janie: "Yeah, it looks just like a star. I see the lines and the points." She points to these features as she describes them. They continue enjoying each other's company like this until the call for snacktime.*

### Listen to Janie

"I love to talk with children and hear what they think and have to say. I believe if they can express themselves, they will feel comfortable to speak up and learn from that. I use my own curiosity to talk with them and to notice together: 'What happened?' 'How are we going to solve this?' 'What will we do next time?' It is so much fun to be with children in this way. You never know what will happen or what new discoveries or learning will take place."

### Reflect

It's not unusual for children and teachers to sit together at the playdough table, but the care with which Janie conversed with Tomas is more unusual. She pays close attention to his ideas and actions, naming what she sees, imitating him, asking him for further clarification, and sharing her ideas in response to his. She trusts the direction he takes to be most pertinent for his learning. With her comments, Janie doesn't try to teach Tomas about measuring, but instead provokes him to think through his own ideas. As he does this, he is challenged to build new concepts and vocabulary. Through this experience, Tomas is learning that he has important ideas to express and can make a contribution to the learning of others. This easy exchange fosters Tomas's relationship with Janie. Knowing this task is important to Tomas, she wants to challenge him to recognize the ideas he is pursuing and take them further. Within this trusting relationship he will feel safe to take up any new challenges Janie may offer for his learning. ■

### Tender Tommy

*Oona has recently transitioned from the baby room into the toddler room and Tommy instinctively knows what's needed. He joins Oona at the window, and sharing their two-year-old perspectives they begin to form a friendship.*

*Tommy: "I'm two and a half."*

*Oona: "I'm two."*

*Tommy: "You want to play at my house?" He gently puts a hand on her shoulder.*

*Oona: "My mommy says you can come to my house too."*

Martin Luther King Jr. Day Home Center

## •PRINCIPLE•
## Support Children's Connections with Each Other

Children have a huge capacity for offering support and also for accepting and benefiting from the gifts given by others. Human beings are born with an instinctive drive to reach out and connect with one another. Yet teachers often try to learn as many skills and strategies as you can to manage children's behavior, and then focus on teaching children how to behave and get along. Imagine, instead, seeing children as already possessing the gifts for developing relationships and our role being to help them express this. Children are compelled to connect with one another, and genuinely fascinated with one another's words, ideas, and actions. This presents ripe opportunities for developing in-depth curriculum experiences.

We can turn to the theories of Lev Vygotsky to support an emphasis on relationships as the source of energetic learning processes. This involves making meaning together, rather than acquiring facts. The study of meaning involves children and adults working together to explore ideas and processes in order to come to shared understandings. Approaching learning in this way is dynamic and often spicy, as the group can have disagreements while they learn to work with multiple perspectives and negotiate their differences. Diving in together helps children see that there are many ways of thinking and expressing themselves, and that different perspectives are worthwhile for solving problems and creating new thinking. The group comes to see that learning can be exciting and fun.

Teacher actions can call attention to different points of view among children. You might describe children's words and work to each other, highlighting how their ideas and approaches are similar and different. You can also suggest that the children talk about each other's work, ideas, and assumptions, inviting challenge and negotiation. When a child has accomplished something meaningful and shows pride in her work, request that she show and tell another child how to do it and what she figured out. All of these actions enable children to share what they know and, in the process, better understand it themselves. Many teachers work in multi-lingual, multicultural classrooms where an emphasis on helping the group see and understand each other is especially important.

### Bubble Experts

As you read Sheila's story, notice how her acknowledgement of the details of the children's actions fostered connections among them.

*One day at the water table, the children were immediately drawn to the soapy water and egg beaters, spending a long time trying to figure out how they worked.*

*They paid close attention to the different ways they could turn the handle, watching the blades spin as the handle was turning. As they worked, their teacher, Sheila, restated what each child said and pointed out what they were doing.*

*"Look, Raul is showing us his beater turns really fast."*

*"Lilia says hers is easy to turn."*

*"Many of you see that the blades stick when you turn the handle too fast."*

*Sheila's attention seemed to bring out the children's curiosity so that they kept trading beaters and excitedly telling and showing each other how the beaters worked.*

*"Mine is really fast. Look how I do it."*

*"Mine has this kind of handle. I turn it and the wheels move."*

*After about ten minutes of play and discussions on the workings of the beaters, the children turned their attention to how the beaters changed the soapy water. Roberto put the egg beater directly into the water and turned the handle to see what would happen. He did this a few times and then put the beater into one of the bowls filled with water, and turned the handle again. He showed the other children the bubbles he was making. "Look at this," he exclaimed as he turned the handle and watched the water change into a pile of bubbles in the bowl.*

*Sheila imitated his actions, asking, " Is this how you do it, Roberto?"*

*Many children began to do this as well and repeated the action several times, until Roberto said, "I'm going to make a lot and a lot and a lot and a lot of bubbles—watch." As he worked, Sheila singled out and named the steps he was following to make the bubbles. She asked him if he could slow down and show each thing he did so the other children could know how to do it too. As he demonstrated, Sheila named the steps he was taking for making the bubbles.*

*"Step one, you fill up a bowl with the soapy water.*

*"Step two, you put the beater into the bowl.*

*"Step three, you begin to turn the handle."*

*As Roberto turned the handle, he said, "You have to go really, really fast to make a lot and a lot of bubbles."*

*He squealed with delight as his bubbles began flowing over the side of the bowl.*

*The entire group had their attention on Roberto's steps and were able to follow them because Sheila had put them in the spotlight. The children were so pleased to be able to share this discovery, and Roberto was grinning from ear to ear as the children kept asking him, "Roberto, is this how you do it?"*

Sedro Woolley Head Start

Sedro Woolley Head Start

### Listen to Sheila

"I'm always looking for ways to help the children see themselves as learners and also as teachers for each other. There are a mix of languages spoken by this group: Spanish, Russian, and English. Since I have been pointing out their actions, they are building more connections with each other. They are beginning to thrive on being a group and supporting each other. I love that I can help them."

### Reflect

Sheila uses close observation of the children's actions with the intent of helping them see their own thinking as well as learning from one another. Children don't automatically reflect on their actions, so teacher talk that illuminates children's actions will often provoke self-awareness. Becoming self-aware and thinking about your own actions and ideas is the foundation for learning. Strategies for learning increase as children begin to see each other's ideas and approaches. In fact, children often learn more from one another than from adults, so referring them to one another is a worthwhile approach. Sheila is alert to the importance of this as she works with her group. ■

## Babies with Babies

Cristina works with very young children. How does her scaffolding reveal the remarkable insights these early toddlers have?

*Cristina observed her group of one-year-old children play with the baby dolls and related props in the room. They imitated the actions from their own experiences, such as deliberately trying to fit the bottles in the dolls' mouths and covering the babies with the blankets. Cristina observed them closely so she could imitate their behavior and play alongside them, describing the details of what unfolded among the group.*

*"Kiran is feeding his baby a bottle."*

*"T'Kai is gently putting his baby to bed."*

*"Hannah is rocking her baby to sleep."*

*"My baby is crying, I'm going to give her a hug."*

*The children attended to Cristina's comments and tried out what they saw her and each other do. Oona, one of the older children, extended her play to a sequence of actions as she fed her baby, wrapped it in a cloth, and then rocked it to sleep. She noticed the other children were following her and repeated this play script over and over.*

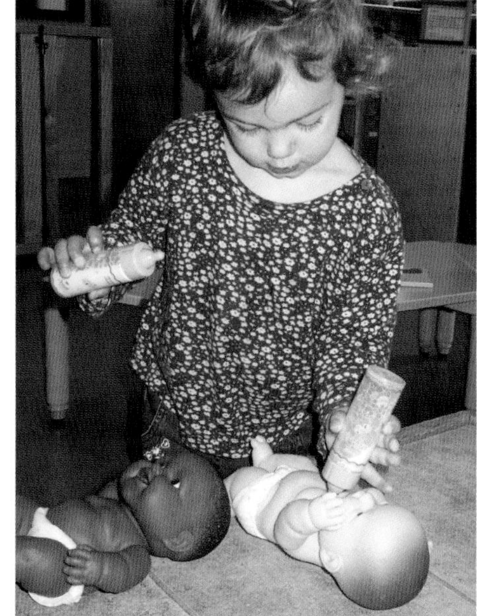

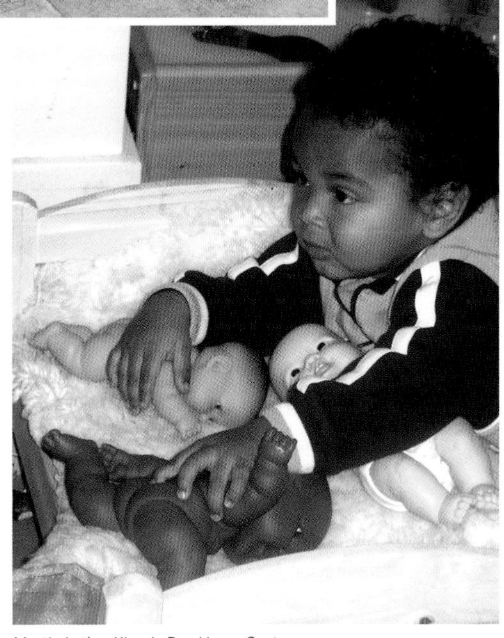

Martin Luther King Jr. Day Home Center

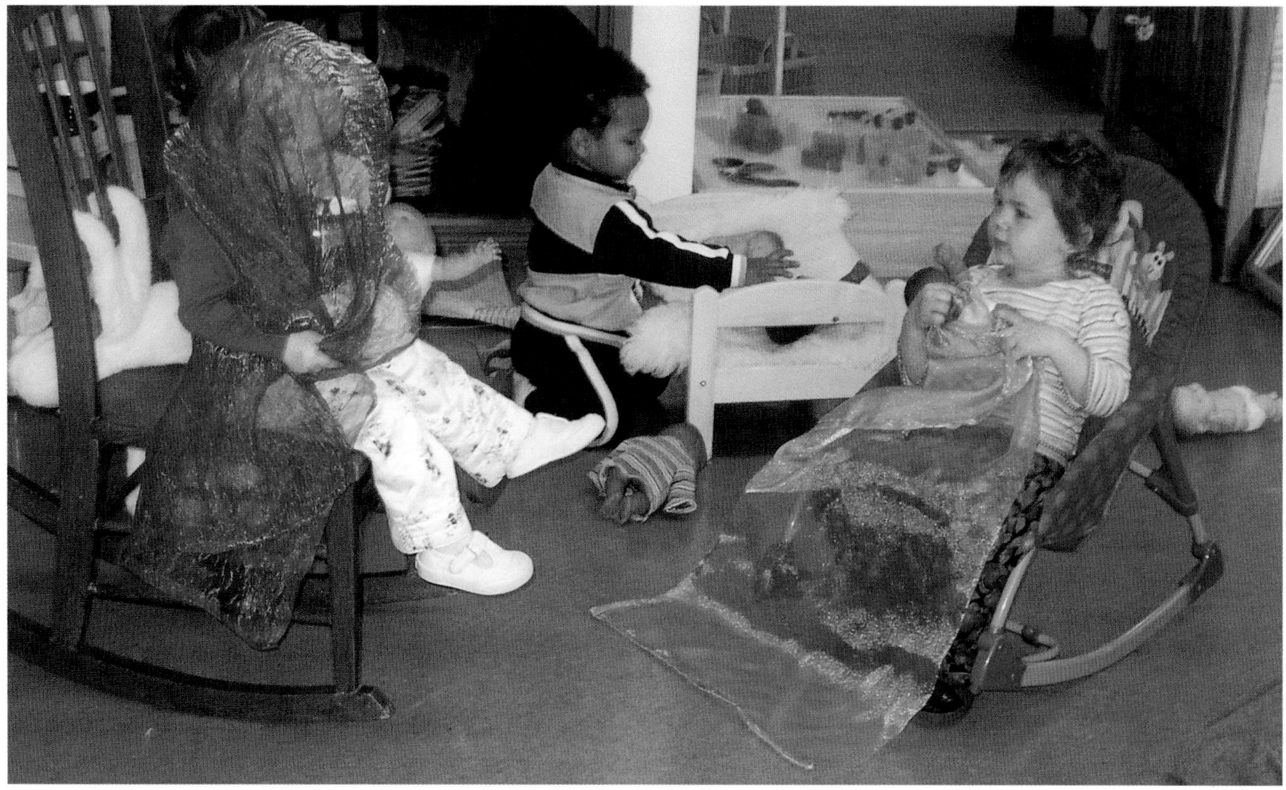

Martin Luther King Jr. Day Home Center

### *Listen to Cristina*

"It has been delightful and fascinating for me to watch the children imitate the familiar caretaking activities from their own lives with our dolls and props. I love to make guesses about what they might be thinking as they play. As I describe the details out loud, the children seem to pay more attention to one another's play and often try what I have pointed out. Today I saw something new. As the children began playing together, they were watching and interacting with each other more than usual. I know it is a stage in their development to move from parallel to cooperative play, but it seems that my broadcasting of their actions helped them make a leap in their thinking. I particularly noticed this with Oona's play. The other children eagerly followed her lead as she was playing with her baby. She noticed the other children's attention to her, and I think it enabled her to see herself and her actions in a new way. A dreamy look came into her eyes and a satisfied grin came over her face. She seemed at that moment to understand the power of her imagination. It was such a profound experience to witness her growing awareness of her ability to create her own magical world of make believe."

### *Reflect*

Cristina isn't just using a teaching technique here, but rather bringing her own enthusiasm and curiosity to her interactions with the children. Along with Cristina, we can wonder about the remarkable development going on with her group. Is this baby play beginning symbolic representation of children's family experiences? Does watching one another's pretending introduce the children to the power of their imaginations? Is it the foreshadowing of dramatic play that will bring them such delight later? Are we seeing Vygotsky's theory of social constructivism in action? How does commenting on their play contribute to deepening the children's experience and enabling their collaboration? When you immerse yourself with the children as they play, you can illuminate for them the amazing process of human development you are witnessing. ■

## •PRINCIPLE•
## Take Action on Behalf of Children's Strengths

*It occurred to me that we are teachers not by chance, but because we are exploding with intentions. Just like children and babies, we are seekers of meanings. Making meaning is different from acquiring knowledge. While knowledge is static, meaning making is the process that moves us to act. What are we going to do after we gain knowledge? Although this way of being with children liberates us from having "the right answers," as we embrace uncertainty and open ourselves to dialogue, we gain a sense of freedom, but with this freedom comes responsibility—the responsibility to act and to change.* —Iris Berger

As Iris Berger suggests, at the heart of responsive teaching is a dive into what is happening with the group, making meaning of it together, and using what you create to learn and live more fully. Young children bring this open, eager disposition to your life and your challenge is to figure out how to offer your adult wisdom without taking over in this learning journey you are taking together. At the center of the meaning making process is the belief and understanding that children have a deep desire to show their competence and make a contribution to their community. This is how they develop a positive identity and learn what they need to know to function in the world. Teachers can best support this process by responding to children with attention to their competence. The task is to look for and accentuate children's participation and "know-how." This responsive relationship is a cycle that builds on the children's and teacher's strengths. If you come to see the children's competence, you will take the time and patience to coach them. When you do, then children come to see their own abilities and positive attributes. The foundation of this cyclical process is the belief that all of us can live up to our fullest capacity for working in partnership toward a common good. Could there be a more pertinent purpose for education in today's world? These may sound like lofty goals, but opportunities for living this way are in the everyday moments you have with children.

### Binkie Love

As you read the following story of two eighteen-month-old children, notice how the teacher works with the children's capacity for sharing and helping each other instead of jumping in to solve their problem.

*Today as she got absorbed in her play, Wynsome dropped her binkie and forgot about it until she saw the one in T'Kai's mouth. She went up to him, yanked the binkie out of his mouth, and put it in her own mouth. T'Kai started to complain loudly. Teacher Sandy responded to this bumpy moment by suggesting that the children work together. "T'Kai, let's go find Wynsome's binkie so you can have yours back." T'Kai accepted this idea readily and they searched the play area together. When they found Wynsome's binkie, Sandy suggested they go to the sink to wash it off. Wynsome, listening to the exchange, eagerly joined them at the sink, bringing T'Kai's binkie with her so it could be washed too. Wynsome willingly gave the binkie back to T'Kai and with the binkies in their rightful owners' mouths the children spontaneously gave each other an exuberant hug.*

Martin Luther King Jr. Day Home Center

### Listen to Sandy

"T'Kai and Wynsome both love their binkies and would chomp on them all day and night if it was okay with their mamas. From my earlier observations I have come to understand that these two share a strong connection around their binkies. They know firsthand how important binkies are and must associate their own feelings with the other. I've seen them offer a binkie to each other when they are playing side by side. I also think that sometimes taking the binkie from the other is about trying to get closer by climbing inside each other's experience. It seems that Wynsome wants T'Kai's binkie rather than *a* binkie or *her own* binkie. It was such a sweet moment when they hugged each other. I've heard that children this age are self-centered, but when I think about what is underneath their behavior, that just doesn't ring true. The reason Wynsome willingly gave T'Kai his binkie back was her interest in sharing the task and being connected with him."

### Reflect

Many teachers in this situation would try to help Wynsome learn she shouldn't take other people's things or teach T'Kai to "use his words." Sandy doesn't mediate this conflict by responding to the children's self-centered behavior to have their own binkie. Instead she calls on the children's innate desire to be in relationship when she suggests to T'Kai they find Wynsome's binkie. Wynsome shows that Sandy is on the right track when she eagerly joins in. This story challenges Piagetian ideas that children are egocentric and unable to take another person's perspective. In fact, when we offer a way for children to live into their positive attributes and abilities, social skills are reinforced. ■

## Traffic Jam

It's important to cultivate your mindset and ability to see children's strengths and offer them strategies for learning to use them. Sometimes it takes strong intervention and perseverance, as the next story demonstrates. Notice the forceful and consistent action Ann takes on behalf of the boys' potential to play together cooperatively.

Urban Village One, Neighborhood House Head Start

*In the block area, it wasn't clear what Juan and Joseph wanted to do because they just started pulling all the blocks off the shelves and throwing them on top of each other in a scramble on the floor. This seemed exciting to them as they added explosion sounds to the crashing of the blocks as they hit each other. Seeing this, teacher Ann quickly gathered a basket of trucks and cars and asked, "Are there any road builders here today to make a place to drive the cars and trucks?" Juan and Joseph immediately began lining up unit blocks end to end.*

*Joseph: "Let's make it a really long road, all the way there . . . long, long."*

*Juan: "Here, here, go here."*

*Joseph: "No, no, it needs to go long here. I want it to be long here." He took some of Juan's blocks and put them at the end of his growing road.*

*Juan screamed in protest: "NO! NO! HERE! HERE!" He kicked apart Joseph's road, scattering the blocks.*

*Ann quickly offered a clipboard and said, "I'm drawing the road you made out of blocks." She then handed the clipboard and pen to Joseph. "Will you draw some of the blocks for our map? That way we can remember how the road goes. We can use this as a map to help us rebuild. Our drawing tells us where the blocks should go."*

*Ann stood the clipboard with the finished drawing up on its side and Juan looked at it repeatedly as he began replacing the blocks end to end.*

*Ann: "Let's add cars to the map. Can you two work together to draw some cars?"*

*The boys negotiated their own turn taking and their drawings showed not only the road but the movement of the cars, and they also told the story of themselves at play.*

### *Listen to Ann*

"This was a loud and volatile situation as the boys' conflict could easily have grown into a big fight. I've been trying to help them see each other's ideas and offer them ways to work together. I try to figure out what they are individually trying to accomplish and then help them work with the ideas they share. Their first reaction is to bump up against each other, but if I stay with it, I can usually help them work together."

### *Reflect*

Ann takes strong actions on behalf of her belief that these children are capable of working through their differences and collaborating. Rather than approaching this potentially volatile situation with techniques for turn taking, threatening time out, or banning their use of the materials, she sees their initial energy as a positive sign of their enthusiasm for working together. She seeks to capture the boys' collaborative spirit by inviting them to connect their ideas and actions through the challenging and focused task of building and drawing a road for their cars. Through this work, the boys come to see their own and each other's competence and feel the reward of working on a shared task. ■

### Your Turn

Observe children working together in a popular play area of the room and document their activities through taking notes and photos with the following emphasis:

- What specific things do the children do and say that indicate they are connecting with each other and building relationships?
- How do they use the objects or materials in their play to communicate their ideas?
- What challenges or conflicts occur? What do the children do and say to resolve their differences?

Use your documentation to make a homemade book with a title such as *We Know How to Work Together.* Include specific photos and details of what the children say and do that reflects what they know about working together. Regularly read this book with the children and invite them to add more ideas over time.

Use these questions to explore what you've learned:

- What am I seeing that reinforces my view of children as eager to connect and capable of working through their differences?
- How does revisiting their experiences help their ideas and actions change and grow?
- What other ideas do I have for illuminating children's relationships?

# Coach Children to Learn about Learning

*But it's not just learning things that's important. It's learning what to do with what you learn and learning why you learn things at all that matters.*

**NORTON JUSTER**

One of the most rewarding outcomes for an early childhood teacher is when the children in a group initiate their own play, work well together, and keep at it for an extended period of time. Teachers often feel proud when learning is so focused and fun that the children don't really need them. When you value these experiences for children, you might become adamantly opposed to interrupting the children's play with your or other people's agendas. Or perhaps you are puzzled about what your role should be when children are involved in sustained play. To feel like a "real teacher," you might feel obliged to seize upon emerging themes in children's play and plan a "curriculum unit" around them.

The value of child-initiated play can hardly be overstated. This understanding has been at the heart of early childhood education since the inception of our profession. Children thrive when they have significant amounts of time to pursue their own ideas through play using open-ended materials. Elizabeth Jones and Gretchen Reynolds (1992) say that children who have these opportunities will become "master players," which they assert is one of the most crucial outcomes for early education, since master players are motivated and successful learners.

In discussing the importance of teacher actions, we never want to inadvertently diminish the vital importance of sustained child-initiated play. Rather than interfering, taking over, or overwhelming them with too much instruction, the actions you choose should *support* children's learning. Instead of insisting that children do things your way, for example, offer helpful suggestions. Teachers walk a delicate line between challenging children to work at the upper end of their abilities while not frustrating or discouraging them. Lev Vygotsky identified this as the "zone of proximal development," which he defined as the distance between what a child can do at her current level of development and what is possible for her with support from adults or peers (Berk and Winsler 1995). He called this support (the actions teachers can take to help children reach the next level of possibility for their learning) "scaffolding." Engaging in this process with children is one of the greatest rewards of teaching.

Coaching children to learn about learning is an important aspect of the scaffolding process. When you coach children to build upon familiar experiences, or offer the next step after long periods of open exploration, the scaffolding process is most successful. When you see children involved in activities where they might benefit from mastering a skill, this is a teachable moment. You have to believe they are capable and deserve more support or it won't occur to you to offer something more. And with each coaching session or demonstration, children need ample opportunity for practice to make this a part of their own repertoire for learning.

In the previous chapter, we explored how teachers can notice and enhance ordinary moments as part of everyday curriculum. In this chapter, we explore more fully the teacher's role in extending children's activities through offering ideas, know-how, and wisdom. You can utilize the following principles to enable children to go further as you coach them to learn about learning.

- Help children see learning as a process with distinct components they can practice
- Invite children to assess their own learning
- Coach children to use tools and strategies for learning
- Plan coaching sessions separately from playtime
- Help children use reference materials to support their learning
- Teach children to look closely
- Teach children to draw in order to see more clearly
- Offer stories and dramas as tools for coaching
- Support children to learn from their friends

## Teach Me Something

*While sitting next to Deb at the art table one day, four-year-old Priya (who had been in Deb's preschool program for a couple months) said, "I really like coming to preschool and all of the things that we play with here, but when are you going to teach me something, Deb?" This wasn't the first time Deb had heard this sentiment from a child. Children who had graduated from her preschool class and returned from kindergarten for a visit would proclaim how much they were learning now that they were in "real school." Deb tried not to be defensive when hearing these comments, but instead she tried to understand the child's point of view. Eventually, Deb came to understand that the children's attitudes were similar to many adults who had thoughts such as "You don't learn when you play. You learn when you go to 'real' school and the teacher teaches you something." These experiences got Deb thinking about how powerful it would be for children if she could help them learn about their own learning. From that day on she developed strategies and engaged in conversations to explore with the children how and what they were learning through their play.*

Burlington Little School

### •PRINCIPLE•
## Help Children See Learning as a Process with Distinct Components They Can Practice

Have you ever wondered what young children think about learning? They absolutely understand that they don't have as much information or as many skills as adults and older children. Yet, they continually strive to reach the next level and proudly let others know of their growing competence. You often hear two-year-olds fiercely say, "I'm not a baby anymore!" Preschoolers claim their size and age with bravado, knowing that being bigger and older has more power and privilege in the world. What if you harnessed this self-assurance and drive for competence, and steadily helped children take charge of their own learning?

Teachers plan for children's learning, but they rarely let them in on their thinking. Children don't often get to see the why behind what you do. Teaching requires reflection in order to understand what is occurring and to see all the possibilities for extending and deepening learning. But the daily life of providers and teachers allows little time away from children to do this reflection. In addition, when teachers do make time to revisit their work, they seldom investigate what the learning experience was like for children. Instead, you might make general evaluations about the children's interest in your curriculum and whether you met "your" teaching goals. What if you invited the children to be part of your reflection process, becoming your partners in identifying what is worth learning and the best way to go about it? When children can say, "I know how to learn something," they see themselves as capable, become more confident, and don't get defeated by setbacks.

To help children see how learning unfolds, you can draw upon the theories of "multiple intelligence" (Gardner 1993), "the hundred languages of children" (Edwards, Gandini, and Forman 1998), "social constructivism" (MacNaughton and Williams 1998), and "making learning visible" (Project Zero and Reggio Children 2001). As you integrate understandings from these resources into your teaching, you can introduce them to children as a natural part of your classroom culture and learning protocols. How might this look?

As children play, adults can call attention to the many ways they are learning. You create an expectation and awareness that they are here to "get smarter," not by reminding and instructing, but by describing and inquiring about what is unfolding. For instance, a teacher might make comments and ask questions like these:

- "When you do ______ you are learning about ______."
- "What are you thinking about when you do ______?"
- "As you work, how will you know when you are done?"
- "If you want to learn more about ______ here is what you might do ______."

You can integrate concepts of learning theories into your interactions with children. Children naturally have multiple approaches to learning as they play, but they aren't necessarily aware of their process. When you offer children a framework for thinking about their actions, they can decide how to pursue their learning. They see what works best for them and are challenged to try new things. Over time, children come to know this is the way they learn. When you make the following concepts explicit, your time with children is focused accordingly.

- When you want to get smarter about something, look closely at what you have done and think about your ideas.
- You can tell someone your ideas through a conversation, through dictation, or by creating a story.
- You can teach someone what you know, or the steps you followed.
- Writing our ideas on a chart or in a book reminds us what we have been learning. We can come back to these ideas again without having to start from scratch.

- Another way to get smart is to create drawings of our ideas and actions.
- We can use different materials to explore the same idea. We could build or sculpt how something looks, create a dance, write a story, or make up a drama about it.
- Inviting others to join us in thinking will make us smarter. Our friends, our families, people in the community, or books might give us more ways to think about our ideas.

Here are some explicit comments you might use to incorporate these concepts into your teaching.

- "Tell me your ideas and I'll write them down."
- "Tell me the story or the steps. What comes first? Then what?"
- "Let's make this into a book or a chart."
- "Let's draw what you have been doing or making. I see ______. What else can you put in the drawing?"
- "Let's find some other materials to use for making this same thing."
- "Who else can join us to explore this idea?"
- "Are there books or other people that might be of help?"

A look at preschool teachers incorporating these concepts into their daily curriculum will shed light on this process of learning about learning.

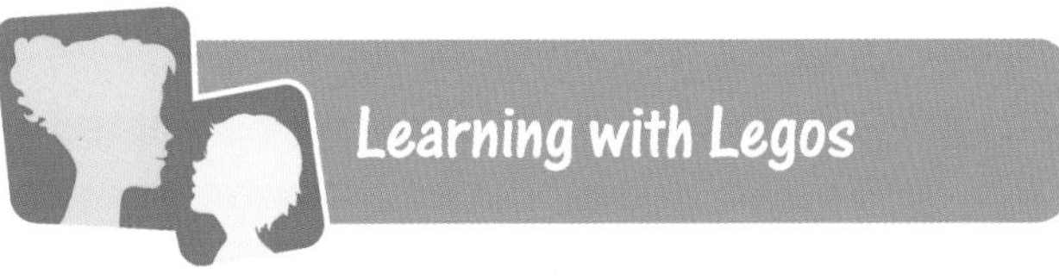

## Learning with Legos

In the following example, look at the ways that Kirsten helps the children see how they can keep learning by using their passion for building with Legos.

*After many days of shared excitement over building with Legos, Kirsten approached the children with a clipboard and a pen. Josh was the first to take up her offer and dictated a story as he pointed to the parts of his Lego construction.*

*Kirsten: "You've been working on that a long time, Josh. If you tell me the story of it, it will help you get smarter."*

*Josh, pointing to each part of his structure: "This is the garden that my dad made in our yard. These are the trees and plants. My dad is mowing the lawn. This is me. I'm riding on a sled at the back of the yard."*

Burlington Little School

*Kirsten: "Let's look closer and see if we can draw it."*

*Kirsten repeated the story that Josh had told her as she carefully drew each part. Josh gave her directions, suggesting more details as she worked on the drawing.*

*Josh: "I have a hill back there that I ride my sled on."*

*When she invited Josh to draw his own Lego structure, he declined, saying he didn't really think he could do it. Kirsten assured him that he would keep learning and maybe later take up this challenge.*

*After a couple of weeks and many experiences of talking about his Lego structures and watching the teachers draw them, Josh became quite skilled at drawing the details of his Legos. He eventually loved re-representing his Lego constructions, initiating the drawings on his own.*

*As Lego mania continued in Kirsten's room, she kept offering new ways for the children to make their work more complex. When some of them began flying Lego rockets around the room and pretending they were pilots talking over their radios, Kirsten put out butcher paper and drew roads and land forms, offering this as the landing pad for the rockets. As the children took up this suggestion, an extended drama unfolded over the weeks that followed. The children used markers to add their own ideas to the landing pad and a detailed airstrip was created.*

*On another day, Kirsten suggested the children make rocket ships out of recycled materials. A number of children spent the day working on this challenge. In the coming days, the children incorporated straws and flubber (a borax, glue, and water mixture sometimes called gak) to design and build a fueling dock for their Lego drama. The flubber became the fuel and straws were used as hoses to fuel the rockets.*

Burlington Little School

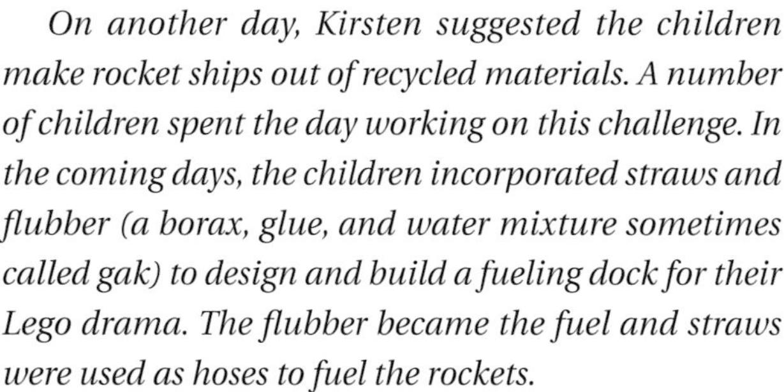

Burlington Little School

Burlington Little School

## Reflection & Action

***How might issues of culture, family background, or popular media be influencing this situation?***

*

***What learning domains are being addressed here and what other learning domains could be addressed?***

*

***What theoretical perspectives and child development principles could inform my understandings and actions?***

*

***What values, philosophy, and goals do I want to influence my response?***

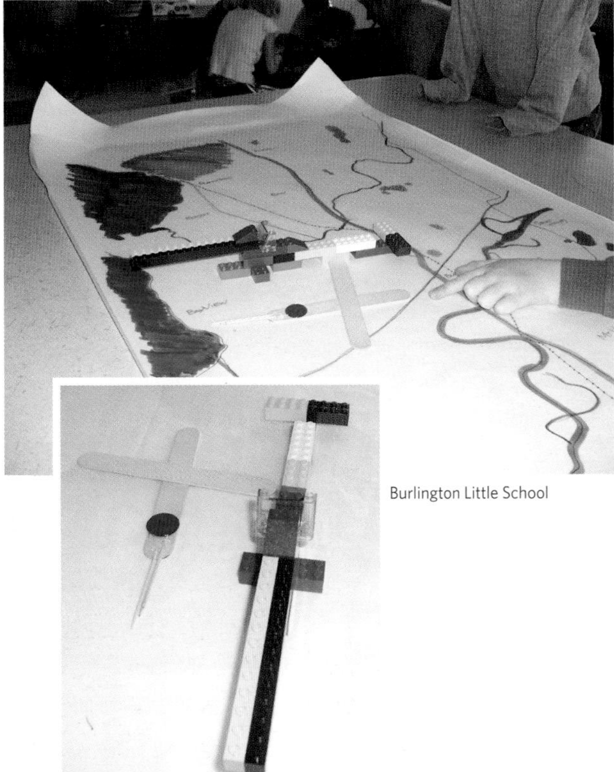

Burlington Little School

### *Listen to Kirsten*

"Many of the children in my group spent a big part of our playtime sitting next to each other and building with Legos. Sometimes they would talk or play together around their Lego constructions, but that was as far as their play would go. My instinct was to try to get them to move somewhere else to play so they could be exposed to more tools and materials. Instead, I decided to try to use their competence and interest in Legos to challenge them to work together and learn something more. At first I wasn't comfortable taking such an active role when the children played. I have learned that I shouldn't interrupt their play. But I found if I stayed focused on the details of the children's work, urged them to think and talk about their interests, and encouraged them to join their ideas through a shared task, they jumped right in with me and each other. This has become an ongoing habit for all of us now; as the children play, we all pay attention to the details and use them as the source for more conversation, activities, and learning."

### *Reflect*

Have you found yourself worried about children in your group who play in the same area with the same materials day after day? Kirsten's story shows how to use the children's obsessions to expand their play and introduce multiple strategies for learning. Did you notice the language and suggestions Kirsten used to encourage the children to see and expand on the learning that their play offered? As Kirsten works with the children over time, talking about their ideas and helping them explain their actions to each other and use other materials to revisit their work, she helps them learn a protocol for learning while pursuing their own interests and passions. Utilizing multiple strategies for learning becomes central to the daily life in this classroom for individual children such as Josh, as well as the larger group. What better outcome could we hope for children than acquiring the skills and dispositions necessary for being independent as well as cooperative, lifelong learners? ■

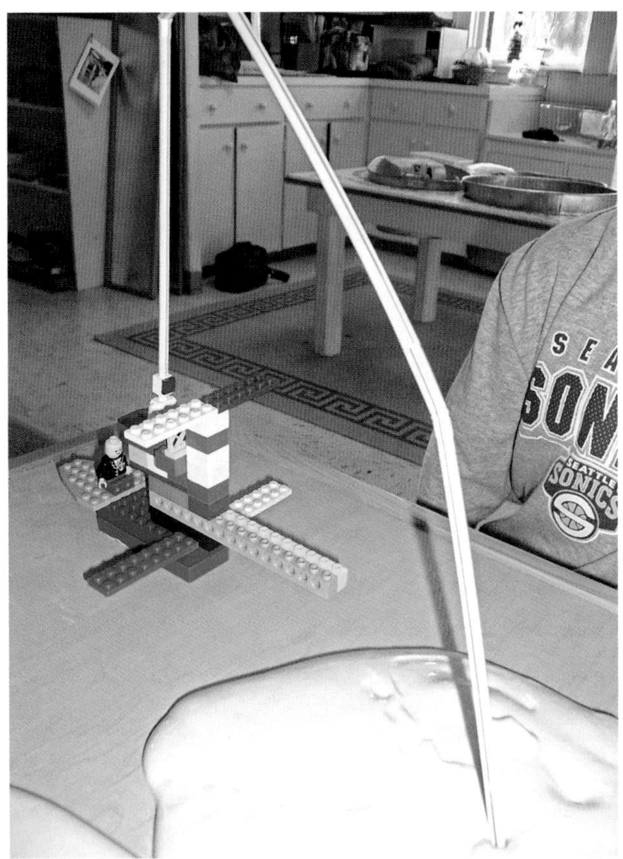

Burlington Little School

## •PRINCIPLE•
## Invite Children to Assess Their Own Learning

Another strategy for focusing children on their own learning is to engage them in assessing what is worth putting into their portfolios, displaying in the room, or sharing with parents. With some guiding questions, children can begin to reflect on their work and how it does or doesn't represent things they are learning. Questions to consider when looking over work samples and documentation of their efforts could include the following:

- Which of these shows us what you have been trying to figure out as you've played this week?
- Does one of these (pictures, stories, papers) capture something you have been trying to learn?
- Do you see something here that makes you know you are learning things while you are here?
- When you look over these collections, can you think of something you would like to learn next? How could you go about that?
- Who knows about this and might help you?
- What will you do tomorrow to get started?

### Whose Learning Is It?

Read the following story of the routine that teacher Brian has established in his class to help the children assess and appreciate their own learning.

*Each Monday morning, Brian displays a collection of the work his group of four-year-olds completed during the previous week. He places observation stories, photos of the children's play, and artwork on a table for review. Brian sits at the table during playtime, working with small groups of children as they eagerly come to hear the stories of their time in child care. They look things over and talk about what they did and what they learned. It's the children's job to decide what work to add to their own portfolios. The children spend time with their current work, but also love poring over the many other items that have been collected throughout the year. Brian suggests that the children study the current items carefully to determine which work best represents how they have been learning.*

Burlington Little School

### *Listen to Brian*

"I used to feel so overwhelmed by the emphasis our program places on assessing children's learning. Filling out checklists and doing observations for each child's portfolio took so much of my time and took me away from relaxed time with the children. This changed dramatically when I started to think of ways to involve the children in this process. After all, it is their learning that I am tracking, and they should be a part of that. What I do now is make my observations and assessments of their play into stories with photos for us to study together. We have come to love this activity as a routine for starting our week. We constantly talk about learning, and these conversations have become a vital aspect of our time together."

### *Reflect*

Can you imagine how powerful it is for children to engage in an ongoing reflection of their own learning process at such a young age? After all, young children's entire life is about learning. Brian's weekly routine takes advantage of this simple fact, offering children insight and ownership of the learning process. It's not just experiences that children need in order to learn, but also reflection on those experiences brings about the deepest learning. And as we can see in Brian's story, children are eager to hear about themselves and their friends, so this activity also encourages collaboration and infuses a sense of joy in the learning process. Additionally, involving the children in this process brings more joy to a task that Brian dreaded in the past. ■

### Your Turn

As you reflect on your group of children, are you aware of how much they know about their own learning process? What indicators do you have of this? How often do children talk about a plan for what they want to do? How is new learning acknowledged in your group? Do the children notice this or do you point it out?

Use your answers to these questions to begin conversations with the children about their learning. Try developing a simple learning plan with individual children or a small group and work together to document and assess what happens.

### Now I Know What Learning Really Is!

*When children spend their preschool years learning about learning, they come to new realizations. For example, remember four-year-old Priya from earlier in this chapter? At the end of the school year, Priya had another conversation with her teacher Deb. Deb was bringing closure to their preschool experience by asking children to reflect on the year. She asked a number of questions, including: "Can you tell me what you've learned that you didn't know at the beginning of the year? What do you want to remember about your time here in preschool?" Deb reminded Priya that at the beginning of the year she had said, "I really like coming to preschool and all of the things that we play with here, but when are you going to teach me something?" Deb wondered what Priya thought about that now. Priya responded, "Oh, that was before I knew what learning really is."*

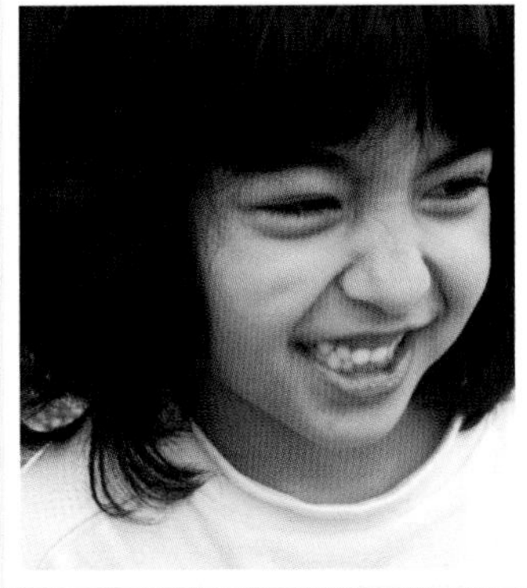

Burlington Little School

## •PRINCIPLE•
## Coach Children to Use Tools and Strategies for Learning

As we make the learning process visible to children, we can further their learning by coaching them to use tools, materials, and specific strategies. Children are keen observers of the adult world and they are eager to learn and gain greater control over making their ideas and actions understood. Historically, child-centered teachers in the United States have been reluctant to offer models or demonstrations for fear of limiting children's creativity. "Discovery" has been our mantra, and our sacred guideline has been to let children figure out what works and what doesn't. Exploration and discovery *is* an important aspect for children's learning. Nevertheless, some kinds of learning require instruction, support, and challenge. It's unfair to ask kids to communicate ideas without showing them how to use tools to do so. When we take the mystery out of tools, skills, and processes for learning, children will gain the confidence and ability to pursue their interests.

The following stories show different teacher approaches to coaching children.

## Scissor Skills

This story reminds us that even the youngest children want access to the power of tools. Teacher Deb offers the children in her group scissors to cut flubber (also called gak). What is your reaction to her decision to teach babies to use scissors?

*One day when her toddlers were exploring flubber, Deb remembered her work with preschool children, and how easy it was for them to cut flubber with scissors. She decided to try teaching her one-year-olds how to use the scissors. The children watched her demonstration in earnest, as she showed them how to hold one part of the scissors in each hand and move them back and forth to cut the flubber. The children were captivated by this serious task, concentrating hard to practice what was demonstrated. Deb held up the flubber so it dripped down in a long drop, and the children worked at using the scissors until they were able to successfully cut the flubber. Oscar watched Deb's demonstrations of the two-handed way to use the scissors. He then confidently took the scissors in one hand and proceeded to cut with ease, even turning his wrist and hand to meet the task.*

Martin Luther King Jr. Day Home Center

Martin Luther King Jr. Day Home Center

Martin Luther King Jr. Day Home Center

### Listen to Deb

"Every day the toddlers I work with surprise me in the things that they can do. They are always so interested in the adult world and the tools I use in the room. They love to clean with the sponges and want a broom to help sweep when they see me sweeping. I have responded by having enough tools for them to participate in the real work of our room. Today I took this a step further. One of the things they are enticed by is the scissors. They always seem to find the scissors that I keep in the room for adult use. Today when we were exploring flubber, I remembered my work with preschool children and how simple and satisfying it was for them to cut flubber with scissors. It occurred to me at that moment that I could teach these one-year-olds to cut. At first I giggled to myself and thought about what most people would think of the idea of giving scissors to a one-year-old. People also often worry about giving children substances like flubber. However, I've come to know their determination and abilities, and I stay right with them during activities that need supervision, so I decided to go for it. When I suggested we could learn to use the scissors, the children seemed astounded. They remembered that I usually take scissors away. They watched me with intense concentration, then worked diligently to learn to cut. I had another shocker when I showed Oscar the two-handed way to use the scissors. He looked at me like I was nuts, took the scissors in one hand, and proceeded to cut like a pro. I've had four-year-olds who couldn't do what this twenty-month-old did with the scissors. I've come to see that children of this age haven't yet been convinced that they are incapable of participating fully in the world, and I am finding out that they are right! I will continue to take seriously the challenges they offer me."

### Reflect

A critical aspect of becoming a coach for children's learning is the belief that children are capable and deserving of the skills and information that adults have power over. Deb's belief in her group spurred her to take the time to break down the task into steps that the children could manage, clearly demonstrating what they needed to learn, and then watching and waiting patiently. This story is a clear example of Vygotsky's theory of scaffolding. The children (except Oscar!) needed support to be able to use scissors safely and with success. Their eager disposition and determination along with their growing small muscle skills created a zone of proximal development that allowed the children to work at a higher level with Deb's help. Challenge yourself to consider what additional tasks the children in your group are eager to learn and capable of learning with your coaching. Imagine the satisfaction on both your parts when you spend your days together working with increasing challenge and skill. ■

## Memory Lane

Coaching children to use thinking strategies can also help them take on more complex learning as part of their endeavors. Here Ann coaches Kierra to use her memory as a strategy for mastering a game she is playing.

*Kierra spent most of one morning playing a lotto matching game. She laid out the cards of children's names in long rows. Then she dove into the effort of finding cards that matched, turning over one card, then another, and another, and another, until finally—a match! Other children briefly joined and quickly left the game, intrigued for a short while by the playful element of searching for the hidden surprise of a matching card. After watching this unfold, teacher Ann decided to offer some coaching to the one child still playing the game.*

*"Kierra, I'd like to play this game with you," Ann said. "Will you teach me what you know about how to play this game?"*

*"You go two times, then it's my turn," replied Kierra. "We hafta find a match. But first we gotta fix the cards, because they got broke. They hafta go in a line." She*

Parklake Two Head Start

*gestured toward the cards that were lying helter-skelter on the carpet. Together Kierra and Ann straightened the cards, laying them in neat rows, creating order from the chaos.*

*Kierra let Ann have the first turn. Ann flipped over one card, then another, reading the names aloud; they didn't match, so she set them back in their original places in the row, commenting, "I'm going to put these right back in their places so I can remember where they are next time."*

*Kierra took a turn, and was careful to set the cards back in their spots, echoing Ann's words: "That's Alex's place. That's Ana's place."*

*Back and forth they traded turns, searching for pairs of cards that matched. Ann offered, "Okay, Kierra, remember that Jonathan is right here—we may need him later to make a match!" Later, she said, "Hey, we saw another Prudencio already—do you remember where he was?" Name by name, they matched up the cards, working their way up and down the neat rows until all the cards were paired.*

### Listen to Ann

"As I watched the children play this game, the cards became more and more jumbled; kids lifted a card to see what it held, then set it back down in any random spot on the carpet. Most of the children soon tired of the random "hide and seek" quality of the game and left it to Kierra, who was stalwart in her efforts to master this game. I wanted to expand the possibilities that the game held for Kierra by suggesting strategies for playing the game that would deepen the intellectual effort involved. I hoped to move the game from "hide and seek" to "remember and find." Kierra quickly embraced the strategy I offered, keeping the cards in well-organized rows and paying close attention to the location of each name. I was thrilled that with this strategy, Kierra mastered the game, brilliantly maneuvering through the long rows of black rectangles, finding cards exactly where she'd put them, creating a game of memory and skill."

### Reflect

Notice how Ann asked for Kierra's thinking about this game as the launching point for the coaching she wanted to offer. We can see from Kierra's comments that she had her own understanding of this game and could clearly describe it. Ann picked up on Kierra's description of the game being "broken" and used that as the place to begin her suggestions. Ann played right alongside Kierra, talking out loud to coach her toward the thinking strategies that would enhance Kierra's learning as they played the game. It takes close observation, a strong desire to understand children's perspectives, and lots of practice to determine the most effective interventions for coaching children toward deeper thinking. But as you can see in this example of Ann and Kierra, the outcome is deeply satisfying for children and teachers. ■

## •PRINCIPLE•
## Plan Coaching Sessions Separately from Playtime

If you want children to initiate their own activities and play collaboratively, show them possibilities for using tools and materials. But rather than interrupting their open playtime to offer coaching, set aside separate times for these special lessons, perhaps during a small group time, or as part of your circle time. During these coaching sessions, demonstrate the many possibilities for using everyday materials, such as blocks, paint, playdough, and manipulatives, and then provide time for the children to work with the materials, try out what they observed, and add their own ideas and actions. Don't insist they do it your way, but instead suggest the many possibilities with the emphasis on how they can invent more. As children work with the materials on their own, take photos and write down their words, turning these into pages for binder books to be kept in the related area of the room. Continue to document and add these documentation pages to the binders. You can even keep the same binder in the room over a number of years so children can revisit what they did when they were younger, or see what their siblings did when they were in preschool.

## Blocks and Bridges

Here is an example of how Cindy coaches children in using blocks through carefully planned lessons.

*The children enthusiastically gathered around the tables and block platform for block building lessons. Cindy began by describing the kinds of building she had observed the children doing lately. "I have noticed that a lot of you have been building roads by putting the blocks on the floor, connecting them end to end to make a long line." She demonstrated what she had seen and showed some of the photos she had taken. "Today I wanted to teach you how you could build a bridge with these blocks to add to your roads." A few of the children confidently claimed that they already knew how to build a bridge. Cindy said, "Great, you can help me teach the others." As a part of the demonstration, she held up each different block, asking the children to name what they noticed about the shape and size. She described and demonstrated how the children might fit the various blocks together to form a bridge and other structures. After this ten-minute demonstration, Cindy invited the children to jump in and try bridge building. They eagerly worked, copying what Cindy had done, but also adding their own ideas, calling out, "Look what I did!"*

Burlington Little School

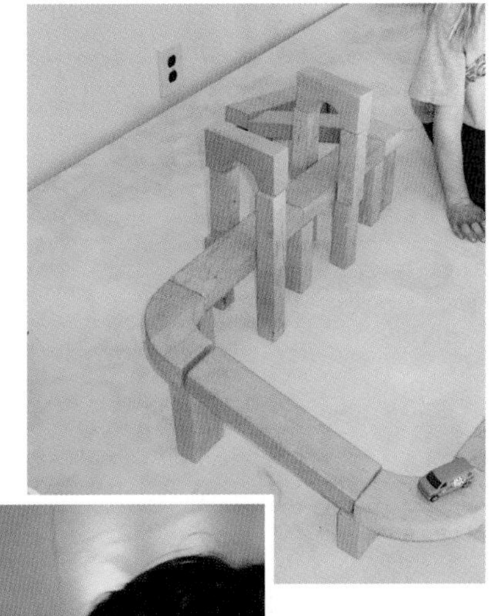

Burlington Little School

Burlington Little School

### *Listen to Cindy*

"The children have been excited about our block building lessons and very eager to try out the new ideas I offer. Because they have gotten really good at building roads with the blocks, I wanted to demonstrate the possibility of adding bridges by building up and attaching tunnels and archways. The children feel so confident in their block building ability that they think I'm silly for trying to teach them more. But I notice that these lessons really do help them use the blocks in new ways. The children often start with what I demonstrate, but then add their own ideas and inventions. I believe that their familiarity with the blocks propels them to new understandings and actions, so these coaching lessons are the perfect thing to do. I've created a binder book that highlights each of our lessons and shows the remarkable roads, bridges, and tunnels the children have been making. I'm excited to see them regularly use this book as a reference during playtime."

### *Reflect*

This story shows how the children's ideas and actions can become a source for coaching them in new skills and strategies. In her coaching lessons, Cindy breaks down and describes the discrete elements that she has seen the children use in their constructions and then builds on this by offering information and strategies that connect to the children's current work. You can see the immediate impact this has on expanding the children's use of the blocks. Cindy's demonstrations, the children's hands-on work, and the binder book are all concrete tools for coaching the children to learn and practice these new skills and concepts. Along with these rich experiences, you can see the literacy learning available as the children follow a sequence of steps and practice reading as they use the binder book as a reference tool. ■

## Boss of the Paints!

Here is another story of coaching lessons, this time in the art area. Deb decides that because the children have had many opportunities to explore paint on their own, offering a lesson in mixing colors will be most pertinent.

*Deb created a chart identifying a sequence to follow for mixing paint and planned a lesson to teach the children how to use the chart. Deb started the lesson by saying, "I'm going to teach you how to be the boss of the paints." Deb explained this could happen if the children used the steps in the chart, so they would have control of the paints, rather than watching the colors blend together in the jar. She used a paintbrush and paints to carefully demonstrate the sequence on the chart of "wash, wipe, dip, mix, paint." After the children watched her demonstration, Deb invited them to try. The children dove right in, excitedly calling out their new discoveries to each other: "Look, I made orange." "Wow, look at this! I turned it into green."*

### *Listen to Deb*

"I knew that the invitation to be 'the boss of the paints' would get the children's attention because they are always so interested in the power of being a boss. They felt really good about themselves as they successfully followed the sequence on the chart. But I was shocked when the children were so surprised with the results of their paint mixing. They have been painting all year and mixing is their favorite thing to do. Their reaction was like they were making an amazing new discovery. From that day on, the children have been revisiting the idea of mixing colors, at first to discover the control they can have over the change, but now they are carefully mixing the color of paint they specifically want for their work."

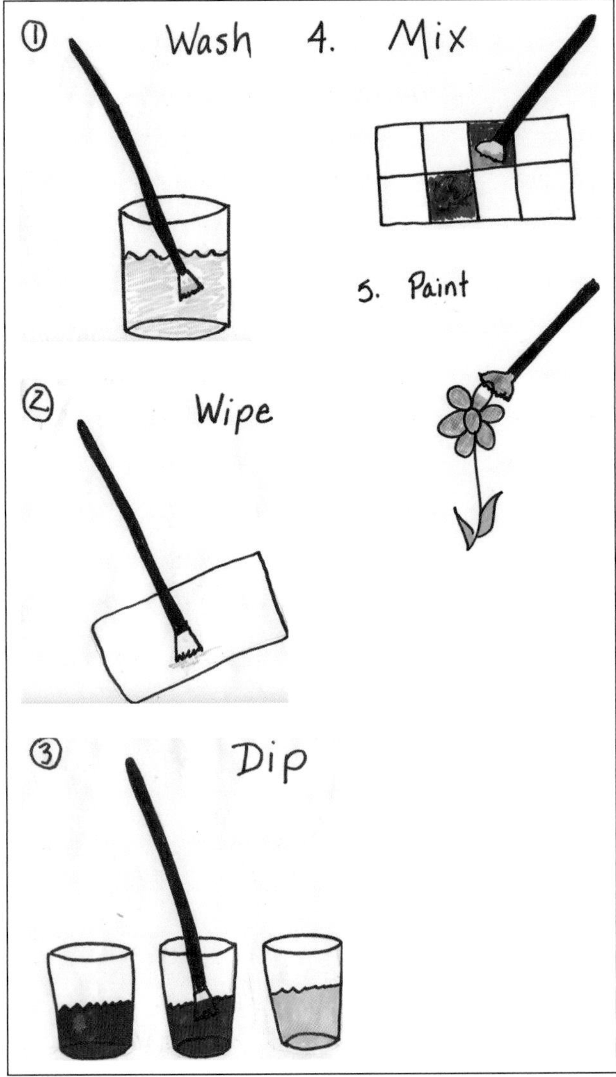


Burlington Little School

Burlington Little School

### *Reflect*

The children's delight and amazement in response to mixing the paint colors came about because, although they had mixed paint colors repeatedly in their own explorations, they had never thought about controlling the process. This story shows the power of extended explorations followed by your role as coach and documenter to enhance the children's skill and confidence. In addition, when children are coached to follow a sequence of steps and a process, they acquire an important tool for learning to learn. ■

### Your Turn

To learn how to coach children in using new materials and tools, gather together some basic supplies for working with wire as a sculpting medium. You will need wire of 18 to 22 gauge, wire cutters, and tools for shaping the wire. Masking tape and perhaps clay or Styrofoam to use as a base to hold the wire could also be helpful, but not essential. These supplies can be found at craft or hardware stores.

Sit down and explore the properties of the wire, how it feels to work with it in your hands, and the different strategies you can use to create shapes with it. Think about discrete skills, information, techniques, and terms that would help children use the wire and tools successfully.

Reflecting on your experience with wire, plan a coaching session or demonstration that you can offer children. This might include a chart with steps for becoming "the boss of the wire," guidelines for safety, and vocabulary related to the tasks of engineering, sculpting, and the work of an artist. Try this out with children, noticing what happens, and revising the way you might coach in the future.

## Flubber Bubbles

*Children find blowing bubbles with flubber fascinating. It is a challenging undertaking, and often only one or two children are successful flubber bubble blowers, while others struggle. To help the children in her group learn the best strategies, teacher Anna Maria worked together with the children to document their discoveries and create a book containing photos and step-by-step instructions (dictated by the children) on how to blow flubber bubbles. This year, two different methods for blowing flubber bubbles were identified, so they have two books of directions, to which the children regularly refer for help. Through this effort, the children are coming to see each other as resources for new learning, as well as learning to use reference books.*

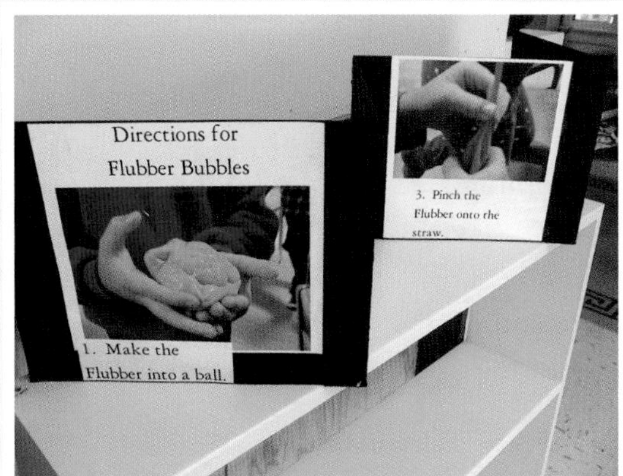


Burlington Little School

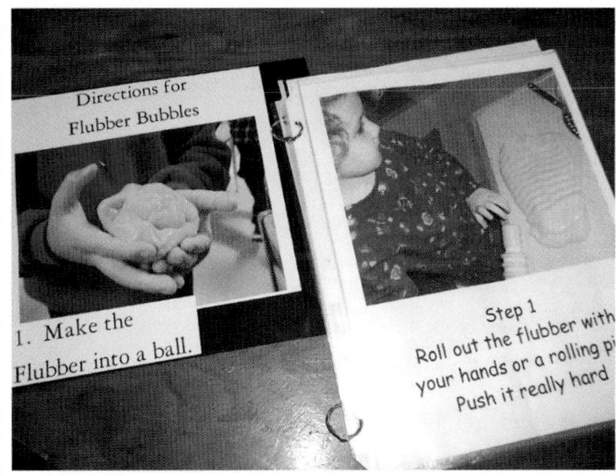


Burlington Little School

**•PRINCIPLE•**

## Help Children Use Reference Materials to Support Their Learning

Pictures, directions, and charts can spark ideas in children and can show them the steps and practice skills for using materials. Following a pattern or a diagram to accomplish something is both challenging and satisfying for children, but hard to do without some initial coaching. Study the following stories to see how these teachers offered reference material to encourage children's learning.

### Stone Sculptures

Sometimes just including a reference book as part of an invitation will serve as an entry point for some further coaching. Notice how Miss Dee Dee undertakes this with an interesting book on the playground.

*One day Miss Dee Dee placed a book about stone sculptures in with some of the rocks on the playground and stood back to see what would happen when the children discovered it. Jamilla and Rochelle were the first to pick up the book. They held the book upside down, but showed no sign of realizing this. They studied the pages and exchanged some words that Miss Dee Dee couldn't hear so she approached the children and asked what they were noticing.*

*Jamilla: "They got some really big rock pictures."*

*Miss Dee Dee: "Yes. Look at those tall rock structures. Actually, if we look closely, we can see that an artist took some smaller rocks and stacked them on top of each other to create these big structures."*

*By this time, Samara had joined in, peering over their shoulders.*

*Samara: "I'm an artist. Watch. I can make those stack up."*

*Samara spent the rest of the outdoor time experimenting with different ways to create towers of rocks that wouldn't fall. At different points, children would come to watch her and she would describe what she was discovering.*

*Samara: "The big ones are easier. Those little ones don't stay. See, these got more flat parts. You gotta get the flat parts to line up. The most I got so far is seven."*

Martin Luther King Jr. Day Home Center

Martin Luther King Jr. Day Home Center

### Reflection & Action

***What details stand out that I can make visible for further consideration?***

*

***How are the environment and materials impacting what's unfolding and what changes could be made?***

*

***What theoretical perspectives and child development principles could inform my understandings and actions?***

### *Listen to Miss Dee Dee*

"I'm often looking for interesting books so children will come to see them as references for their ideas. Books that connect children's activities with the work of artists are especially appealing to me. Putting the Goldsworthy book next to some actual rocks was a useful strategy to provoke their interest and offer an example for the children to pursue. They often use the rocks for building and design, so I thought this book would be very useful to them. I loved how they connected with each other and worked together around this interesting activity."

### *Reflect*

You can see Miss Dee Dee's goal for the children's use of the book come to life in this story as the children readily moved between working with the book and working with the rocks. By reinforcing the notion that the book reflected the work of an artist, she helped the children to connect to the bigger world and to see themselves in this way. Samara displayed this when she confidently proclaimed, "I'm an artist." It's also easy to see how this activity can meet learning outcomes in math, science, and spatial relations as the children study the shapes and sizes of rocks, and work with strategies for balancing their rock designs. ■

## The Challenge of Using a Model

In the next story, Shauna sees how the children step up to the challenge of following a model to enhance their block play.

*Shauna noticed the children's avid interest in and their attention to the details of the small, different-shaped blocks they had been working with for over a week. She decided to introduce the diagrams that came with the blocks to provide the children with a new way to use them. The children homed in with rapt attention to the details in the diagrams and the blocks, determined to make what was illustrated. Shauna pointed out to the children how the illustrations had taught them more about the blocks and suggested that they make illustrations of their own work. The children readily took up this task, drawing their own diagrams of the structures they created. Shauna put these drawings together in a binder to leave on the shelf near the blocks for the children to refer to.*

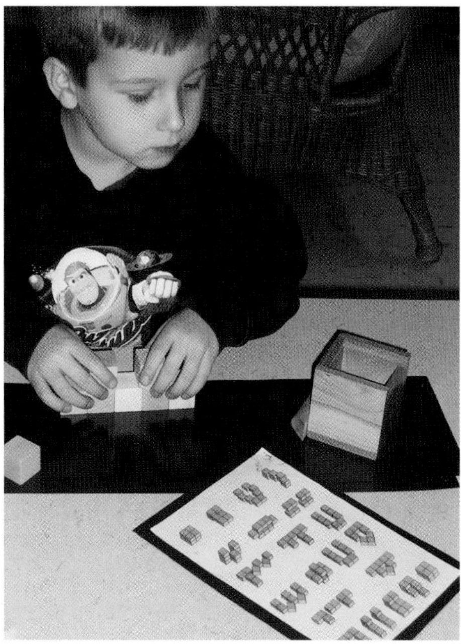

Burlington Little School

Burlington Little School

Burlington Little School

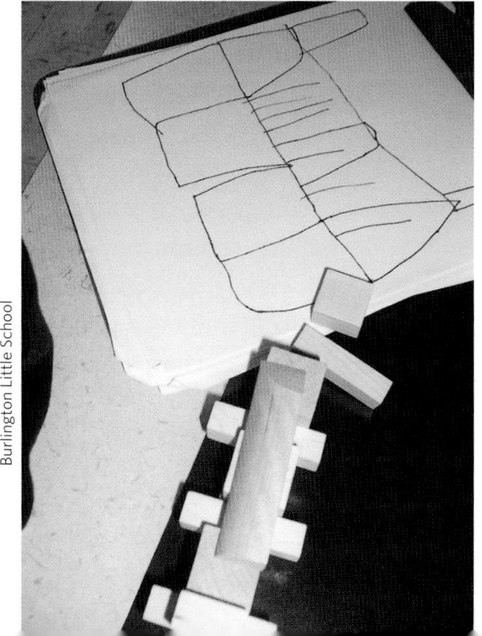

Burlington Little School

### *Listen to Shauna*

"I learned in my early childhood classes never to give children a model to copy. When diagrams came with the Legos, I threw them away to ensure that children drew on their own creativity. What I realize now is that when children have lots of open time to play, they are ready for new challenges. Working to replicate a complicated model can be extremely rewarding. I gave the children a wonderful collection of small blocks of different shapes and sizes, which came with diagrams for building, using the unique features of the blocks. After the children had played with the blocks for over a week, I thought it was time to challenge the children by offering the diagrams. I was excited to see how engrossed they became in duplicating the patterns and structures in the diagrams. What was even more impressive was their willingness to make their own diagrams!"

### *Reflect*

Can you see the difference between leading children through an activity where everyone duplicates a model of, for example, the same paper plate bunny, and using the kind of complex diagram for enhancing block play described here? All too often, professional guidelines become rules that teachers follow without thinking. Our purpose in offering stories like this one is for you to see the powerful role you can play in children's learning when you thoughtfully use your wisdom and skill to help children access and develop their competencies.

Models and diagrams offer children opportunities for careful study, for learning to follow steps and sequences, and for working through complex problems. Reference materials with pictures and diagrams provide young children with concrete experiences in literacy development as they practice reading and using symbols for their thinking and learning. Think about the children you work with—meeting a challenge and working through it successfully is among the most satisfying learning experiences for them. ■

### Your Turn

Gather books or reference materials from your current collection of adult or children's books that could be used as a reference for children's learning. Assess the books with the following questions in mind:

- Do these books have inspirational and clear pictures that show possibilities?
- Are there diagrams or steps to follow that the children could understand?
- Could children use these books or reference materials on their own or would they benefit from some coaching in their use?
- How would the books or reference materials be useful if you added them to areas of your room?

Choose one of these books or reference materials and combine it with some related materials as an invitation for children's discovery. As you observe the children using the reference materials, notice what teacher actions might be helpful. Take action and reflect on what occurs.

## •PRINCIPLE•
## Teach Children to Look Closely

If our goal for coaching is to enable children to become self-directed, cooperative learners, then they need to sharpen their listening and observation skills. Children are typically disposed to notice details and we can assist them in making use of this for their learning. Paying attention to what is around them will help children with their collaborative endeavors, reading body language and social cues, and discovering the ideas and perspectives of others. Coaching children in observation skills taps into their eagerness to sort, classify, and see how things are alike and different. Noticing details helps them with spatial relations, drawing, and literacy skills. Coaching children to observe closely will also aid them in reading facial expressions and body language (emotional intelligence), distinguishing letters on a page (literacy learning), and looking at objects under a microscope (science learning).

A camera is another good tool for coaching children to notice what they see. Because children regularly see adults taking photographs, they are keen to use the camera themselves.

## Through the Looking Glass

*Using a magnifying glass or jeweler's loupe is a useful way to teach children to look closely. The advantage of a loupe is that it is held right up to the eye and blocks out all other distractions. Whichever tool you use, children benefit from some initial coaching to help them recognize when something is in or out of focus.* The Private Eye: Looking and Thinking by Analogy *(Ruef 2005) offers a curriculum using loupes, including a companion guide to introduce prekindergartners to the process of looking, drawing, and theorizing with 5x loupe magnifiers. The author suggests that teachers initially use a slide projector or overhead projector to teach the concept of "blurry versus clear." Then you can move on to coaching the use of loupes or a large magnifying glass that comes with legs. Encourage the children to describe what they are seeing when they look through the loupe or magnifying glass and what it reminds them of. Have them draw what they are seeing. For instance, children looking closely at a leaf have said the veins of the leaf remind them of bones in a hand. If these drawings are put on transparencies, they can be projected on the wall to change the scale and help the children identify new details.*

Children First

## Zoom Lens

In the following story, Amber has a camera solely for the children's use. What insights can you get from this story about how children see the world?

*"Can I take pictures?" the children in Amber's classroom frequently asked as they saw Amber take photos of their work. She decided to get a digital camera exclusively for the children's use. When given the camera, the children often used the zoom feature for close-ups of textures and angles of different items around the room. They also took close-ups of different parts of people. They loved looking at each photo on the LCD screen on the camera right after taking a picture. Because she wanted the children to notice and describe what they were drawn to, Amber created a routine of downloading the photos onto the computer and having discussions about them with the children.*

*Blake couldn't wait to show Amber the details he had captured with the camera. He and Amber turned the viewing of the photos into a game where Amber had to try to figure out what the image was by looking closely at the textures, colors, and shapes on the screen.*

*Blake: "Amber, look at this, look at this!"*

*Amber: "Umm, what am I seeing? I see translucent colors and different shapes."*

*Blake: "Yes, yes, and this is the open part of the glass. Can you tell what it is? Come over here." He took Amber by the hand and pulled her over to the table where the color blocks were located. "See, I took a close picture of these."*

*They continued this game with every photo. After all the images had been viewed, they erased the photos on the camera and Blake eagerly started the game again.*

Burlington Little School

### *Listen to Amber*

"I had always been curious about the images that ended up in my camera after one of the children had used it, so I decided to get a camera that the children could use throughout the day so I could study their photos more closely. I notice that the children consistently take close-up photos of discrete items, like a wheel on one of the toy cars or the weave of the carpet. They also take a lot of photos of faces and body parts, using the zoom lens so the parts are almost unrecognizable. I haven't been sure if the children are purposeful in what they select to photograph, or if they just like using the zoom. Today Blake gave me some insight when he invented a game where he took close-up photos and I had to guess what they were. He was very purposeful in his picture taking, and loved showing me these distorted views."

### *Reflect*

Amber's descriptions of the children's photography and Blake's photos in particular leave interesting questions to consider. How do children see the world around them? Do they notice the smaller details more than the fuller picture that adults see? Is this another indicator of adults' tendencies to make quick meaning of what is around us and children's ability to be present to the many possibilities? When we offer children the opportunity to use cameras and explore what they see around them, we can coach them in heightening their awareness and their ability to see, and in the process share in their rich view of the world. ■

## •PRINCIPLE•
## Teach Children to Draw in Order to See More Clearly

In addition to giving children plenty of open-ended time for drawing and painting, we can use these activities for learning to look closely. The goal is not to create exact representations, but rather to help children see details for their learning. Mona Brookes (1996) offers useful strategies for this. In *Drawing with Children*, Brookes provides worksheets to help children practice copying shapes. The notion of copying a drawing has been traditionally discouraged in early childhood education, but here it is used as a coaching strategy for seeing, rather than producing, art. Helping children see the elements of design—lines, shapes, sizes, and patterns—enhances their aesthetic development and their ability to represent.

George Forman (1996) describes the value of drawing to learn about something. When children have to transfer onto paper what they see as a three-dimensional object, or represent an idea they have in their mind, they are confronted with problems to solve. Simple drawing lessons will help children in these ongoing endeavors.

Here are examples of how teachers have worked with children to draw the details of what they are seeing.

## Look a Little, Draw a Little

In the following story, notice the explicit ways Cathy coaches the children to draw. Her goal for them is not only drawing, but also understanding how to observe closely and how to work with thought and purpose.

*Every week Cathy offers a drawing lesson. She gives the children special drawing pens that are used just for these lessons. She begins her coaching by suggesting that the children look closely at the details of the object while she describes what she sees as she moves her finger over an object. For example, when they were drawing self-portraits, Cathy said, "I see this oval shape that outlines your face. At the top of your oval face I see some of your hair. Can you see a row of hair growing above your eyes? Those are brows, and yours curve down a little. If I look closely at your eyes, I see a round, dark shape in the middle, your pupil, and then another circle around that." As they work on their drawings, Cathy coaches the children to look a little and then draw a little, and then look and draw again.*

Burlington Little School

Burlington Little School

### Listen to Cathy

"I have not been trained in art and I don't see myself as an artist, but I have always had a great desire to learn to draw. Recently I read that in the Victorian era, everyone had instruction in drawing and was expected to learn to draw. You weren't considered well educated unless you could render the human figure and draw a still life. This information led me to the idea that the children and I could learn to draw together. I've studied various books about drawing, ones geared toward children and others toward adults, and I've attempted to share the lessons from these books with the children. What I notice is that children's work is always unique to them. We may all be drawing the same flower, but children emphasize the different aspects of what they see. The drawing lessons direct their attention to looking closely and their drawings always reflect the details they are seeing. We often revisit our line drawings with watercolor paints, so we add the aspect of color to what we are seeing. Or we will work with watercolor alone. I'm always amazed at the beauty, care, and attention the children give to this work."

### Reflect

Most children love to draw and it is a more accessible medium for their representation than writing or even talking. Even the youngest children can use drawing to communicate movement, experiences, and feelings (Kolbe 2005). But drawing with children, as Cathy describes, is more than art and creative expression. If children gain skills and confidence to draw what they see around them, they will be able to express ideas, tackle problems, and learn through their drawings. Children can learn drawing skills by practicing with particular objects that they can easily see, such as ladders, bicycles, and pussy willows. The objective of these drawing lessons isn't just to learn to draw, but to coach children to look closely to learn to see. ■

### Colorful Coral

*Black-and-white drawings help children capture details. In this photo, however, teachers Fran and Nicole also help the children notice and represent the colors of the sea life present in their community. To begin their investigation of sea life, the children looked through a reference book featuring images of the Great Barrier Reef. The glossy photographs of the colorful coral were alluring and the children were keen to discuss the colors, shapes, and interesting names of these coral formations. The teachers offered a palette of brightly colored chalk pastels alongside images of a variety of coral species. They helped the children notice shape and color, and to make choices about the coral pieces they preferred. The children took care to blend the chosen pastels to achieve the desired hues they saw in the coral. Fran and Nicole helped the children notice each other's blending techniques, from the use of several fingers together to merge larger blocks of color, to the intimate engagement of a pinkie fingertip to delicately smudge color and line.*

Earlwood Children's Centre

### Your Turn

In order to help children cultivate their ability to see, you must develop your own keen awareness of the details around you. Try "drawing to see" using the following guidelines.

Find an object to draw that has simple lines, shapes, and textures, such as a flower with a stem.

Place the item where you can see it, but far enough away from your pencil and paper so you have room to draw.

Looking only at the item and not at your paper, draw the details of what you see. Allow your pencil to draw what your eye sees, rather than trying to draw with a particular idea of the item in mind.

For more practice with this kind of contour drawing, turn to the book *Drawing on the Right Side of the Brain* by Betty Edwards.

•PRINCIPLE•

## Offer Stories and Dramas as Tools for Coaching

Teachers can coach children by telling stories and using props to convey ideas they want children to grasp. Stories captivate children's attention, and playing out the details with dramatic play and props helps them internalize the concepts and strategies. Read about how teacher Sarah invented "teacher theater" for this purpose.

## Dino Theater

As you read the children's responses to Dino Theater, notice how many social skills and strategies they come up with. How might Sarah use their ideas in the real conflicts that emerge in the classroom?

*At one morning meeting, Sarah acted out a story using three rubber dinosaur toys. In this story, two of the dinosaurs were building a castle out of blocks when a third dinosaur came along, hoping to join their game. The first two dinosaurs said, "No, you can't play with us," and the third dinosaur felt sad and didn't know what to do. At that point Sarah stopped the story and asked the children what they thought the dinosaurs could do to solve their problem. The children generated a host of ideas, which Sarah then had the dinosaurs act out. Sarah had the dinosaurs "talk" about their own thoughts and feelings as they interacted. Here are a few of the suggestions the children had:*

*Tess: "They could change their mind and let the other dinosaur come to the party."*

*Elaina: "The one could go ask his mother for help."*

*Taylor: "The longneck won't like them."*

*Maria: "The longneck could build its own castle."*

*Siri: "The longneck could ask if they could come over to her house. They could play a little while at her house and then they could go to the castle. Then they could connect them."*

*Ruth Mabel: "The longneck could ask the dinosaurs if they could move over a little bit."*

*Maile: "Maybe they could go to a party—all the dinosaurs. That yellow one could say 'There will be a really big cake with five candles,' and they could sing 'Happy Birthday' to the yellow one."*

*Alex: "If they change their mind, they could join her into their game."*

*Ira: "Maybe they could go to a movie about dinosaurs called* The Dinosaur Movie *and they could watch the longneck."*

*Ezana: "Dinosaurs don't eat the same food."*

*Kintla: "He could talk: 'Please can I play?' "*

*Sarah left the animals out for the rest of the day so the children could play and replay the various scenarios on their own.*

### *Listen to Sarah*

"Teacher theater is a tool I use often to coach the children to work through common issues or problems that arise in the classroom. The kids are full of good ideas and creative solutions to help the protagonists in the dramas. They particularly love it when my co-teacher and I act out a situation for them to consider. I choose the topics for teacher theater in response to a particular or recurring interpersonal issue that is happening in the classroom. By having teachers or animals act out the situation, the kids involved can revisit their problems and receive some coaching without feeling

Hilltop Children's Center

Hilltop Children's Center

singled-out or criticized. Teacher theater is tremendously popular, and the kids always ask me to replay the scenario again and again and again. Replaying the drama with the props we leave out is also very popular. It's fascinating to watch the children act out what they have learned from the story and discussions."

### *Reflect*

Whenever children are invited to pretend, they seem to be able to access skills and concepts that are more difficult for them to grasp when they are in the middle of a real situation. The practice of teacher theater coaches children to think constructively about social problems, because the issues are one step removed from the emotion and intensity of their own play. Teacher theater also coaches kids to collaborate on generating ideas and offers them words and solutions that they can try the next time they find themselves in a similar situation. ■

For a more in-depth view of coaching kids through stories and dramas consider the book *Kids Like Us: Using Persona Dolls in the Classroom* by Trisha Whitney.

## •PRINCIPLE•
## Support Children to Learn from Their Friends

Children learn not only from their teachers' demonstrations and coaching, but also from their peers. In fact Vygotsky's theory of scaffolding makes note that children often learn more working side by side with friends who are operating at the top end of a similar zone of proximal development (Mooney 2000). Children often use similar language and understand things in the same way, so coaching them to learn from each other is a useful approach. To support children in learning from one another, teachers can plan specific opportunities for children to help one another or work together, and suggest that children teach other children what they have done or know about.

## Be My Friend

In the following story, notice how Benny's teachers help him share his good idea and become a teacher for his peers. Pay attention to how Ann continually finds opportunities to refer children to each other.

*Ann, a consultant in a Head Start classroom, watched with amazed delight as Benny turned paper towels meant for cleaning up splashes from the water table into pouches for holding water. Impressed with his ingenuity, she took the following photos to capture the sequence of actions that Benny used as he made pouch after pouch full of water. She planned to use these photos to revisit this work with Benny and to highlight Benny's work to his friends, teachers, and family.*

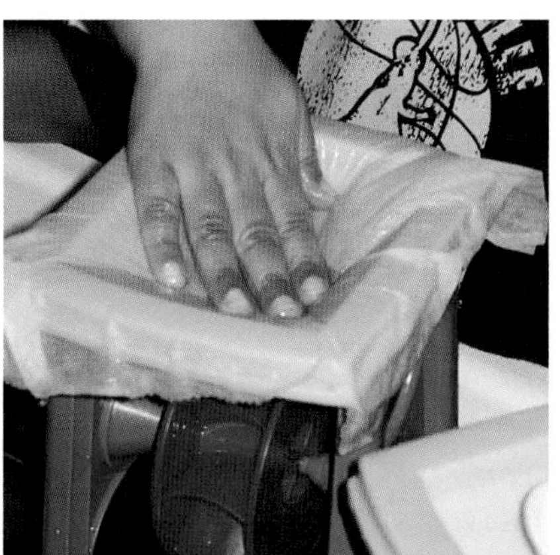

Parklake One Head Start

**Benny pushed the paper towel down a little into the water wheel.**

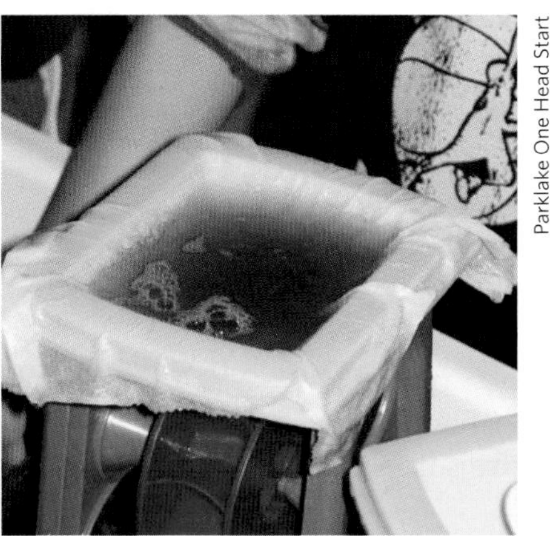

Parklake One Head Start

**He filled the towel with water all the way to the top.**

Parklake One Head Start

**He carefully lifted the edges of the towel to make a pouch.**

Parklake One Head Start

**He lifted the pouch up into the air. "You can watch it drip—or you can squeeze it and make the water swoosh out."**

*Ezra, Benny's teacher, and Ann alerted the other children to Benny's good idea about the water pouch and asked Benny to teach the other children how to make pouches. With splashing, laughter, and joyful pride, the children followed Benny's step-by-step instructions on how to turn paper towels into sturdy water pouches.*

*Soon after witnessing Benny's invention, Ann visited another center run by the same Head Start agency. There, Cedeena was playing at a table full of birdseed. Ann told Cedeena the story of Benny's invention and said, "I wonder if Benny's idea would work with birdseed?" She showed Cedeena the photos she'd taken of Benny's work on the screen of her camera. Cedeena eagerly accepted the challenge. She invented a pouch for birdseed! She practiced and practiced filling a paper towel with birdseed and lifting it up without spilling the birdseed.*

*"Benny ought to know about this!" Ann exclaimed to Cedeena. "You could write him a letter to tell him about your invention." She offered Cedeena the clipboard she was using to take notes about Cedeena's play, and her pen. She helped Cedeena start her letter: "We can begin the letter by writing, 'Dear Benny,'" Ann said. "Then what should we tell him about the pouch you made for birdseed?" Cedeena dictated words and Ann wrote; then Ann handed Cedeena the pen so she could draw her pouch so Benny could see it.*

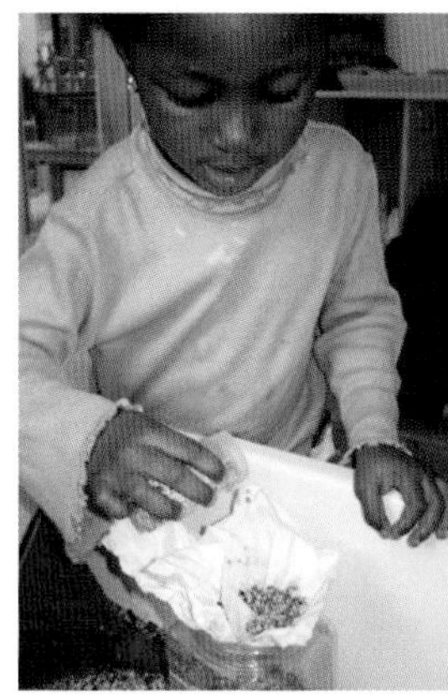
Parklake Two Head Start

Parklake Two Head Start

Dear Benny,
First you put the towel in the cup, then you put bird food in, and then you have to wrap it up and then you maked a pouch. That's how to make a pouch with birdseed! You have to wrap it really tight. Then you pour it into the jar.

*Ann delivered Cedeena's letter to Benny and his teacher, Ezra. Benny was delighted, laughing a big belly laugh and eagerly gathering a marker and paper to write a letter back to Cedeena. After dictating a letter to Ezra, Benny added a diagram of the birdseed invention, a way of letting Cedeena know that he understood her idea.*

Dear Cedeena,
Be my friend. Thank you Cedeena.
Be your friend. Benny
"you put the bird seed and it goes round and round in the cup."

*When Cedeena received Benny's letter, she hurried to her journal where she drew a picture of her friend Benny. Then Cedeena practiced making her birdseed pouch some more. Cedeena thought about Benny while she worked with birdseed. "Does Benny like to go fast on the tire swing?" she asked Ann.*

*"I don't know," Ann replied. "You could write him a letter to ask." And she did.*

Dear Benny,
We can play outside. Do you push fast on the tire swing? I do! I love fast and I say "woo-hoo!" Have fun. Play with me at water table and play with me at blocks.

*"Does Benny like my blue skirt?" Cedeena wondered as she wrote her letters.*

*"I don't think Benny knows what you look like," Ann answered.*

*"I'll draw him a picture so he knows who I am," Cedeena decided.*

*Benny and Cedeena's correspondence planted the seeds for a friendship that continues to grow. Their teachers have arranged a field trip for the two children's classes to meet at a park near their school, a park with a tire swing. Benny and Cedeena can cement their friendship with the joy of speed!*

**Reflection & Action**

***How do I understand the children's point of view in this situation?***

*

***What learning domains are being addressed here and what other learning domains could be addressed?***

*

***What theoretical perspectives and child development principles could inform my understandings and actions?***

### *Listen to Ann*

"A core value in my teaching is to nurture relationships among children. I watch for opportunities to help children grow connections with each other, ways that I can invite them to see each other in new ways, to collaborate, and to deepen their friendships. Benny was new to his classroom, and hadn't made many connections with other kids yet. I wanted to help the other children see his competence and creativity, and experience his leadership—and I wanted to help Benny see himself as a good buddy to other children, able to offer them his ideas and inventions. When Benny's teacher, Ezra, and I asked Benny to teach the other kids how to make pouches for water, Benny stood a little taller; his pride was tangible. He didn't say much, but demonstrated each step. His demonstrations engaged the other children—who spoke a number of languages—and launched the whole group into a shared adventure. And the shared adventure of making—and popping!—pouches full of water strengthened the relationships among this group of children.

"My decision to share Benny's story with Cedeena also grew from my core value about growing relationships among children. It was powerful for me to see two very young children (both these kids were barely four years old!) grow a solid connection to each other without meeting, by sharing their stories in writing and images. This experience affirmed the power of literacy—writing and drawing—as a tool for relationships."

### Reflect

Ann's coaching offered abundant opportunities to integrate literacy, sequencing, and representational work for Benny and Cedeena's learning. But there are larger implications in this story. As Benny and Cedeena heard about each other's pouch making, they began to imagine the other person's experiences, taking each other's perspectives and wondering about each other. Building from their shared experience of pouch making, they invited each other into other games—pushing each other on tire swings, using blocks together, being *friends* with each other. As they came to know the other person, they also came to know themselves more deeply—as inventors, teachers, writers, and friends. Their offerings of warmth and friendship radiate from their exchanges. This shows how coaching is more than teaching techniques, how it can foster genuine interactions that deepen our relationships and the quality of our lives together. ■

## Engineering Teams

Cindy and Vicky decided to challenge the children in their group to learn from each other by outlining a specific activity and designating the children who would work together as a learning group.

*Because a majority of the children in their group constantly played together in the block area, Cindy and Vicky wanted to challenge them to use their ideas and skills to teach each other more about block building. They divided the children into three "engineering teams." Each team had a different set of building tools and a different objective—to build a horse arena, an airport, or a ramp. The teachers decided on these activities based on the building they had observed during playtime. After a few moments of adjusting to the fact that they would be teaming with kids they didn't typically play with, the children took up the challenge and began to show each other what they knew about how to build with the blocks. When the building work came to an end, the teachers asked the children to take their building one step further by drawing what they created. Using clipboards and pencils, the children began to draw. Some of them drew the constructions by looking at them. Others drew by tracing the blocks. The children compared their strategies for drawing and building as they showed their drawings to each other.*

Burlington Little School

Burlington Little School

## *Listen to Cindy and Vicky*

"Most of the children in our preschool group have been very focused on building and construction over the last month. Each of them uses the blocks in unique ways and as a result they have mastered different skills. We wondered if we could help the children see and learn from each others' work if we gave them a few challenges and encouraged them to work with new partners. We directed the formation of the groups and helped the children work through their bumpy times. After the team building projects, we challenged the children again and asked them to draw their structures. Our goal was to introduce the idea of depiction, and that you can translate a three-dimensional idea into a two-dimensional one. The children were thrilled to take up this challenge. Later in the year, we'll ask them to draw their structures before they build them. We might even suggest that they do a collaborative drawing. We are excited about this idea of dividing the children into smaller groups to coach each other about their ideas and skills. It provided a wonderful opportunity to build new relationships and collaborate. And they really did teach and learn from each other!"

## *Reflect*

Many teachers think that child-centered curriculum means that teachers don't direct anything. You can see in this story that Cindy and Vicky's plans are all centered on the children's interests and ideas. But they are also claiming an active role to challenge the children to work at a more complex level in their relationships and with the materials and activities. You can see the careful thinking and planning in the structure for teamwork that they offered the children. This created a purposeful space and time to coach children in problem solving and conflict resolution. Unlike "heat of the moment" conflicts, the children anticipate the teacher's coaching because they have been alerted ahead of time that working with new people might be difficult. It is also apparent how closely they observe and listen to the children so they can use these details to build on their ideas and strengths. These teachers have tentative plans for future challenges, which indicate the possibilities for the children's growth as well as their own. ■

### Your Turn

Observe your group of children and make note of the different skills each has mastered. Look for an opportunity to arrange for one child to teach someone else what they know. You could have her or him talk another child through the steps, make a chart with the sequence to follow, or offer a demonstration to the group and have the group make the chart. Reflect on how this process worked and what changes you might make to incorporate this into your ongoing teaching practice.

CHAPTER 6

# Dig Deeper to Learn with Children

*What if we were to assume that children came to school more, rather than less, able to communicate their thinking about the world? Why not assume that when the child enters school, he or she presents us with an enormous number of innate tools to acquire knowledge? What effect might this assumption have on our approach to what the languages of learning are?*

**KAREN GALLAS**

Throughout *Learning Together with Young Children*, we have urged you to draw on children's strengths and competencies as the focus for the teaching and learning process. Karen Gallas (1994) reminds us that children bring "innate tools" to this process. If teachers believe this to be true, how will this affect the way you respond to children's actions? Rather than seeing children's self-initiated pursuits as a distraction from planned curriculum, teachers can use these pursuits as a vehicle for deeper learning. The challenge is to notice the details of how children are communicating their thinking as they play, sing, use their bodies, engage in dramas, build and construct, and make up games, so that you can support them to go further. Sometimes this involves introducing a related idea in a conversation with children about what they are exploring. At other times, teachers may challenge children to re-represent their idea with another material, for instance, drawing their block structure, or using objects from the natural world to explore a concept. When Gallas speaks of "the languages of learning" we are reminded of the renowned poem "The Hundred Languages of Children" by Loris Malaguzzi (Edwards, Gandini, and Forman 1998), which has inspired the world to see children as remarkably competent. Both Gallas and Malaguzzi remind us that children's expressions of knowledge and tools for learning should not be reduced to adult agendas and narrow academic outcomes.

Working with children's natural approaches to learning isn't a new idea in the early childhood profession, but judging by today's trends in education, it is out of favor. Teaching with deep respect for children's competencies requires you to engage your mind with theirs. You notice what is unfolding and then determine the support and challenge that will invite them into deeper study. Your actions might lead to extended curriculum projects, but in many cases, your comments and actions in ordinary moments with children are the source of the most meaningful learning.

To gain insight for extending children's pursuits, consider your work with them as similar to that of an improvisational theater artist who must develop a scene with other actors without a script to follow. Improvisational actors approach each idea offered as an invitation they must accept. Their rule of thumb is to respond to each invitation with "yes and . . ." For instance, picture the following situation.

Actor 1: "Oh look, it's raining."

Actor 2: "Do you want a peanut butter sandwich?"

Do you see how offering something totally unrelated to rain, like peanut butter sandwiches, leaves no direction to go? Now consider another response.

Actor 1: "Oh look, it's raining."

Actor 2: "Let's jump in these puddles."

Here actor 2 uses the "yes and . . ." rule. "Let's jump in these puddles" acknowledges that noticing the rain is an offer worth taking up, and then responds with new and interesting possibilities to keep the scene going. Bringing this simple "yes and . . ." mindset to your teaching repertoire suggests that you are looking for the children's thinking; you take their ideas seriously and believe they can take up new challenges. How might this look between a child and a teacher?

Child: "Yeah! It's raining. There's a puddle I can jump in."

Teacher: "Stop, don't jump into that puddle, you'll get all wet and might catch cold."

Do you see how this response stops any possibility for using the child's idea for a deeper experience? Consider another response.

Child: "Yeah! It's raining. There's a puddle I can jump in!"

Teacher: "Let's find your rain boots so you can jump in every puddle you can find."

This teacher says yes to puddle jumping, challenging the child to do more with her exuberance, while assisting her to stay dry and comfortable.

In this chapter we help you consider the innate tools and passions children bring to the learning process with examples of teachers saying "yes and . . ." to expand the children's experience. Can you see how the "yes and . . ." rule is another way to think about Vygotsky's theory of scaffolding children's learning (Berk and Winsler 1995)? The following principles will help you know what comes after the "and . . ." as you accept children's many promising offers.

- Challenge children to go a step further in their pursuits
- Help children represent their ideas with multiple materials
- Tap into children's love of songs and music
- Draw on children's deep fascination with drama and magical thinking
- Harness children's instinctive drive to use their bodies
- Build on children's attention for the natural world
- Explore children's theories for deeper learning
- Reflect children's ideas back to them with documentation

## •PRINCIPLE•
## Challenge Children to Go a Step Further in Their Pursuits

To uncover children's theories and challenge them to dig deeper, you must look closely at their actions and seek the underlying concepts they are exploring. As you work alongside them and study your observations, you can discover their interests to spark further investigation. Children's actions and words also help you see what they already know, and you can use this awareness to support them in new challenges. Sometimes children have inconsistencies, gaps, or "soft spots" (Duckworth 1996) in their thinking that can be taken up for further study. It is useful to offer only one next step, aligned with the children's pursuits, rather than initially planning numerous activities or a unit to study.

## Opening the Doors to Learning

In the following story, notice how each of Bekah's small challenges grows her moments with the children into a longer investigation.

*Bekah put out geo boards with rubber bands, encouraging the children to make geometrical shapes and patterns by stretching the rubber bands across the nails on the boards. Three-year-old Sage found them fascinating. Sage used the rubber bands to form a rectangle and announced, "Look, Bekah, I made a door."*

*Bekah said, "You did make a door. I bet you could draw a door too." Bekah moved her finger along the rubber band lines, outlining the rectangle shape, and explained, "See, you can make lines with a marker that look just like the rubber band lines." Bekah found a marker and paper and demonstrated how to draw the lines while Sage watched. She handed the marker to Sage, who took up the challenge. With much deliberation, even looking back and tracing the rubber band lines with her marker, Sage drew a door.*

*The older children next to Sage became very interested in her work, proudly declaring that drawing a door was really easy. Bekah responded, "Here's some markers and paper. Go for it!" The group all began drawing doors, teaching and showing each other their completed work. This went on for the rest of the afternoon and continued into the next week. Making doors became a shared activity among the group. The children drew pages and pages of doors. At one point Bekah offered another challenge to the group of door makers: "What's behind all these doors?" The children immediately wanted to figure out how to get their doors to open. Bekah responded by offering X-Acto knives and coached the children to carefully cut open the doors with the knives, using necessary safety precautions. Once they mastered cutting the doors, the children spent the next few days drawing pictures of "surprises" that were behind the doors.*

Burlington Little School

### Reflection & Action

***How are teacher actions impacting this situation?***

*

***What learning domains are being addressed here and what other learning domains could be addressed?***

*

***What theoretical perspectives and child development principles could inform my understandings and actions?***

Burlington Little School

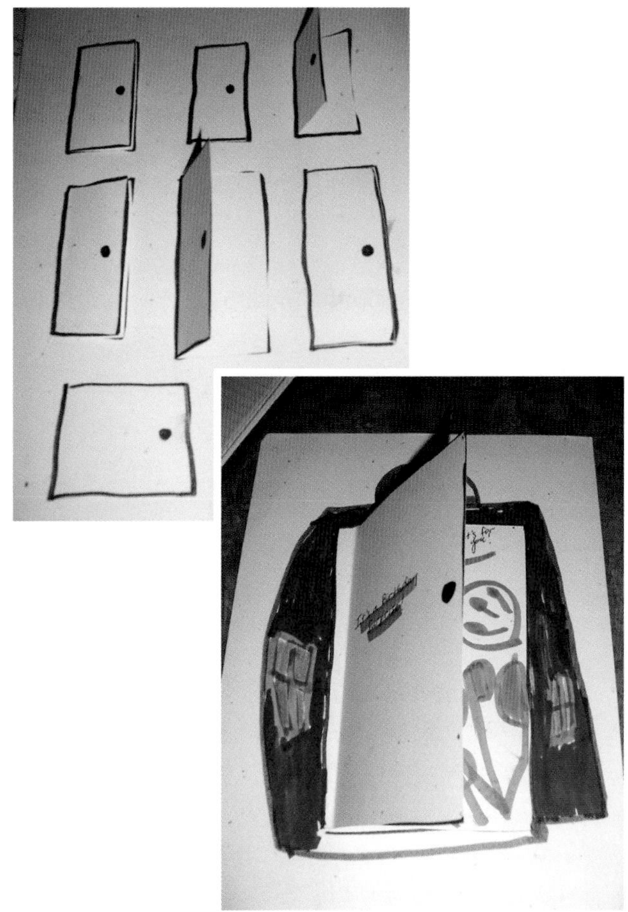

Burlington Little School

### Listen to Bekah

"When Sage announced, 'Look, I made a door,' it launched an interesting exploration with the entire group. The fact that she discovered and named her shape a door made me think she might be interested and able to learn to draw the door. The older children usually have all the ideas and take the lead, so I wanted to challenge them to follow Sage's lead to see where it went. I was delighted with how this opened the door for all the children, both literally and metaphorically. As I think about this, I am seeing many more possibilities for the door as a metaphor to offer back to the children. What is so interesting about doors? Why have the children been drawn to them? What else can we do to keep thinking about doors?"

### Reflect

Bekah's story illustrates how the use of appealing, open-ended materials and teacher actions aligned with children's interests can connect children to each other and expand their learning process. Making a door with rubber band lines and then drawing it provided experiences with symbolic representation for Sage and the other children. Bekah believed the children were capable of safely using an adult tool and she carefully demonstrated and coached them in the process. This expanded their skills and investigation. Think about what might have happened if Bekah chose, instead, to focus her actions solely on teaching Sage the name "rectangle" to identify the shape she made with the rubber bands. Consider what might have occurred if Bekah had suggested that Sage make something else with the rubber bands. Do you see how the timely comments and suggestions Bekah offered built a bridge to each new activity and encouraged collaboration among the group? The questions Bekah poses at the end of her reflection show teacher research in action. What strategies or materials could she offer next to learn more about the children's thinking related to doors?

Even the youngest children in our programs benefit from challenges to pursue their ideas and questions. In the following story, notice how the teacher's attention to the simple actions of a child reveals opportunities for enhanced learning.

## Floating Leaves

Julia's ordinary moment of exploration on the playground lead to a deeper investigation when her teacher noticed and took her actions seriously. How might you pay close attention to these kinds of details with your group?

*While on the playground one morning, Ann watched Julia act on her appetite for scientific exploration. Julia found a leaf and put it into the tube on the fence and then looked to see what would happen. The leaf didn't move. Then Julia blew into the tube, but the leaf still didn't move. Julia put more leaves into the tube. She blew into the tube again—and this time, one of the leaves swooped out of the bottom of the tube. When they went back inside the classroom, Ann offered Julia another tube and some leaves to continue her exploration. Julia put a leaf in the new tube, and it didn't go through this tube either. Julia blew hard on the tube, but the leaf still didn't budge. Ann demonstrated an idea. She held a leaf on the palm of her hand and blew on it. The leaf floated to the ground. Julia put a leaf in her hand and blew on it. The leaf floated to the floor, and Julia clapped her hands.*

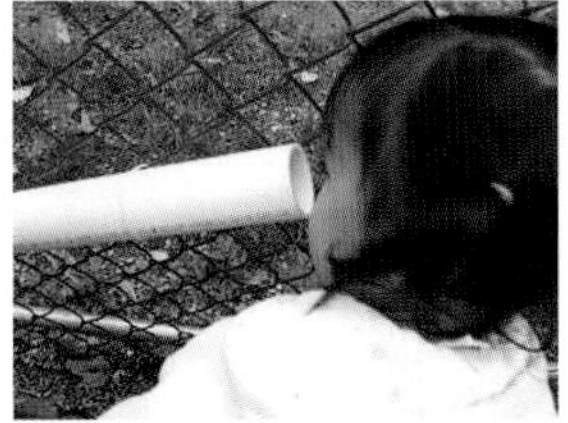

University of New Hampshire Child Development Center

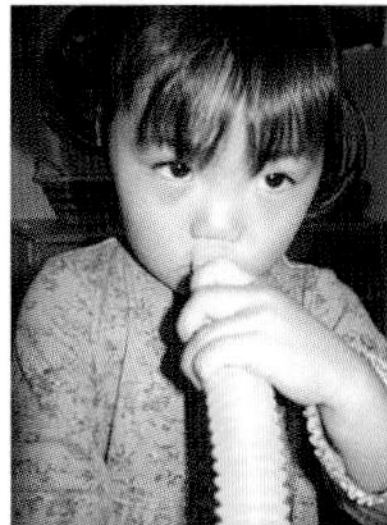

University of New Hampshire Child Development Center

### Listen to Ann

"Julia loves to blow bubbles. From bubble blowing experiences she knows that the power of her breath can move things through the air. Did she draw on this knowledge today as she explored the leaves and tube? How do we make meaning of Julia's interactions with the leaves and tubes, and how might we extend or challenge the thinking she did today? Can we understand her work as an investigation of cause and effect? Our hypothesis is that, indeed, Julia's work with the leaves today was an inquiry process. 'What happens when I blow on leaves—through tubes and on my hand?' To honor her inquiry, we'll offer Julia other objects with which to experiment: objects that move easily with breath, and objects that will resist breath. We'll arrange materials near our heater vent so when the air moves up through the vent, it will move the materials. As we continue to watch Julia's encounters with these invitations for further inquiry, we will challenge her to carry on her pursuits and we'll learn more about her understandings and questions."

### Reflect

Do you see how Ann's action of demonstrating the consequence of blowing on the leaves was in line with Julia's initial pursuit? If Ann hadn't seen the essence of Julia's experimentation, Julia might have gotten frustrated or abandoned her inquiry. Notice how Ann poses questions to herself to deepen her own understanding of the meaning of this play for Julia. She draws on her observations of Julia's previous experiences blowing bubbles to decide on the next challenge. She plans the next step to "honor" Julia's quest, and to find out more, not just to teach Julia a physics lesson. ■

### •PRINCIPLE•
### Help Children Represent Their Ideas with Multiple Materials

As teachers discover children's underlying interests and understandings, you can routinely invite children to explore their ideas by representing them in other ways. In the larger educational arena, students represent their learning with a paper, a test score, or a demonstration of mastery. However, representing what children know doesn't merely demonstrate their learning; it also enhances it. Different mediums such as drama, drawing, or sculpting provide children with additional perspectives to reflect on an idea or understanding and then confront what isn't yet clear (Forman 1996; MacNaughton and Williams 1998). Each medium helps children practice different skills and recognize different aspects of the ideas they are pursuing. As they study a representation together, observant teachers can guide children to recognize their ideas. When you observe children's representations of their thinking with different materials, you can see what they are trying to figure out. From that, you can offer a new avenue for additional inquiry. The stories throughout this book reflect a curriculum approach that continually highlights and revisits experiences to enhance learning. Here we want to offer more discussion and examples for how to put these ideas into practice.

## Facial Relations

In the following story note how teacher Maya seeks what the children find so fascinating about their faces and the innovative ways she offers different materials for them to represent their interest.

*Face painting materials are always available in the art area of Maya's preschool room. Several times a week, a number of the children were using the mirrors and oil pastels to paint their faces. They worked carefully, looking at themselves for a long time in the mirrors and studying the many photos Maya took of them. They focused on covering particular areas on their faces instead of painting a mask or a design.*

*Noticing the children's interest, Maya printed large black-and-white photos of the children's faces and offered these for them to paint on. The children eagerly took up this work, asking for multiple copies of the black-and-white photos to keep painting. Again their focus was on painting over distinct spaces and lines on the photos of their faces. At one point, the children decided to add to their work and paint on each other's photos.*

*The next week, Maya gave the children wire and demonstrated how they might follow the lines and shapes of their faces by bending and shaping the wire. This was a difficult task, but the children were challenged to revisit these interesting aspects of their faces, so they kept with it.*

*Maya continued to offer materials for the children to re-examine their interest in the spatial aspects of their faces. She introduced them to Picasso's unusual paintings that highlight and distort facial features. The children delighted in these, which led to cutting up the photos of their faces and gluing them back into different configurations.*

*This work continued off and on over a number of weeks. There was a long stretch where the children used mirrors and fine line pens to draw pictures of their faces. In this work they began to represent the details of their faces in their drawings, which depicted eyelashes, eyebrows, and ears.*

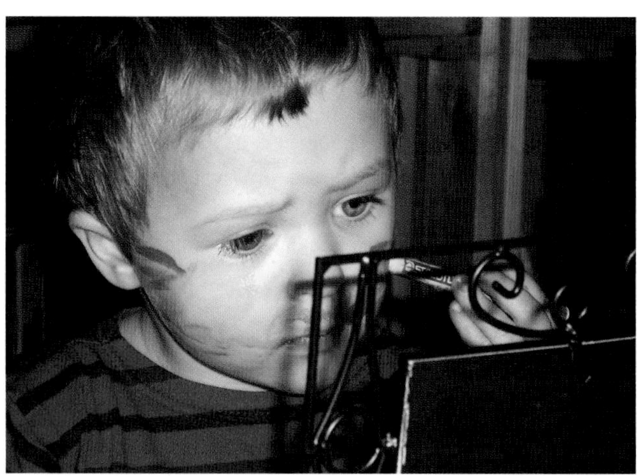

Burlington Little School

Burlington Little School

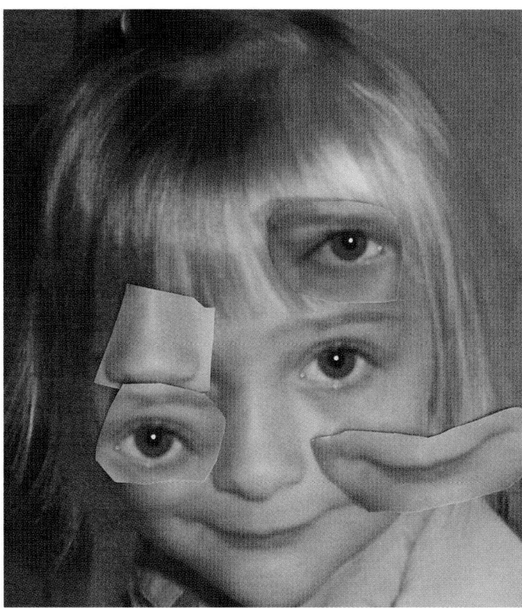
Burlington Little School

Burlington Little School

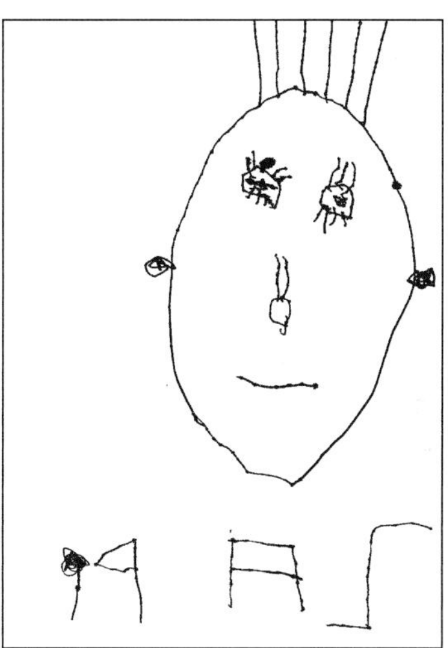
Burlington Little School

### *Listen to Maya*

"This year a small group of children in my room was captivated with painting their faces. It was evident that they took this work seriously and delighted in exploring their faces in many ways. They loved to show each other what they had done and have a photo taken of their altered faces. When I printed out the photos and studied the collection of them, I got really curious about the children's face painting. I found it interesting to look closely at each of their faces to see the purpose and detail in their work. It was fascinating to see the different facial expressions the children had behind the face paint in each of the photos. The photos reflected the children's deliberation and careful work with design, shape, and color. I began to ask myself what they were exploring as they used the paints in this way. Did they feel the magic and power of altering their identity? Were they revisiting the contours and spaces of their faces by coloring over them? I decided to give children more opportunities to explore this fascination with their faces. And they dove right in with everything I offered. They continued to study the spatial aspects of their face for a long while, but with each new material, their study shifted to other aspects of their faces. I loved how they worked with each other's faces too. I'm certain that these extended experiences of re-representation allowed them to look deeply into human faces and see many things."

### Reflect

Maya didn't jump in and turn the children's interest into a unit on faces, but instead looked for the underlying fascination the children demonstrated through their work. As a result, she focused on offering different materials for children to re-represent their focus on the spatial aspects of the shapes and lines of their faces. As you reflect on this story, what other materials could you present to continue the children's re-representation and study of faces? What guesses do you have about how the children would respond and what they would do with this new offering?

Drawing on the work of Vivian Paley (1990), teachers can use story dramas to give children multiple experiences with re-representing their ideas in different ways. Story dramas invite children to go through a process of dictating a story, drawing it, and acting it out as a drama. This creates a habit of mind for thinking in multiple ways, which can be carried over into other activities. It's an especially useful tool for children less inclined to draw or dictate their ideas.

## Story Dramas

In this story, notice how story dramas spread like wildfire in this child care program. Can you see how the children were motivated to participate by the prospect of acting out their story with their friends?

*From the beginning of the year, Deb's group of three- to six-year-old children were passionate about acting out dramas with whatever tools or materials they happened to be using. In order to frame and further this natural interest, Deb decided to introduce them to story dramas, an activity she adapted from inspiration from Vivian Paley. Every week in Deb's class, she set aside a table for creating story dramas and invited the children to participate. At first a number of the younger boys didn't show much interest. But once they understood that they would be acting out their drawings, they dove right in.*

*One day the children eagerly visited the table and each drew a picture of a story they wanted to tell. Some of the drawings were simple illustrations and stick figures. Other drawings were very complex, depicting every detail of the story. Next, the children dictated the story to go with their drawings while Deb wrote down their words. The last component of the process was for the children to act out their stories. All of the children gathered around the stage. One by one, the authors*

Burlington Little School

*went up on the stage with their story and drawing and chose the part they would play. The story was read carefully for the group to notice each of the roles before the rest of the cast was decided. Deb helped cast the parts, making sure everyone who wanted to be involved had a role to play. The children eagerly raised their hands to be the flowers, grass, sun, and ocean as well as the animals and people in the stories. The group did a quick dress rehearsal where Deb invited the children to demonstrate and practice an action, sounds, or words that depicted their part. Then they quickly and exuberantly acted out each story. Here are some of the stories that the group worked with.*

Burlington Little School

**The princess looked at the sun. Then she got trapped in a jail. Then she saw a different color sun. And that sun was blue, so she was confused. That's it.**

**Greta, age 3**

Burlington Little School

**The princess scuba diver and the knight scuba diver dived in the sea. Then the bad guys said, "I'll get you my creatures." Then the big, big, big transformer said, "Turn into a bulldozer." Then the tiger said, "I'm a sleepy cat." Then Denton threw the transformer down into the ground. And he got the bad guy creatures to melt and melt and melt. Then Denton said, "Watch out, princess." Then she moved to him.**

**Denton, age 4**

Burlington Little School

**Andrew and his two brothers Jered and Lered were holding onto logs while kicking their feet in the water. They were trying to escape from Fobat the evil pirate, slave owner. Fobat was chasing them in his pirate ship. Lered said to Andrew, "Kick harder." Jered said, "Yeah, kick harder." So Andrew said, "I'm kicking as hard as I can." Meanwhile Fobat was making one of his crew walk the plank to get food for them. And they set the anchor down and two people were practicing fighting with their swords. Fobat had a sword himself, but he stealed it from Andrew's father. Andrew's father had gone away to fight another pirate, which was Fobat's brother Forat.**

**Max, age 6**

### *Listen to Deb*

"The steps my children follow for story dramas spill over into other parts of their day. They are more willing to draw, engage in dramas, and talk about their ideas. Even the children who are the most reluctant to hold a marker or pencil work earnestly on these story drama stories because they know what's coming—they get to act them out! Over time, I have seen the children's drawing skills grow by leaps and bounds. I have also discovered that dictating stories really helps the children learn language and the form and function of reading and writing. The younger children who are just beginning to work with these concepts learn that they must slow down so I can write each word. The older children, who understand initial concepts about literacy, practice phonemic awareness as they carefully pronounce the sounds of the words that they dictate. I have delighted in the way they play with their understanding of what makes a good story through the words and phrases they choose for dialogue, action, and the passage of time. The children love to put each other into their stories and I can see the influences they are having on each other's storylines.

"Acting out the drama is the most engaging aspect for most of the children. It is usually very short, sometimes chaotic, but always exciting. The children have been adding props from our classroom to enhance the dramas and they often take up the storyline of one of the story dramas in their free play. The children have powerful feelings as a result of seeing their words and drawings come to life through their friends on the stage.

"I have continued to add other elements of re-representation to this activity. Sometimes the children draw their pictures onto transparencies and then we project them on the wall above our stage with an overhead projector. The drawings become the scenery that the actors use in the drama. To extend this process to other media, I have begun to ask children to dictate a story about their Lego constructions or block structures and then we cast the parts and act them out."

### *Reflect*

There are many layers of learning through representation and re-representation reflected in this story. Can you see language, literacy, creative expression, math, and spatial skills as well as significant cooperation and problem solving through the use of story dramas? When children draw their ideas and the actions involved in their stories, they are confronted with many challenges. They must decide the most important elements of the story and the relationships of the characters to the action. They must work with spatial and visual concepts as they depict the details. In the story development and dictation process, they construct the understanding that letters make up words and that words become sentences and then whole stories can be read back and enjoyed. All of these actions are foundational for learning to read and write.

The children's work in these story dramas portrays the struggles that all human beings have with good and evil, love and hate, fear and bravery, danger and rescue, allegiance and betrayal, and life and death. The stories have happy endings where the good guys come back to life, and evil is defeated, as the hero saves the day. Working out feelings of fear and powerlessness through dramatic play has long been considered important for children's emotional development (Hoffman 2004). As you study the above children's stories, can you see the array of human emotions and experiences found in the myths, fairytales, and literature throughout many cultures of the world? It is astonishing how much these very young people know about complex human themes. ■

### Your Turn

To better understand the value of having children re-represent their ideas in a different medium, try this activity adapted from one invented by Tom Drummond.

**Step 1.** Gather together a few friends or colleagues, along with an object that you are familiar with but about whose inner workings you don't know much. Possibilities for this include a kitchen timer, fax machine, staple gun, wind-up toy, or Jacob's ladder folk toy.

**Step 2.** Without peeking inside or dismantling the object, explore how it works and begin to make note of what you are curious about.

**Step 3.** Make a quick list of questions that come to mind about this object.

**Step 4.** Discuss your theories about how you think this object works with the others in the group.

**Step 5.** Make individual drawings showing your theory of how the object works.

**Step 6.** Compare your representations and see if they illuminate the inner workings or if there are still outstanding questions.

**Step 7.** Decide on another material (such as blocks, recycled materials, wire, or clay) to create a collaborative representation of your theory of how this object works. Refer to your drawings in the process and make note of any new insights that occur as you translate your theory from your drawing to a new material.

**Step 8.** Use your drawings and new representation to explain your theory and discoveries to someone else. As you consider your learning process, consider whether you have deepened your understandings of the following concepts.

- Exploring to learn (physical knowledge)
- Hypothesizing to learn (theory making)
- Drawing to learn (symbolic thinking and consolidating knowledge)
- Collaborating to learn (social constructivism)
- Making thinking and learning visible through multiple representations (multiple intelligences)

As you think about the new understandings this activity illuminated for you, what will your next step be? How can you incorporate what you learned into your curriculum planning?

## •PRINCIPLE•
## Tap into Children's Love of Songs and Music

Listen to preschool children at play and you will often hear them humming a familiar tune as they work. When you turn on the music, watch a toddler's body move in time to the beat. Children are naturally drawn to the rhythms and sounds of music. They easily remember lyrics because they tell a story and are connected to a melody. Why not draw on this enthusiasm for music to help children take pleasure in learning. As Tom Hunter suggests in the spotlight story here, don't just use songs for the purpose of teaching a lesson. Instead, offer music for the joy and liveliness it can bring to the children's and your life.

### Sing a Lot

*The following words of wisdom about using songs with children are from Tom Hunter.*

Song Growing Company

*"We turn songs into teaching resources too quickly these days. In a way it makes sense—children learn a lot when they sing, so why not teach them using songs? The problem is the delight of the song itself gets lost to whatever it is we want to teach children. The song no longer exists as a song inviting a range of responses. It's become a lesson, one-dimensional, often with the vitality wrung out of it. Teachers should sing a song with children many times before using it to teach anything. Play with it—faster/slower,*

*louder/softer. Wonder out loud about it. Change the words. Let it belong to the children and become part of their lives with all the connections they will naturally make. Then it becomes even more valuable, the learning it brings coming not only from what teachers want but what the children find.*

*"Children surrounded with lively oral experiences (songs, finger plays, nursery rhymes, conversations) will likely master early literacy skills fine. What's the bottom line? Sing a lot so the song is first a song and then a teaching resource."*

## Enticing Fred

Family provider Billie loves to sing with her children, who have become mesmerized by the storyline and rhythm in a song about a turtle. Listen to her story of how the children take serious steps to re-create the song for their own lives.

*"My Turtle, Fred" (Hunter 2004) is a song that Billie and her kids listen to and sing often. It tells the story of a stray turtle that wanders into and eventually out of a kid's yard. One spring, three of the school-age boys in Billie's program decided they were going to create a turtle habitat that was so inviting that Fred couldn't resist and would end up wandering into their yard. They did some research and came up with what they thought turtles needed to survive and then set about creating "turtle paradise," as they called it. They dug little ponds, created shaded areas with pine branches, and built lovely rock gardens, climbing apparatuses out of tree bark, and other features that only turtles could fully appreciate. The final touch was when Billie took them to the pet supply store and they picked out several turtle replicas (made of resin and stone) to place strategically around the habitat. Their reasoning was that if Fred should wander into the yard and see all these other "friends" then he would be more likely to stick around for a while.*

Heart and Home Family Child Care

### *Listen to Billie*

"The story and melody of the song 'My Turtle, Fred' seemed to touch something deep inside these boys in my group. They listen to the lyrics and take them very seriously, worrying about Fred and where he might be living. Their concern for Fred has led them to this wonderful collaborative project to create a habitat to lure him to our yard. I think on one level they understand that Fred won't really come to live with us. But they also believe he will. So far, we haven't spotted any visitors to our turtle paradise, but the children haven't given up hope that their carefully thought-out plan will eventually work . . . and neither have I!"

### *Reflect*

Billie uses songs in her program all the time because she knows their power to reach children at a deep level. She takes the children's interests seriously by tapping into their love of this song to pursue the many opportunities for the joy and learning it provides. The music and lyrics of the song inspire the boys to expand their thinking to take the perspective of the turtle. How can we create a beautiful place where a turtle would like to live? Who would the turtle like to live with? Their answers show their attention to the significance of relationships as well as their understanding of the importance of protective habitats. What is your response to the boys' tenderness, creativity, and their ability to make plans and carry them out as they design, construct, and sing about this habitat for Fred? ■

Using songs to revisit ideas and information draws on one of the multiple intelligences (Gardner 1993) that children can bring to their learning. The following story reminds us, even if we don't have any formal musical training, that music can become an integral and lively aspect of our daily life together.

## Silly Songs

As you read the story of Deb's approach to songs and music, think about the music you enjoy in your own life and how you can bring this to your work with children.

*Deb sings all of the time with the children in her child care room. They sing songs that other people have written and also make up their own songs. Deb spontaneously invents operas during moments of adventure on the climber or when children are emoting from the drama area. They sing greetings to the sun and the rain and the changing of the seasons. And they make up ditties to go along with their daily routines. One year, the songs about routines were particularly delightful to the children. Because the children were making up and singing out so many verses to the songs as they worked, Deb suggested they make a song book with words and illustrations. The children turned it into a silly song book as they laughed uproariously at the twisted lyrics they created about their routines.*

*"Go to your cubby . . . and take a shower."*

*"Turn on the lights and . . . don't get in fights."*

*"Look for your lost underwear . . . in your hair."*

*The children looked through the book each day, singing about the simple pleasures of their days in funny, new ways. The book was over three inches thick by the end of the year.*

Burlington Little School

### Listen to Deb

"One of my favorite childhood memories is my dad's singing. He would sing in the shower, sing along with the radio, and the best part was singing together with me. He never had any formal music training and neither have I, but this hasn't stopped me from enjoying music in my life and in my classroom. Following my dad's example, I sing all of the time with the children. The children are learning so much from their love of singing and making up songs. They draw pictures and dictate the silly lyrics all the time for our song book. I see them reading it to each other throughout the day. But more importantly I know that I'm passing along the same pleasure and wonderful memories that my dad's singing gave to me!"

### *Reflect*

As Deb suggests, the song book she and the children created together is an excellent example of literacy learning. As the children dictate the lyrics, they come to understand that words and sentences can be used to write songs and books. The children come to see that print has meaning and is useful and enjoyable for their lives. Additionally, did you notice the phonics practice they engaged in when they made up lyrics that rhyme? You can also see in this story the power of humor to enhance children's thinking. Native American communities with rich oral traditions have long understood the role of humor in the teaching and learning process (Momaday 2007). The unrelated images and words the children invent and put together for the lyrics show they understand that when they contrast two opposing but interesting ideas, it can be funny. When children work at shifting their perspectives in this way it boosts their cognitive development (McGhee 2003). ■

## •PRINCIPLE•
## Draw on Children's Deep Fascination with Drama and Magical Thinking

Young children's use of make-believe play and magical thinking to make sense of the world is a delightful aspect of spending our days with them. Children regularly act out dramas and offer profound observations, relating their own experiences and view of the world to other people, animals, and even objects. The technical terms for some of this thinking are "animism" or "personification," which refer to giving human personalities, thoughts, or movements to natural or inanimate objects. Rather than seeing this world view as merely cute or dismissing it as undeveloped, why not draw on children's unique perspectives to extend the learning process?

Teachers can create dramatic play opportunities that specifically reflect children's interests and encourage them to represent and further their understandings through their pretend play. Whenever children say, "Let's pretend," a new landscape of possibilities for learning is revealed. When children pretend, they try on new feelings, roles, and ideas. They stretch their minds along with their imaginations.

### Bird-Watchers' Park

Study this story from Australian colleagues Fran and Nicole describing how adding dramatic play props related to the children's deep interest in birds extended the study and learning over a long period of time.

*The provision of one reference book about birds invited four-year-old Lewis and his peers to become engrossed in the world of ornithology and they began researching birdlife at every opportunity. Responding to this interest in birds, the teachers, Fran and Nicole, established a small area that included several other reference books and storybooks along with sticks, stones, feathers, bird figurines, and a real nest. The children immediately took this interest to the outdoor area. They became avid bird-watchers, using the reference books to help them in their bird hunts.*

*The teachers decided to establish an outdoor dramatic play area in order to facilitate further exploration and extend the play. Soon the children were checking in to the bird-watching office the teachers created and taking binoculars and clipboards on their hunts to record their findings on identification charts. The drama extended to using tents and turning the outdoor BBQ facilities into the "Earlwood Bird-Watching Park." The children eagerly immersed themselves in the play. However, it soon became apparent that there were not many birds to actually find. The children decided that it must be because the birds could see and hear them coming.*

Earlwood Children's Centre

Earlwood Children's Centre

Earlwood Children's Centre

*The group decided a bird-watching house was required and Fran and Nicole and the small group of friends worked on converting the existing outdoor cubby house into a bird-watching house. They attached bamboo to the exterior of the house and painted it in tones of brown and green in order to camouflage their position. They discussed plans for their new bird-watching house as they painted, excited about the prospect of seeing a wide range of birdlife once they were suitably concealed within this new vantage point. Riley also decided that leaving birdseed out might help entice the birds to the area—he sprinkled seed with the other children and eagerly checked on the progress of attracting birds. The children also sketched colorful parrots in chalk pastels, which were laminated and mounted around the bird-watching park as another lure.*

### Listen to Fran and Nicole

"The power of the peer group is remarkable. The passion friends have for a particular subject matter can become infectious within this community of learners. We came to understand that the children certainly possessed a wealth of knowledge about birds, which became the basis for their practical ideas about what would attract birds to the area. The most popular suggestion was the bird-watching house, which became a focal point of play for this group of bird enthusiasts for many, many months."

### Reflect

This story reflects something very different from traditional prop or theme boxes that teachers offer arbitrarily for children's play. Can you see how the children's appetite for fantasy and the provision of these particular dramatic play props launched this group into more study and collaboration around something they were already engrossed with? The children took this "make-believe" play seriously, as they knew the possibilities it held for engaging their minds and emotions. The children didn't just play or learn facts about birds. Instead, they used the props to express and construct new understandings about birds and many other things. Through their bird-watcher play scripts, the children furthered their dispositions to be careful observers and use reference materials. They developed skills for recording and analyzing their findings and practiced problem-solving to meet the challenge of how to attract birds to the outdoor area. The children used the props to invent and construct the bird-watching house and stretched their thinking by taking the birds' perspectives. Along with all of this, they strengthened their identity as learners and collaborators. The teachers, Fran and Nicole, took this dramatic play seriously as well, offering support and adding complexity to the drama while marveling with the children at the ongoing possibilities for this pursuit. ■

Planning opportunities for children to draw on their innate tendencies toward animism is another way to engage them in complex learning processes. Children eagerly engage and learn with a character they can have a relationship with. These characters invite them to pretend and explore in ways that teachers can't.

## Rat Habitats

The following story shows how Lindsay helped her group learn to care for their pet rats by helping them talk together. What is your response to the children's point of view about the rats? Can you see why they would be drawn into a relationship with these energetic creatures?

*The children in Lindsay's child care room gathered in small groups near the rat cage to hold the rats, and to talk about them. As they observed the rats, the children spent a lot of time talking about the rats' point of view, what they might like and not like about the children's treatment of them and their cage. Lindsay extended the children's shared interest in the rats' perspectives by making stick puppets from photos of the rats and inviting the children to have a conversation with them.*

*Furry rat: "I like it when you hold me gently and most of all when you let me run around."*

*Zoe: "We have to make sure we hear the cage click otherwise you will get out and chew the cords and you can break the electricity and climb on wire fences."*

*Furry rat: "I do like to chew on things."*

*Olivia: "Is it why your eyes are so big, cause you're scared?"*

*Furry rat: "Sometimes I get scared when you bang on my cage."*

*Zoe: "Can you climb big poles and swim in the water? I heard that on a show about rats."*

*Furry rat: "I do like interesting things to climb on. And yes, I can swim."*

*After many meetings with the rat puppets, Lindsay invited the children to think about their conversations with them to design and build habitats for them. As they used recycled materials to build the habitats for the rats, they talked about how the rats' perspective influenced their work.*

*"The rats like colors, so we have to have many colors in the habitat."*

*"They run around a lot. That's why we need to make it big."*

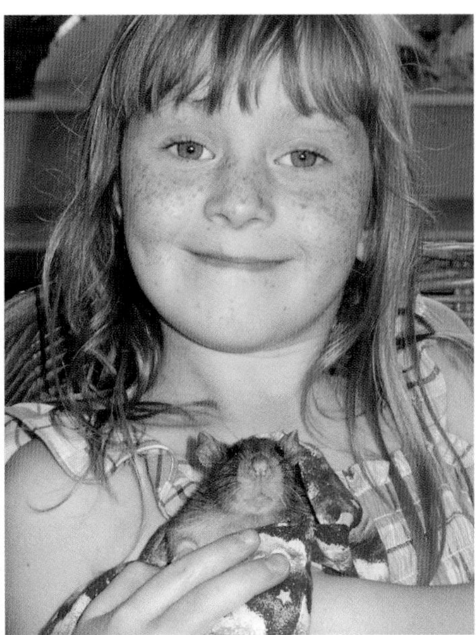
Burlington Little School

*"The rats love to be in cozy spaces. They need a blankie. They need a carpet to be soft and cozy."*

*"I'm putting in two chairs to sit in. Rat chairs. Cozy chairs."*

*"The rooms the rats need are a living room, eating room, hallways, and a bed in a bedroom."*

*"They need doors between the rooms so they can get in the room."*

*"I'm using this screen for the door, so the air can get in and the rats can breathe."*

*"All of the rooms in the habitat need air holes."*

*"Remember, they like it best when they get to run around."*

*"When we put all of the rooms together the rats have lots of room to run around."*

*"We can make windows in the tops of the rooms so we can watch them in the habitat."*

*Over a few weeks' time, the children created an elaborate habitat for the rats. They observed the rats closely in their new habitat and continued to remodel it based on their observations.*

Burlington Little School

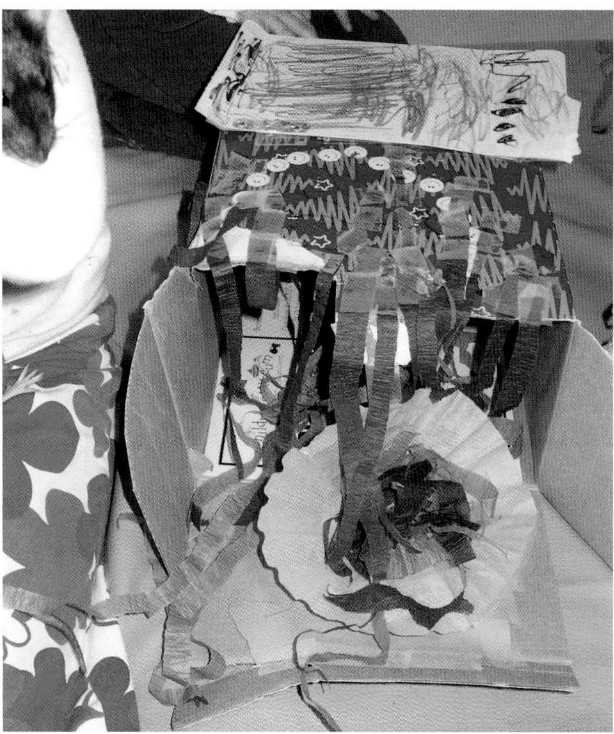

Burlington Little School

## Reflection & Action

*What details stand out that I can make visible for further consideration?*

*

*How might issues of culture, family background, or popular media be influencing this situation?*

*

*How do I understand the children's point of view in this situation?*

*

*What learning domains are being addressed here and what other learning domains could be addressed?*

### Listen to Lindsay

"Since the beginning of the year, the children in my group have been infatuated with the rats living in a cage in our child care room. Their shared interest in these small, friendly creatures has led to a big, collaborative project. The children lit up when I introduced the rat puppets. I was surprised at the genuine way they took up the conversations with the rat puppets. They seemed to be able to think more creatively when they pretended to talk with them. We could see the children's amazing ingenuity for using what they observed and understood about the rats in order to make them a comfortable, beautiful, and fun habitat. They were so excited to show the rats their new habitat and knew they must introduce them to it in a calm and gentle way to keep the rats safe. I've noticed that their tender concern for the rats has spilled over into their interactions with each other. As they are thinking about what it takes to make friends with the rats, they are making friends with each other."

### Reflect

Can you see how the children's magical thinking about the rats led to serious scientific investigation and study? Their imaginary conversations with the rats motivated close observation of the rats' behavior and in turn elicited rigorous thinking about the design and construction of the elaborate habitat. Lindsay didn't approach the children's interest by offering lessons or facts about rats. Instead she extended their conversations, knowledge, and work by inviting the children to make believe they could really talk with the rats. Her actions encouraged them to use their imaginations to boost their interest and learning.

To see the world the way that children do, teachers must be able to hold on to their adult view of the world and at the same time use children's logic to offer new ideas. It may mean practicing magical thinking yourself by applying your human thoughts and feelings to objects and creatures and joining with the children in pursuing the possibilities. In the following story, the teachers invite the children to bring their unique perspectives to learn more about the physics of water.

## A Water View

In this story, notice how easily the children are able to use their view of the world to immerse themselves in new understandings. As you study the children's ideas, try out their way of thinking about the water to see what you learn.

*During their play at the water table one morning, four children began articulating and drawing their theories about why some objects sink and others float.*

*Jonah: "Rocks make things sink."*

*Lucy: "Because they don't have enough air."*

*Eric: "Right, rocks don't have enough air in them and then they sink."*

*Felix: "My Lego boat floats because the water is strong enough to float it."*

*As they talked, they tried to make their theories visible to each other, offering each other the rock and the boat to hold and weigh, pointing out the way the rock fell quick and sure to the bottom of the table, and bending close to the water's surface to study the way the boat floated on the water. Teachers Nick and Ann met regularly with the children over several months to investigate the original, loosely formed theories and to explore the complexities of new theories generated as the children worked with a range of materials and a tub of water. After a few rounds of prediction, experimentation, and analysis with objects, Nick and Ann decided to ask the children to think about the experience of sinking and floating from the water's perspective. They posed various questions to provoke the children's thinking. Ann began the exploration of the water's perspective by taking the voice of water in a story about a lake's encounter with a rock and a pinecone. As she told the story, she invited the children to help her articulate the water's thoughts and feelings.*

*Ann: "How do you suppose the water feels as the rock lands on its surface?"*

*Jonah: "The water would feel tired."*

*Ann: "And when the pinecone lands, what would it feel then?"*

*Lucy: "That felt nice, because the water could feel it scratch where it had itches."*

*Eric: "When leaves go on the water, it feels tickled."*

*This story launched the children into broader consideration of the water's perspective:*

Hilltop Children's Center

*Jonah: "Do you know how to say 'sink' in sign language? Like this." He scrunched his face into a grimace of effort, and clenched his hands tight, making his arms shake. "That means the water is so strongly trying to hold something up that is very heavy. It's just too heavy. The water has to work hard but it can't do it."*

*Ann: "And what is the sign language word-sign for 'float'?"*

Hilltop Children's Center

*Jonah lifted his hands above his head and smiled. "That means that the water held it up! It was easy for the water and the water was happy that it was so easy."*

### Listen to Ann

"As we watched the children's focused investigation of sinking and floating, we wanted to encourage their theory-making and testing, and to challenge them to move their thinking into ever more complex terrain. We decided to invite the children to meet formally as a "work team," a group experience in our program where children and teachers come together to investigate a question over time. In the children's initial play around the water table, Felix had suggested that water has an active role in sinking and floating when he'd said, 'The water is strong enough' to hold a Lego boat. This sparked our decision to help the children think about this idea some more by exploring the water's experience, to take an unfamiliar perspective and to examine the theories they'd been sharpening through a new lens."

### Reflect

These teachers' intention wasn't to "teach" the children about "sink" and "float," density and water displacement, or other elements of physics. Instead they wanted to invite the children into a cycle of investigation and inquiry, creating an opportunity for the children to revisit and revise their initial theories about air and weight, and to articulate new theories based on further study. The simple story of a pinecone, a rock, and a pond of water sparked insightful consideration by the children and a new way to understand the experience of sinking and floating. They eagerly let go of the perspective of the objects in the water, and took up the invitation for a new way of seeing. They built a relationship with the water, acknowledging its effort, extending compassion for its experience of being overwhelmed by a heavy object, and celebrating with a grin and arms outstretched its experience of holding an object lightly on its surface. The children's understanding of "sink" and "float" became more complex, and they certainly did learn about physics. The invitation to take the water's perspective deepened the children's investigation by engaging their emotions and their intellect more deeply. ■

## •PRINCIPLE•
## Harness Children's Instinctive Drive to Use Their Bodies

Everything we know about how young children learn points to the fact that children bring their bodies with them wherever they go and use them for learning and expression. Yet, there has been a trend in education to take away dance, movement, and physical education in favor of a focus on "seat work." Physical education is thought of as a way to build the body, not the mind, when in fact, children readily use their bodies as tools to explore ideas and feelings. Teachers spend a lot of time reminding children to "use your walking feet," "sit criss-cross applesauce," or "get your wiggles out," thinking of children's natural exuberance as interrupting their attention and learning. What if instead you saw children's physicality as one of their innate tools or languages of learning that you might harness to expand the learning process? Here is an example of a teacher working with this mindset.

## Big Body Playdough

Have you ever thought of playdough as a large motor activity? Neither did the teacher in this story until she began to observe closely and let go of her limited views. Notice how teacher Kristin honored and extended the children's natural desire to move big.

*Kristin created a playdough invitation for children by setting out five black trays, each with a ball of dough in the middle. Everyone jumped right in and the room was filled with sounds of laughter, banging, and slapping as the dough hit the trays. The children were using a lot of force as they worked with the dough. They literally used their whole bodies to press into it. They stood on chairs to get more leverage. They pushed and squeezed and pounded with all their might. They used hands, fingers, fists, chests, foreheads, and elbows to flatten and shape the dough. As Kristin continued to offer this invitation over the coming days, the children added more body movements in their play. After studying a video of the children working with the playdough in these ways, Kristin and her co-teachers decided to put the playdough on the floor to make more room for this big body playdough work.*

*The children dove right in and continued using their entire bodies and strength. Being on the floor allowed them to spread out and use their bodies in different ways. They lay down and stood up, using their feet on the dough. They used the design tools with greater force to press into the dough to create the greatest impression.*

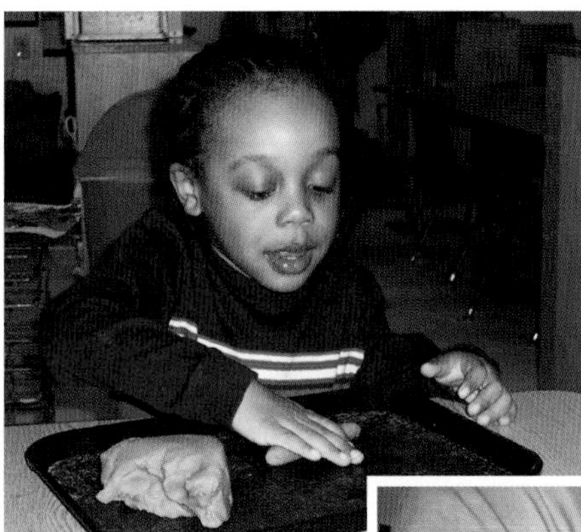

Denise Louie Head Start

Denise Louie Head Start

Denise Louie Head Start

Denise Louie Head Start

### *Listen to Kristin*

"As we observed the children work with the playdough, we noticed they were using mostly big body movements as they played. My coworker, Cathy, exclaimed, 'I never knew playdough was a movement activity!' When the suggestion was posed that we put the playdough on the floor, I thought to myself, 'That's not an option because, of course, playdough has to be done at a table, right?' When the children had left for the day, we put the playdough, along with the design materials, onto platters on the floor. We then got down and imagined rolling the materials gently with our feet, or combing the sides of a dough mountain with a comb. We decided that yes, this is how we would offer the materials next week, on the floor.

"Being on the floor indeed allowed the children to spread out and use their bodies in different ways. I was impressed by the way the children pushed and pulled with all their might while using the materials with respect. My impression was that now that the children had been freed to use their entire bodies, they needed much more room than I had given them. They were bumping into one another and, I thought, less able to focus on their work as their personal space was less defined. But, as we were preparing the setup for the next group to come in, a child looked at me and said, 'We do this again. Here! (pointing at the floor) Not there,' he added, pointing at the table. I was surprised to see that when I added additional mats to the floor to allow the children to spread out, they stayed in groups, working very physically close to one another. Certainly the extra room was used when the children had an idea that called for it, but mostly they huddled together, forehead to forehead, comparing their work. The notion that bumping into each other was problematic was how I saw the situation. The children did not seem to mind so much. The dough and the design materials are now in the room on an open shelf that is connected to the large open floor area and also near a big table. That way the children can have access to the materials and use them on either surface. I realize I am seeing children in a new light, learning things about them that I had not previously seen. And it has proven a bit of a challenge—a positive one—to look for meaning and ponder how to expand upon a material that is so well known to me."

### Reflect

What is your response to the idea of children working with playdough on the floor? Kristin saw the underlying interest the children had in using their bodies in big ways and took the risk of offering them the chance to do more. Notice how she challenged her own preexisting ideas about the use of playdough, and the children's ability and interest in negotiating their play space. Because Kristin was willing to "see children in a new light" and take action on their behalf, big things happened, both literally and figuratively. ■

Children constantly use their bodies, trying new challenges, using their muscles, and moving in a variety of ways. It follows then that asking children to think about and study their bodies is a logical place to extend their thinking and learning. Notice how the teacher in the following story does this when she offers a way for the children to reflect on their bodies and how they move.

## Moving Bodies

In this story, read how the children take up the teacher's delightful invitation to play with moving bodies. How did using the dolls to represent their own body movements enhance the children's understandings of their bodies? How did it extend the learning process?

*The children in Gloria's preschool group loved to move their bodies. They were constantly dancing, climbing, and running both indoors and out. To capture this interest, Gloria gathered together a collection of wooden dolls that artists use as models and some books about dance and body movement. She put these on the table for the children to discover as they came in the room. The props sparked new investigations. The children manipulated the dolls in many ways, studying the movement of the arms, legs, neck, and torso. They studied the photographs and arranged the dolls to match the people in the photos. They tried to mimic the movement of the figurines and the photos using their own bodies. Some of the children studied the photos in the alphabet book and attempted to "write" the letters of their names with their own bodies.*

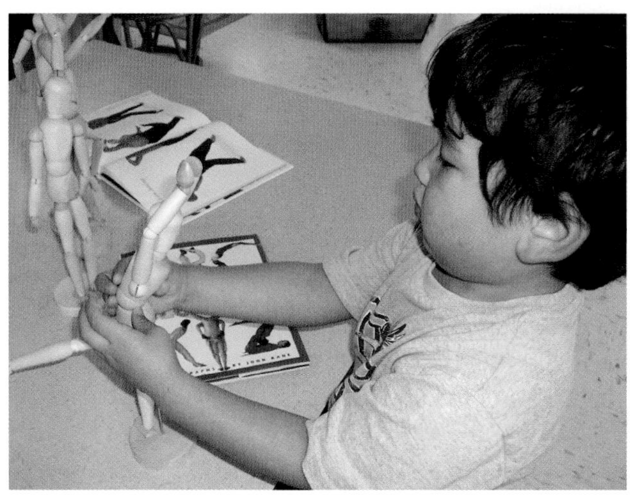

Burlington Little School

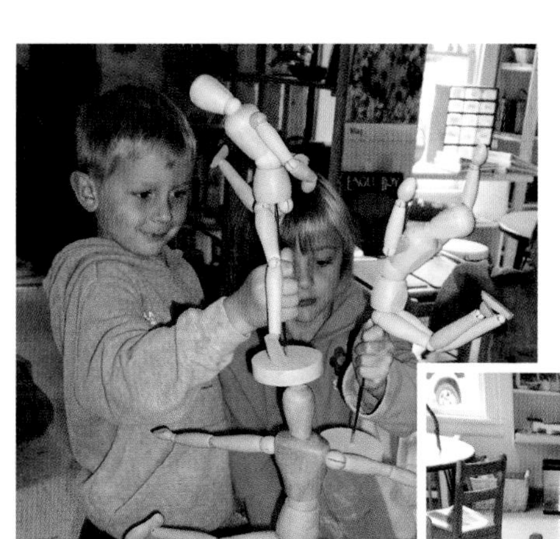

Burlington Little School

### *Listen to Gloria*

"Because we have such an active group, my co-teacher and I thought it would be interesting to offer the children a different way to study and represent the ways that bodies move. The children were captivated by the wooden dolls and spent a number of days playing with them. It was great how a lot of their play was having the dolls interact with each other. They had the dolls stand on each other's heads, wrap their limbs around each other, and pretend they were dancing. Of course it didn't take the children long to use these ideas with their own bodies as they copied the movements and positions of the dolls and studied the photos in the books. We had a great literacy lesson as the children worked to spell their names with their bodies, as they saw had been done in the human alphabet book. We decided the next thing we could offer is paper and pencils for the children to draw the models, just like artists do. It will be interesting to see if they will use their own bodies to re-represent their drawings."

### *Reflect*

Gloria's innovative idea of using the artists' wooden models for children to study moving bodies is a great example of how re-representation can provide a new window for children's thinking and understanding. By manipulating the movements of the small dolls, the children had a more focused view of something that they do often but probably don't think about. Once the children practiced the movements on the dolls' arms, legs, necks, and torsos, they switched quickly to try these movements with their own bodies. It was a powerful learning tool for them to be able to go back and forth between studying the models and then themselves for this investigation. What do you think of Gloria's idea to invite the children to draw the models next? Do you have any guesses about how the children might respond? Do you see how this active group might be enthralled with more opportunities to explore their bodies? ■

## •PRINCIPLE•
## Build on Children's Attention for the Natural World

We would be remiss if we neglected to acknowledge the importance of children's relationship with the natural world as a significant source of learning and expression. Mud, sticks, and stones are often used by children to create constructions, dramas, and whole new worlds for relationships and negotiations. Howard Gardner recently added the naturalist intelligence to his theory of multiple intelligences (1999). Thoughtful, observant preschool teachers immediately understood his reasoning. Most teachers have known children who never miss a tiny creature in the vicinity of their play. They have first-hand experience with children who learn through their instinctive understanding and deep relationship with nature. So, rather than see the outdoors as only a place to let off steam, you can see it as a place for rich investigations and opportunities for revisiting and re-representing concepts from other learning domains. Here is an example from a teacher who took the children's investigation outdoors to revisit many other concepts.

### Millions of Pods

The natural world offers more than just studying it for itself. It also provides an abundance of loose parts with interesting textures, colors, shapes, and sizes. Wanda takes advantage of the learning possibilities when the children in her group begin collecting pods that have fallen from the trees on her playground.

*Nolan, Zoe, and teacher Wanda were walking around the play yard when they noticed the great quantity of tree pods that were on the ground, reflecting the wonderful fall season. The children wanted to collect them, so Wanda gave them a bunch of plastic bags for pod gathering. The group had conversations about what these pods were and how they got to be so big and wet. The children described the colors, textures, and shapes of the pods, noticing these aspects as they found each one. It took them the rest of the afternoon to complete the pod gathering task. When it was time to go inside, Wanda suggested they would continue to explore the pods.*

*The next day, Wanda set up a table with trays filled with pods and baskets for sorting. The children quickly remembered their interest in the pods and began sorting and counting and continuing to discuss the texture, weight, and dampness of the pods. One of the children said, "I think we should keep these forever." There was a chorus of assent but then many recognized that if they were to keep the pods, they must dry them out. The ideas the children came up with to dry the pods were baking them in the oven or heating them in the microwave. There were many questions and theories about what changes would happen to the pods as they heated up.*

Burlington Little School

*"What will happen when they are in the microwave?" Wanda asked them.*

*The children replied:*

*"They will get kind of big and they will get small slopes on them."*

*"They will turn into fries and cakes and ice cream."*

*"They will get bigger bristles around it."*

*"They will get drier because of the heat."*

*"They will get powdery, because they will get puffy and explode."*

*Then Wanda asked, "What will happen when they are in the oven?"*

*"They will get a little bigger with bigger bumps."*

*"They will get dry, bigger and dry."*

*"They will burst in the oven cause it's hotter."*

*A number of the children were fascinated with watching the time count down on the microwave oven. They counted with it and also kept suggesting that more time needed to be added.*

Burlington Little School

*When they finished heating the pods, they examined them closely and discovered that they were not much different. Some of them were less soggy, but not much. For the rest of the afternoon, they had the pods on the table with a variety of sizes of baskets and tongs for the children to sort and classify.*

Burlington Little School

## Reflection & Action

***How are the environment and materials impacting what's unfolding and what changes could be made?***

*

***How are teacher actions impacting this situation?***

*

***What theoretical perspectives and child development principles could inform my understandings and actions?***

### Listen to Wanda

"The children were excited about the many pods creating a beautiful, natural carpet in our yard. These interesting, natural materials were soothing and satisfying because of their sensory qualities and the sheer abundance of them. The children's close attention to the specific features of the pods was apparent in their predictions about heating and drying them. Most of the children seemed to think that the heat would cause the pods to get bigger. Is that because they have watched things rise as they bake in an oven? This was truly emergent curriculum growing from the children's interest in these natural items. The wealth and splendor of the natural world presented an incredible learning opportunity for individuals, the group, and for me as a teacher."

### Reflect

This serendipitous event was rich with learning because Wanda took action to challenge the children to pursue and go further with it. She created an opportunity for the children to explore mathematical knowledge when she offered baskets for sorting, classifying, and counting the pods. She encouraged inquiry, collaboration, and problem solving when she invited the children to the kitchen to make predictions and test out their theories for getting the pods to dry out. As you read their predictions, what guesses do you have about the children's understandings and theories? Can you see at each juncture how Wanda used the children's love of the sensory wonders of the natural world to create more opportunities for investigation? ■

In the past, spending time outdoors has always been a huge part of childhood. Most of us remember the visceral, sensory aspect of nature such as feeling fresh air on our skin or seeing the sunlight shining through the buildings in the city where we lived. We remember the feeling of power and adventure as we climbed a tree or rode our bikes down a steep driveway. So much of our identity came from the landscape where we grew up. This is less true for children today. In *Last Child in the Woods,* Richard Louv makes the case that spending less and less time outdoors impairs children's ability to learn as well as increases a multitude of other ailments. Understanding this problem, the teachers in the next story challenged themselves to do more to promote their preschool children's interest and connection with the natural world just outside their door.

In this story, Deb and Kirsten want to help their group of preschool children develop a shared identity around their land, history, and culture, rather than TV superheroes and fast food restaurants. The challenge was finding a way to do this in their early childhood classroom. Notice how they used the children's immense interest in the natural world and an eagle to help them explore the beautiful river valley where they live during a year-long project.

*In the fall, Deb and Kirsten sent home a homework assignment for the children to complete with their families. The children were to go on a walk around their yard and neighborhood to gather things that could be studied. The children were to look for and collect things from the natural world, including leaves, nuts, pods, pinecones, flowers, stones, pebbles, twigs and sticks, shells, and beach glass. They collected these kinds of items in the school play yard as well. The teachers designated a special table with clear plastic containers for sorting the items. The children were engaged with this over a couple of weeks, looking through each container and discussing the items and where they found them. The children's families got involved as well, studying the items and talking with the children about them when they were dropping off or picking up.*

*The next step was to move the children's attention up and outward to their homes and whatever elements of nature they could see from their homes. They sent home a second homework assignment.*

## STARLIGHT ROOM HOMEWORK

We are launching a study of where we live: our homes, our neighborhoods, and the Skagit Valley. To get started, we would like children to bring a photo of their home and answer the following questions together with their family. Taking the time to explore and talk with your child will lay the foundation for our studies at preschool.

- What kind of building do you live in: a one-story or two-story house, an apartment, or a condominium?
- What is the land like around your house?
- Do you live in a neighborhood with lots of other houses or is it mostly acreage?
- What grows around you? Are there any animals or other creatures that live near you?
- What can you see from your home? Are there any mountains, creeks, rivers, lakes, farmlands, the Puget Sound, or . . . ?
- What do you like best about where you live?

On the back of this paper, please draw a picture of your home and what is around it. Bring your drawing and stories of your findings to school next week.

*The teachers put the children's drawings and stories of their discoveries in a book, which was regularly revisited. The children loved looking through the book and talking about the creatures that they could see from their houses. As the weeks progressed, Deb and Kirsten discovered a group called Friends of Blanchard Mountain who were working to save a local mountain from being logged. A woman from that group began to work with the class on this project. She helped develop a map of the valley with images of the animals and land formations, believing the drawings would entice the children's interest in the map.*

Burlington Little School

*Deciding it was time to locate themselves in relationship to the larger valley, the teachers had the children draw pictures of their houses. The teachers printed a small photo of each house and placed them on the map where the children lived. The children looked at the map daily, talking about and pointing out where they lived in relation to each other and to the animals and other natural features near them.*

*To help the children stay engaged in the abstract notion that a map represents the real place where they live, the teachers introduced an eagle puppet named Eaglina to be their guide. They created a story about Eaglina coming from Canada, looking for a tree in which to build her nest. When she flew over the Skagit Valley, she knew this was the place she belonged. At Blanchard Mountain she found a perfect tree to live in, but the animals in the woods told her that the trees might be cut down, so she better not build her nest there. She flew over the map, stopping to look for places to live, describing the natural beauty of the mountains, water, trees, animals, farms, towns, trains, and boats that were a part of the children's daily lives in the valley. The children were enthralled with the stories Eaglina told them each day.*

*The class began to take field trips to some of the places on the map: the tulip fields, the bay, and the river. Before each trip the teachers would revisit Eaglina's stories and explore what the children might see that day. They did representational activities before and after their excursions.*

Burlington Little School

Burlington Little School

*Before the trip to the Skagit River, for instance, Deb and Kirsten offered the children a large piece of paper with an abstract representation of the river and invited them to draw what they already knew about the river. Here's what they said:*

*"The river moves."*

*"You can see lots of fish."*

*"It's dirty because there is mud on the bottom and the mud makes it dirty."*

*"It makes noises from fish, splashes on the rocks, and all kinds of stuff."*

*When they returned from the river, the teachers showed the children the documentation of their group effort to make a river of their own. This same investigation moved to the sandbox outside, where the children dug a trench for the river and poured water to watch it flow.*

Burlington Little School

Burlington Little School

*Before the trip to Padilla Bay on Puget Sound, the group revisited the map and Eaglina's stories again by drawing pictures of what they thought they would see. When they returned, the teachers wanted to help the children extend and revisit the experience, so they created a miniature invitation of elements from the bay such as wet sand, seaweed, and shells to explore in the classroom.*

*The final field trip was to Blanchard Mountain. The children were very excited because they had been learning about the mountain from Eaglina for such a long time. As they drove to the top, a group of eagles soared above them, letting them know that they were welcome. The Friends of Blanchard Mountain were their guides as they explored the trees, plants, and animals that live on the mountain. The highlight of the trip for the children was seeing the beautiful Skagit Valley from the top of the mountain, as this was the view that their friend Eaglina shared with them from her flights high up in the sky.*

*But the children continued to worry about Eaglina building her nest on Blanchard Mountain. They decided to build a nest for her so she could live in the classroom until the mountain was safe. The teachers suggested the children each create individual drawings and paintings of a nest that they thought Eaglina might like. Next they used their individual ideas to design a nest to build together.*

Burlington Little School

Burlington Little School

### Listen to Deb and Kirsten

"Eaglina now lives in a beautiful nest in our preschool classroom. The children have decided she will stay with us until the trees on Blanchard Mountain are safe from logging. We took Eaglina with us on every trip, and a magical and amazing event happened in each place we visited—real eagles came and soared above us! The children's caring relationship with Eaglina and their concern about the trees propelled their intense interest in this investigation. They eagerly took up each invitation to think, talk, draw, and build what we suggested. We are heartened by these young children and their care and concern for the beautiful land where we live and the creatures we share it with. We are gratified to have been able to guide this long-term investigation that has been so significant for all of us."

### Reflect

The teachers used the children's interest in animals and other features of the natural world in many different ways to engage the children's minds, hearts, and bodies. The children worked with concrete objects from nature, had discussions, told stories, and studied photos as well as went on actual visits where they could immerse themselves in the places they were studying. Do you see how the teachers provided many opportunities for the children to use representation and re-representation to make their thinking and experiences visible for further discussion and study? The children's relationship with Eaglina elicited their care and concern for her and the land where she lived and along with their teachers' purposeful offerings, led them through many remarkable learning experiences. ■

### Your Turn

Think about an outdoor place from your childhood where you loved spending time. Then find some materials from nature that will help you tell the story of your experiences in this place. Share this with someone, letting the natural materials speak along with your story. Offer these same materials to a group of children and observe what they do with them.

## •PRINCIPLE•
## Explore Children's Theories for Deeper Learning

Children are constantly trying to figure out how the world around them works. In fact, when you observe them closely, behind children's actions you can see them pursuing their theories about how the world works. The ongoing quest they have to uncover and rearrange the world in order to understand it can be a source of great motivation for deeper learning. When you tap into children's thirst for understanding by helping them uncover their theories and make them visible, the work becomes fascinating for both you and the children. You can ask children to explain their theories, offer materials to help children tell the story of their theories, or suggest they change media to re-represent a theory to expand their thinking. As you work with children to help them pursue their theories you will gain new insight from their unique perspectives.

## How Do Phones Work?

In this story, Emily undertook an exploration with the children in her child care class to discover their theories about how telephones work.

*Aidan asked his mom the thought-provoking question "How do phones work?" They brought this curiosity to school and shared it with Aidan's teacher Emily one morning. Emily wondered if other kids might be interested in this idea as well, and decided to take a small group of interested kids into the studio to explore what they knew, and see what direction they might take to uncover their theories. Aidan and Emily checked in with other kids to see who else might be interested in learning about how phones work. Gabriel, Eli, Cecilia, and Brooke were attracted by the question and decided to join the group. As they arrived in the studio and found a cozy space on the floor, Emily set the stage for the conversation: "We're all wondering about how phones work. What are your ideas about that?"*

*Aidan: "My mom said that the voice goes through a wire into another wire into another phone and the voice goes into another ear. Then another person's voice goes into another wire."*

*Cecilia: "And you can hear it."*

*Aidan: "And you can hear it. After they put back the phone down, the electricity goes out and . . ."*

*Cecilia: "The voice goes out."*

*Aidan: "Then the voice goes out. Voice is electricity. The electricity is on when the voice goes inside the ear."*

*Gabriel: "My dad said that phones really use electricity so other people could use them. You have to put something down so you can hear other people on the phone."*

*Teacher Emily: "What about Cecilia's ideas?"*

*Cecilia: "I can dial because I have a piece of paper that has the numbers."*

*Aidan: "I don't talk on the phone because I'm three . . . I mean four!"*

*Gabriel: "I'm four and I can talk on the phone."*

*Gabriel (to Cecilia): "How do you know what numbers to push?"*

*Cecilia: "You have to match the piece of paper to the numbers."*

*Gabriel: "How do you know what numbers are on the paper?"*

*Cecilia: "I look at the numbers on the paper, then I dial them."*

*Gabriel: "How do you know which number you're calling?"*

*Teacher Emily: "Are you wondering how she knows who she's calling?"*

*Gabriel: "Yeah!"*

*Cecilia: "The paper has the name on it."*

*Teacher Emily: "So, it sounds like to help a phone work, it needs electricity, wires, and you can dial numbers. What else do we know about phones?"*

*Aidan: "When the phone goes into the other ear from the first phone, I notice that it burns the whole house off the ground like a rocket ship."*

*Cecilia: "I don't think so."*

*Aidan: "Well, that's what my phone does at home."*

*Eli: "Does it turn into a space shuttle?"*

*Teacher Emily: "Eli, what are your ideas about how phones work?"*

*Eli: "Electricity comes from the wires."*

*Teacher Emily: "Do all phones have wires?"*

*Everyone: "No."*

*Cecilia: "I have 164 wires."*

*Aidan: "Do you want to know how many wires I have? . . . ONE HUNDRED!"*

*Eli: "I have twenty hundred and seventy thousand."*

*Brooke: "I have a phone that doesn't have a wire."*

*Eli: "It's just pretend, you know."*

*Teacher Emily: "How does a phone work that doesn't have wires?"*

*Gabriel: "Your voice goes through the air in the sky and goes into the other telephone."*

*Next Emily suggested that the children continue this conversation while drawing pictures of their ideas. As they drew their ideas on paper, they added details to their theories about how phones work.*

The wires go into another house. The wires are attached to the phones. One wire's attached to the Seattle phone, one wire's attached to the Washington, D.C. phone. —Cecilia

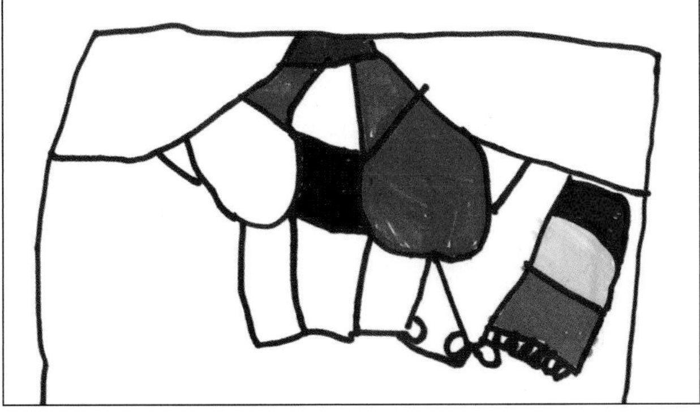

This electricity is underground. I'm making what underground looks like. —Eli

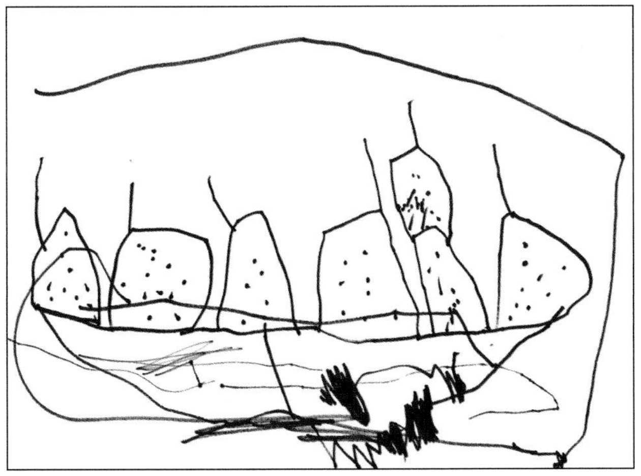

The phone stays on. It needs electricity. The electricity stays in. It's inside a tank. —Brooke

### *Listen to Emily*

"The children brought a lot to this exploration: their real-life experiences, their theories, their imaginations, and their ability to be fantastical. Drawing their theories gave them time to absorb and sort out the ideas that came up in their conversations. I thought that seeing these ideas on paper might serve as a visual communication tool for each other's ideas, stimulate some further language, and extend their thinking. These intricate ideas and their drawings provide a window to the serious thought and developing understandings that children can uncover through a process together. Each child brought their own ideas into this investigation, developed theories based on those ideas, and bounced those theories off each other. They added layers of thinking by continually contributing to the process and listening to each other. I plan to bring this group of imaginative kids together again in the coming weeks to consider what might come next to extend this experience for them."

### *Reflect*

This story shows how excited children can be when thinking through their ideas. Their excitement leads them to a greater investment in the learning process. They want to stick with the task because they are so innately invested in figuring things out. Look back over this story and study teacher Emily's questions and comments. Notice how her responses help the children revisit their ideas, stick to the focus of the conversation, reinforce their thinking, and challenge them to think and say more. Try analyzing the children's comments and drawings for the theories that each child has about how the telephone works. Where do you see their life experience influencing their logic? Where do you see them run into blocks in their thinking that lead them to magical explanations? ■

•PRINCIPLE•

## Reflect Children's Ideas Back to Them with Documentation

In chapter 5 you saw examples of teachers placing books, posters, and photos from their documentation around the room for children to revisit their work. Using documentation with children coaches them in learning skills, steps, and processes. Revisiting experiences helps them become self-reflective. Reflecting on experiences is the source of the most effective learning for both adults and children (Project Zero and Reggio Children 2001). Showing children documentation of their work not only reinforces the children's identity as learners, but gives teachers an opportunity to learn more about the children. Showing children back their ideas sparks further interest, brings up new questions, and stimulates more action.

Documentation for the children to revisit can be placed throughout the room. You can create an appealing display with notes and photos next to the materials that were used in the story. Or you might print photos of the children and their work onto transparencies and project them on the wall where children can use these larger than life images of themselves to launch new pursuits. A simple computer slide show of images from an investigation can be playing as the children begin the day, which encourages them to pick up where they left off, rather than start from the beginning. A slide show of images playing at the end of the day allows children to revisit their learning with their families. All of these opportunities for seeing themselves involved in the learning process reinforce and advance children's knowledge.

## Inventing Our Own Language

Even very young children benefit from reflecting on their experiences. Look for the powerful impact seeing their ideas and actions has on the one-year-olds in this story.

*Deb kept a daily journal and took lots of photos of the unfolding activities that were significant to her and the toddlers she worked with. She studied the photos and notes for her own learning and also began sharing them with the children and their families. Telling these stories to the children and showing them the photos of her observations had positive influences on their play skills. The details from her journal entries about the children's study of flubber demonstrate the power of using observation stories and photos with children to learn from revisiting experiences.*

Martin Luther King Jr. Day Home Center

*One day as the children worked with flubber, Deb narrated their actions and pointed out the things they were doing.*

*"Oh look, when Kiran puts his finger in the flubber, he pokes a hole."*

*"Oona is using the comb to make dots and lines all over the flubber."*

Martin Luther King Jr. Day Home Center

Martin Luther King Jr. Day Home Center

Martin Luther King Jr. Day Home Center

Martin Luther King Jr. Day Home Center

*"T'Kai is carefully putting the lid on the cup."*

*As she described and pointed out these actions, the children copied what they saw and heard. They also stayed at the flubber table a little longer than usual.*

*A few days later, Deb showed the children a homemade binder book containing photos of the flubber explorations they had been doing. She read the book to the children when they came to the flubber table to play. They were engrossed in the story of themselves and the flubber and when she was done reading, a number of the children looked through the book again. The children continued to explore the flubber, trying out the tools and actions that were in the book. As they worked, Deb continued to refer them to the photos and describe their actions. They stayed at the flubber table even longer than before.*

*Later that day Wynsome was sitting by herself looking at the flubber book and imitating the poking action that Kiran was doing in the photo. She was poking the photo with her finger just like he was.*

*When Oscar and Hannah worked with the flubber, Deb used her observations and photos to show them back their work. As they played, she continued to describe what she saw them doing and pointed out their actions. After she took a number of photos, she immediately downloaded them onto the computer and invited the children to look at a "show" about their work. Many other children came over, fascinated to see themselves on the screen. They pointed excitedly, saying each other's names.*

*Oscar was very interested in seeing a photo of himself making an imprint in the flubber with the edge of a plastic container. As he looked at the photo he made a grunting sound and pointed, indicating that he had pushed hard to make the imprint. Deb suggested that he show this action with the real flubber. This time as he pushed hard to make each imprint, he intentionally made the same grunting sound. Hannah showed that she caught on to Oscar's meaning right away. She demonstrated by pressing her hands together really hard and squinting her face as she made the same grunting sound. Both of them continued to make imprints in the flubber, grunting as they worked.*

Martin Luther King Jr. Day Home Center

Martin Luther King Jr. Day Home Center

### Listen to Deb

"I invited the children to begin a study of flubber over an extended period of time because it is a substance that moves and flows and responds to the children's actions. I had used documentation successfully to enhance preschool children's learning, but I wasn't sure what impact this practice would have on my work with one-year-olds. The children eagerly engaged in revisiting their ideas and actions with the flubber through my descriptions and the photos. As I examined the children's responses to the documentation, I wondered if it helped them develop symbolic representation of their actions in their mind. I was thrilled when Hannah and Oscar shared an understanding about making flubber imprints. I believe that the work I have been doing encouraged the children to create a shared language for the hard pressure needed for imprinting. I saw this event as important for the development of their symbolic thinking and language, but I also saw a bigger significance. I got to witness the miraculous process humans go through to develop language."

### *Reflect*

Deb's story shows the power of revisiting documentation with children over a longer period of time. This sustained study extends the children's learning as they practice these skills and concepts through their actions and see these same actions in the documentation. And indeed, as the children have these experiences and come to represent the action of applying pressure with a grunting sound, they develop a construct in their brain for pressure and then don't have to see it or do it to remember it. Tracking the children's work over time illuminates their progress as well as enables Deb to see the impact of showing children back the documentation. ■

### Your Turn

Offer a group of children some interesting materials to play with. While the children play with the materials, here are some things to do:

- Observe closely with a clipboard, pen, and camera. Capture specific details of what you see and hear.
- Ask the children to describe what they are doing and their ideas.
- Point out each child's work and ideas to the others.

Look over your notes and photos and analyze them with the following questions:

- What did the child (or children) do and say? Use descriptive words about specific things, including any quotes from their conversations.
- What were they learning? Compare your documentation with a learning domain list or assessment tool you use.
- What were you curious about? What do you value in this?
- What ideas does the child's family have about this?

Create a homemade book for the children using the details of the documentation you collected and the photos you took. Offer the book to the children along with the materials that are depicted in the book. Observe, document, and photograph how the children respond to the book.

What ideas does this give you for what to do next?

# Adapt the Curriculum Framework for Different Settings

*The best in life comes from a center, something urgent and powerful, an ideal or emotion that insists on its being. From that insistence a shape emerges and creates its structure out of passion. If you begin with a structure, you have to make up the passion, and that's very hard to do.*

**MARGARET WHEATLEY**

The structures and regulations that shape early childhood programs have very little to do with the passions children and teachers bring to their work. Requirements are intended to move children toward standards and teachers toward compliance (Wagner 2002), not mobilize their passions. Nonetheless, when you commit yourself to "teaching with fire" (Intrator and Scribner 2003), you will find ways of working around the barriers in your setting. Your passion and the resources you seek out will help you invent structures that support more in-depth learning for you and the children.

As you've studied *Learning Together with Young Children*, have you found yourself periodically thinking, "Yes, but in my setting, we can't . . ."? The barriers to using our curriculum framework may initially seem formidable. The daily demands of your work don't lend themselves to slowing down and being reflective. Required paperwork, learning outcomes, and assessments may dominate the focus of your limited time. There are constraints related to the logistics of your space, schedule, budget, and staffing patterns. Perhaps your children represent a wide range of cultural and linguistic backgrounds or have families challenged by issues of poverty, violence, or the legacy of racism. You may have children who only come part time or a few days a week, or you have double sessions with two full groups of children and teachers who alternately share your space. Sometimes teachers experience isolation as the only one in their program with an interest in analyzing or writing up documentation stories. Do you find it difficult to choose a focus for curriculum when so many interests are emerging? What about different perspectives and conflicts that have to be negotiated with coworkers or parents? The list of challenges teachers face goes on and on and they are all real. But if you remember why you wanted to be a teacher in the first place, you tap into longings that unleash other possibilities. You can transform frustration into determination. When you taste how your days with children could be different, you will refuse to settle for less. In this spirit we offer you another challenge: move beyond your excuses and fears, claim your power, and invent your own way to deepen children's learning with our curriculum framework.

Claiming your power will look different in each setting. You must engage in a continual process of examining and negotiating the real lives and interests in your classroom with the standards and regulations you're handed (Wien 2004). Ask yourself questions such as: How can my documentation support children's learning and simultaneously help me uncover where standards are being met and what else I might do? What other possibilities and perspectives will deepen our thinking?

Here are some principles to guide you in adapting our curriculum framework for your context.

- Focus your documentation on a process
- Invent new ways to meet requirements
- Expand possibilities for prescribed curriculum
- Document everyday experiences that meet standards
- Make assessments relevant and meaningful
- Seek different perspectives to inform your planning
- Learn from conflicting ideas

## •PRINCIPLE• Focus Your Documentation on a Process

When you make documentation available to children, they see themselves and their peers exploring, discovering, inventing, and learning. This is especially valuable when you are trying to engage part-time children in extended investigations. Project work is difficult to sustain if you don't have a consistent group of students who regularly explore questions together, challenge each other, and learn from each other's ideas. Children who attend part time may have difficulty following the threads of a project topic, feel out of sync with others in the group, or have no consistent relationships to sustain their interest. When different groups of children attend on different days, they may develop different interests or go in different directions with a topic, making it hard for the teacher to know how to focus the overall project.

In part-time programs, teachers may find it more viable to focus extended projects on the *process* of an investigation, rather than a topic. When you show children documentation of the process different groups are engaged in, you connect them with something familiar and help them see they have shared experiences even though they aren't exploring together each day. A process lends itself to deeper learning because it allows children to engage from their own perspective, rather than try to play "catch up" with what they've missed when they weren't there. As you review with children documentation of what others have been doing, you as a teacher aren't focused on a topic, but on getting the group to "see" each other and invest in a process together.

If you are an after-school teacher, you are probably with your group of children for only a few hours each day, and the children probably often arrive to your program wound up or burned out from their school day. Does it make sense to pursue in-depth curriculum in this situation? As you read Rhonda's approach, notice how her choice to focus on a process rather than a topic opened a new line of thinking for her and the children.

*Rhonda has named her group "The Explorer's Club" to reflect her approach to providing curriculum a few hours a day for children who come to her after school. Some children come every day, but others only a few days a week. Rhonda's curriculum is environmentally based with a wide range of interesting things to do around the room. Some materials are always available while others are special invitations she sets out for them to explore for only a few days. Rhonda has mastered the art of observing the details of children's activities, but she struggles with how to offer in-depth project work when children are with her on such a limited basis. Her coworkers are content to just hang out with the kids and show no interest in collaborating with Rhonda to figure this out. Still, Rhonda's disposition is to be persistent in gathering documentation because she delights in revisiting what the children have been doing. She began noticing that more than anything else, the majority of the children in her program gravitated toward process activities, such as working at the sensory table or painting. Rather than just appreciating that, Rhonda decided to experiment with the idea of focusing extended project work on a process rather than a topic. She began offering an invitation each week that focused on an aspect of color mixing, keeping a daily journal of observations, and creating displays of the efforts of different groups,*

Burlington Little School

Burlington Little School

*drawing the attention of the children to each other's work. The children began staying at the color mixing table for longer periods of time, trying to replicate or take further what they saw other children doing in Rhonda's documentation. This created shared connections between children who rarely saw each other in person.*

*Several months into this open-ended investigation of color mixing, Rhonda decided to introduce specific instructions for mixing colors to get different shades and hues. After discussing her documentation about these efforts, Rhonda then suggested the children create a full color palette with documentation of the formula for making each color to share with other children not present. This sparked an ongoing connection between different groups as they studied and expanded on each other's color palettes.*

### Listen to Rhonda

"Until this color mixing project I was beginning to think it was not possible to sustain an interest in a project topic when the group of children changes each day. Finally I realized I had to let go of my preconceived notions of what this was supposed to look like and redefine the concept of in-depth projects for my context. Because color mixing offered so many possibilities for investigation and theory making, I realized that these were the elements of in-depth project work, even though it wasn't a topical theme to pursue. Using my documentation and the same materials with each group could provide a thread to weave between the groups. And this could support my values of helping children experience connections over time and across different groups. What I didn't anticipate was that using my documentation with the children would address my own hunger to have someone to talk with about the details I'm seeing. Indeed, these conversations with the children have provided me with more perspectives, deeper understandings, and ideas about other strategies for extending their thinking and connections with each other. This color mixing project has reminded me that I don't have to give up my longings for more in-depth work and collaboration. I just have to think outside the box."

### *Reflect*

Instead of letting go of bigger expectations for her work, Rhonda let go of the idea that there is one right way to do in-depth investigations with children. Her values and solid practice of creating engaging invitations in the environment, along with her persistent disposition and attention to observing the details in children's pursuits, enabled her to leap over the barriers she was experiencing. Using her documentation with the children was a critical factor in helping them build relationships that influence each other's investigations. Even though many of them couldn't talk with each other or compare their explorations side by side, they were able to relate the process they shared through the photos and Rhonda's stories about the work. This approach also helped Rhonda overcome her own isolation and sense of failure in meeting her expectations. Rhonda's story helps us see in action what might otherwise be abstract theories: co-constructing knowledge and pedagogical documentation. ■

## In the Comfort of Friends

When planning to start a two-and-a-half-hour, two-day-a-week toddler play group, Deb encountered reservations and skepticism among colleagues. As you read her story, how would you describe what in-depth curriculum looks like for this age group and under these circumstances? Notice how Deb focused on the process of building relationships as the focus of her documentation.

*Deb is masterful at setting up environments where children encounter wonder and delight, and the room for her toddler play group is no exception. But she knew that for children twelve to twenty-four months old any interest in her engaging environment would hinge on the children and their families feeling secure and comfortable. As part of her plan, Deb encouraged the parents to linger with the children for as long as possible before leaving the room on the first day. The environment would be new and different for the children so Deb worked to include many things that would feel familiar for them. The first "curriculum plan" she developed was to take photos of the children: a close-up photo of each child's face, a photo of each child with his or her family, and a photo of each child with Deb. By the time the children arrived for their second day with her, Deb had put the photos in little books for the children to look at. The children were also given a picture of themselves with Deb to take home and post on the refrigerator. Deb added pictures of the children with their families in frames and in homemade books around the room.*

Martin Luther King Jr. Day Home Center

*In the coming weeks, Deb placed larger photographs around the room that focused on the children's exploration of the room and each other as playmates. One day she printed the photos on transparencies and watched the children point with recognition and squeal with delight as they recognized themselves, family members, and new playmates up on the big screen. Seeing Kobe's picture projected on the wall, Aiden noticed he was absent that day. "Where Kobe? Where Kobe go?" he asked. The children were clearly making connections with each other. They were also making connections between activities they saw in the photos and what was available in the room. When Sasha saw Shaelyn rolling a ball down the ramp in a photograph, Sasha took a few balls from the basket herself and scrambled up the ramp to roll them down. Soon the children were sending other things down the ramp and in the coming weeks continued their experiments with different possibilities for ramp play.*

### Listen to Deb

"I was so thrilled to be returning to work with toddlers and I had so many ideas I wanted to try. But I have to admit, I was a bit worried as I shared my colleagues' concerns. Would the children be secure enough to part with their parents and enjoy the environment I was so carefully planning? Was the time between days in my program too long for them to recognize it as a safe and secure place? Would they forget about their playmates or have trouble bonding with me? I'm a strong believer in the value of open-ended, self-directed play—valuable in and of itself—so I had to keep asking myself, 'Why would you care about developing some in-depth curriculum?' My initial idea about curriculum was to foster comfort and security with lots of familiar images. Seeing themselves in pictures not only met this outcome, but led to stronger connections among their playmates. I know this isn't how teachers or parents typically think of 'curriculum,' but I have no doubt that helping the children form relations is the essence of in-depth curriculum for this age group. I'm reminded that despite prevailing notions about toddlers, they are capable of sustained attention and have a keen eye for details. They are eager to be together, not just parallel players. Doesn't this suggest that curriculum for them can be far more engaging?"

### Reflect

Deb's story brings to life the implications of research on attachment theory and brain development for toddler curriculum. Because she drew on the idea of emotional intelligence (Goleman 1995), Deb demonstrates that in-depth curriculum for this age group goes beyond planning activities. Instead, Deb focuses on the process of building relationships. Making common threads of experiences visible to children not only deepens their relationships but also enables them to build on each other's ideas. When you see your friends doing things in pictures, it reminds you of what you know. Children will usually enjoy a couple hours a week in a fun environment, but Deb's view of curriculum goes beyond short spurts of entertaining activities. She gives heightened attention to the foundational idea that deeper involvement in learning comes from secure relationships and revisiting familiar experiences to make new connections. ■

## •PRINCIPLE•
## Invent New Ways to Meet Requirements

Many child care providers feel they cannot deviate from a standard approach to curriculum planning because of licensing requirements or even NAEYC accreditation criteria. However, if you are conscientiously planning and have documentation of your work, you can negotiate with monitors and evaluators, and demonstrate how you are meeting the intent of the requirements. Do you feel confident that you can articulate clearly why you do what you do? Do you see yourself as an inventor, risktaker, or challenger of the status quo? If not, you may want to cautiously begin to integrate some of the ideas in *Learning Together with Young Children* and most likely this will generate interest and curiosity from others. Sometimes some simple changes can lead to big things.

## Making the Leap

It's easy to be held captive by someone's interpretation of licensing regulations. But if you understand the *intent* of the requirements, you can demonstrate how you are meeting this intent in a different way.

Notice how Marilyn, a licensor, encourages providers to stand up for what they believe is appropriate. Could you imagine doing what she suggests?

New Hampshire Technical Institute Child Development Center

*Marilyn always approaches her licensing visits with keen eyes, open ears, and her state's licensing code book in hand. She sees her job as not only ensuring the health, safety, and well-being of children, but also encouraging innovation and exceeding the minimum licensing requirements. Marilyn isn't just looking for violations, but appropriate variations on how teachers are keeping the children's best interests in mind. As she walks around the inside and outside of a building, watches interactions with children, and reviews required documents, you will hear her making comments like, "I can see that you have kept our code in mind when you added this new area to your play yard."*

*When Marilyn doesn't initially see evidence of something that is required, she uses this as an opportunity to raise questions, not jump to conclusions. "Can you tell me how you go about meeting our requirement for posting curriculum plans for children?" Sometimes this question opens up a fruitful discussion about the intent of a regulation or a possible variation of how it could be met. As a licensor, Marilyn sees her role as not only a monitor for quality, but a motivator to think through the why and how of important quality components. Her visits are not dreaded by programs. Rather, the staff members appreciate the new eyes and ears she brings, and her openness to their ideas, even as she holds them accountable for standards.*

### Listen to Marilyn

"Licensing administrative codes are legal requirements for child care providers. However, if you read our codes, they are usually very broad. I always tell providers that the key is to be able to articulate and document what they believe, do, and plan for children. Sometimes when providers feel they are being stopped from doing what they want, it is not due to a licensing code, but someone interpreting it in a very limited way. This is when the confident and knowledgeable provider needs to be able to say why she does something the way she does, and justify that she is meeting the codes.

"If you feel you are not being allowed to do what you know is appropriate for children, go to a supervisor in licensing. Do not be afraid to do this. One very emergent-curriculum–styled program fulfilled the requirement of posting curriculum by hanging large pieces of paper on the wall where the teacher webbed the day's activities with the children. Her only change in practice was to save those papers for the licensor and to date them. Now, if a licensor could not make that leap, then I would engage a supervisor."

### Reflect

Licensing monitors and Head Start review teams have an important role in holding programs accountable to quality standards. Marilyn's approach parallels the NAEYC accreditation process in that she encourages programs to self-reflect and set goals for their own improvement. If your licensor is more rigid in interpreting regulations, what could you offer to open her mind?

Start with the assumption that you can have a discussion. Think in terms of friendly negotiations and raising her awareness of other options. Show your licensor evidence of your careful thinking, not just your defensiveness. When all else fails, if you believe what you are doing is truly beneficial for children, follow Marilyn's advice and engage a department supervisor. ■

Teachers often tell us they struggle to make required recordkeeping meaningful in their actual work with children. This is especially true when you are required to fill out curriculum planning forms and turn them in long before the actual days of implementation. If you are using your observations to guide your planning, new ideas may be emerging from the children that will influence the direction of your curriculum. Depending on your comfort level with challenging requirements, you may want to explore new ways to document your curriculum to more closely align your required paperwork with your practice. Or, you may choose to just fill out the required form but not let it hinder your ability to be responsive to children's emerging interests.

## Shuffling the Boxes

A provider can often initiate change by working within a required system rather than challenging it all together. Notice how Kristin's efforts to meet requirements around lesson plan boxes gradually shifted her thinking as well as the expectations of parents and her coworkers.

*Kristin's Head Start program has a required lesson plan form that all teachers must post. During her first year of teaching there, she dutifully filled in the little boxes and tried to conform to the thematic and learning domain focus the form is centered on, even though her approach to curriculum was more emergent than these forms suggest. As she grew in confidence, Kristin had a number of conversations with her education coordinator and director, seeking permission to try something new. While they weren't willing to let her abandon the essence of the form, her supervisors gave Kristin tacit permission to do some experimenting. She started including new boxes on her form, and adding questions to take up with her coworkers at the end of the week when they would sit down to plan. As she began doing more observing and photographing, Kristin's documentation replaced her activity books as the primary source for ideas about what to do next. Over the next few years she moved some of her documentation into the little boxes themselves as evidence of what her thinking and the children's learning was focused on that week.*

### Listen to Kristin

"After my first year of learning the ropes and going along with everything in my program, I started playing around with the layout of the lesson plan form, as well as the required information it asked for. Initially my supervisor and I made some minor changes, like replacing the word "theme" with "focus," and then I added the word "investigation." I experimented with reducing the number of boxes that had preplanned activities and adding boxes that would be filled in with environment changes. Over time, I continued to play with the form, with collaboration from my direct supervisor and a careful eye from the education director, and it evolved along with my own understanding of curriculum. Eventually I added space for reflection, which I titled 'what we found out' or 'what we discovered today.' I added questions like 'What do we want to know about this?' and 'What do we need to help us in our investigations?' The boxes were ever present, of course, and I was still required to write in activities. But those evolved from preplanned activities that had a predetermined outcome, to small group activities that were more invitation focused. Soon those boxes were filled in with things like 'explore clay' or 'review documentation from our field trip.' At the end of each week I invited my co-teachers to review documentation with me and we would discuss where the children might go next, and write in the boxes the invitations

# Kristen's Experiment with Planning Forms

## PHASE I: TOPIC EVALUATION

**What has been happening in the classroom and our community? How did this topic come to our attention?**

In classroom, the children have been very interested in painting. They have been talking a lot about colors. They have been mixing colors to make new colors, and adding glue and collage materials.

**What is the underlying interest in this topic? Why is it meaningful to the children?**

magical—the new colors they make, satisfies curiosity, the way it feels—textures: smooth, rough

**How does this topic support the values of the teachers, parents and our program?**

Supports science exploration, are appreciation and expression vocabulary acquisition, respect for others (taking turns, making choices about paint and materials)

**What possible directions could this topic take? Make a planning web:**

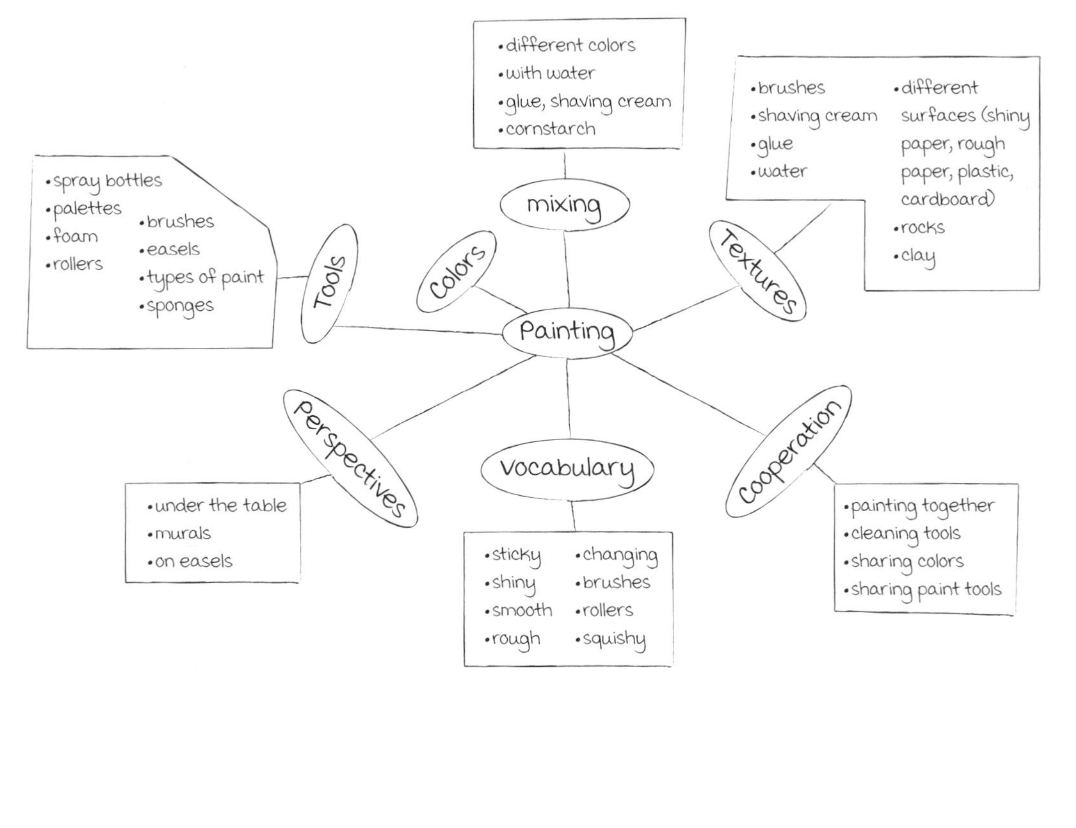

# Kristen's Experiment with Planning Forms

**Our Investigation** Paint!

| | | | |
|---|---|---|---|
| Large Group Meeting: How was your weekend? Revisit documentation panel from painter's visit. movement! | movement! Story: the Pot | Review painting with tools—what was that like? movement! | Review hand-washing week-in-review. movement! |

| | | | |
|---|---|---|---|
| Small Group Meeting: Explore new paint tools: rollers, spatulas | Explore new paint tools: rollers, spatulas | Review painting tools and add new surfaces—easels, the wall | Paint on vertical surfaces—easels, the wall |

What did we find out? Children are excited about making big paintings—covering space.

What next? Offer long rolls of paper, butcher paper, offer paint outside?

we would offer next. After four years I finally stopped filling in the boxes altogether and started putting pictures and stories in those spaces with narrative about what was happening. The parents and teachers all loved it because it was so clear what was really happening in the classroom."

### *Reflect*

Translating a cycle of reflection and action onto a form is a difficult endeavor because it is hard to capture the complexity of this dynamic process on a flat piece of paper. The process easily loses its vitality and life if you try to put it in little boxes. The challenge is to invent a representation of your thinking so that your written plan communicates the mindset of a researcher even as you acknowledge learning goals for the children. If you are saddled with a standard form to use, do your best to integrate your thinking into the words you put in the little boxes. When you write out plans in advance, you easily forget to pay attention to the learning process itself. Kristin shows us how a teacher's experimentation can enhance her own understandings as well as that of others. As she tried to make her curriculum planning form more genuinely reflective of her own thinking process, we see how she was better able to engage others around her. Kristin's shift to using invitations in her activity times with the children became opportunities for the teachers to reflect together with the children about their new discoveries and insights. Her coworkers and the children's families let her know that posting documentation stories had far more meaning for them than words with the names of a song or activity she was planning in advance.

Even if you are required to use a prescribed curriculum with lessons and projected outcomes someone else has designed, you can demonstrate possibilities for deeper learning, as Kristin illuminates in the above story. Keep focused on the *intent* of a particular lesson or desired outcome and consider how to connect that with what is meaningful to the children. Your ongoing observations of children can guide you in this process. ■

### Show Me the Evidence

*"Our licensing code calls for evidence of staff planning. In my mind the important part is the planning, not the form. It can be a web, a chart, a list, or journal notes, as long as the teacher's thinking is made visible. Names of songs and activities in boxes don't really show thinking. I push again and again for a window into the teacher's thinking to demonstrate evidence of planning. This ultimately raises the issue of whether they get paid planning time. We have to show these connections. Teachers can't think about the best interests of the children without planning time. This is part of their job, not something they should be expected to do on their own."*
*—Jean, Child Care Licensor*

Hilltop Children's Center

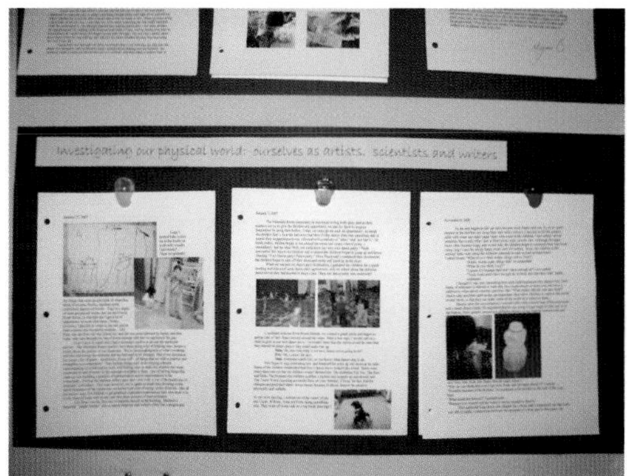

Hilltop Children's Center

## •PRINCIPLE•
## Expand Possibilities for Prescribed Curriculum

Even when teachers have a prescribed curriculum they must follow, there are ways to use our suggested repertoire of teacher actions to enhance the teaching and learning process. Some programs are using a thematic curriculum to teach particular content topics while others have specialty curricula for literacy, math, science, and so forth. If you think about the principles we have offered in *Learning Together with Young Children,* most of them can help you think about how to make mandated curriculum more meaningful for you and the children. You can draw on your observation skills before and during introducing your required curriculum. Most of the teacher actions we recommend work well in any setting.

If you are working with a mandated curriculum with a scope and sequence to follow, your challenge is to make it meaningful for you and the children. You can do this by drawing on different core practices of the curriculum framework and teaching repertoire this book offers. Find other colleagues to brainstorm ideas with. Continue to refine your ability to clearly describe how what you are doing and what the children are learning meets requirements and standards. Take heart from the following stories.

Pat, a consultant hired to train teachers on using a mandated literacy curriculum, found ways to focus the teachers on using observations of children to make the lessons more meaningful. Though this is initially just a small expansion of the curriculum, do you see how it could help teachers do more reflecting and not just use the curriculum in a lockstep fashion?

*When introducing the new literacy curriculum, Pat found the teachers were initially enthusiastic about having a tool to help them navigate the waters of the increasing pressure for literacy outcomes. The selected curriculum is designed with a scope-and-sequence, day-by-day prescription of lessons to deliver to children. It combines learning the alphabet and phonemic awareness along with particular storybooks to enhance language development and introduce literature to children. Teachers are to sequence the books with particular vocabulary to highlight and a script of questions to ask with each book. In her trainings, Pat emphasizes the need for reflection on each lesson. The teachers felt this was impossible because they had no planning time to prepare beforehand or talk afterward about what happened. And literacy is but one of their desired curriculum outcomes. Pat was discouraged that the teachers just did the minimum of what was required, rather than making the lessons their own and planning for more possibilities.*

Home Away from Home

*Instead of just giving up on the idea of using a more reflective practice, Pat created an observation form and introduced this as part of the planning process. The form asks teachers to initially read each of the storybooks themselves and identify the themes that would potentially be relevant to the children. Next she suggests the teachers use observations to identify specific situations in which the children's play is related to a theme in one of the books. As they take up the particular questions and vocabulary lessons for that book, the teachers then tell specific stories of observations of children's activities related to the storyline. For instance, in the book* Old Bear *by Jane Hissey, the animals are trying to work together to solve the problem of retrieving Old Bear. Using her observations, a teacher can tell stories and invite conversations about the times she has seen the children working together to solve a problem. Follow-up activities can build on their experiences as well as using the lessons from the book. With this expansion of the curriculum, Pat breathed new life into literacy teaching for the teachers and the children.*

### Listen to Pat

"What I think would help teachers is not a script to follow, but a format they can use to create their own lessons and make them more meaningful. Because I want observations of the children to be a central feature of all teaching, I decided that introducing a form like this could be universally adapted for any of the storybook lessons. I hope that this approach will carry over into other areas of their curriculum planning, and that the teachers will come to see the value of observations for making lessons meaningful for children."

### Reflect

Pat's approach doesn't disregard the goals of this particular curriculum, but goes beyond its limitations. She devises a simple form to set a protocol in motion for reflection and action based on everyday observations of children. When a teacher introduces a storybook selected by someone other than herself or the children, she can still personalize the content with related stories featuring the children and their playmates. Each of these little steps of claiming your power to do something deeper and more significant in your teaching leads to bigger things. ■

## An Instrument for Change

*Martha is eager to bring her creativity to her work with the children. Her program uses a thematic approach to curriculum planning, infused with social justice and community values. The teachers are encouraged to brainstorm ideas together for their toddlers, preschoolers, and school-age children. When Martha heard about offering children open-ended materials as invitations for curriculum explorations, she helped to plan a workshop for her center. Teachers arrived to a beautiful set of invitations set up around the room and spent time exploring them and considering their possibilities for their upcoming curriculum theme of music and dance. When Martha returned to her classroom to try these invitations with the children, her excitement grew. "I never knew the children would get so involved. It was more interesting for them and for me than how we have been doing our themes. After a few days of the teachers offering the children invitations, the children started offering them to each other. Several made their own musical instruments and spread them out on a cloth for others to see and play with." From this simple experiment a new wave of teacher collaboration is now moving across the program. Teachers are eager to share stories of what the children are doing with invitations and they are giving each other ideas and materials from their own collections.*

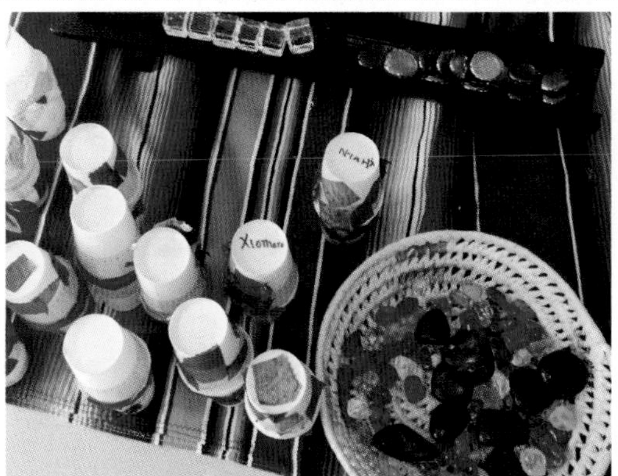

José Martí Child Development Center

Inching their way along, some dedicated teachers and early childhood programs have managed to create supportive structures that unleash tremendous possibilities for teachers to take their work with children into extended, in-depth investigations. Ann Pelo (2007) is one such teacher, and she offers the following guidelines for planning investigations to uncover children's ideas. Her biggest caution: Don't plan an activity, plan how to find out more about the children's thinking.

- Create a protected corner or studio space where children can pursue an investigation away from distractions and where materials can be left out for work to continue over a span of time.
- Revamp your "small group time" practices to form evolving work teams or project groups of particularly chosen children with different but complimentary strengths to contribute to a study or investigation.
- Organize your staffing so that the same teacher can work with the children on the project and also have time to meet with at least one other person to study the documentation you gather during the process.
- Formulate questions and gather materials that lend themselves to children re-representing their ideas about different aspects of the focus you are investigating over time, moving from individual to group work.
- Save work to revisit with the children, along with your documentation and evolving story of what the group has been undertaking and discovering.
- Have the project team regularly report on their work to the whole class, making use of your documentation and their representational work.
- Invite the children's families to study your documentation with you, adding their insights and resources.
- Strengthen your technology resources and skills to include work with a digital camera, tape recorder, computer, scanner, and printer. Stay current with evolving software to economize your documentation work.

Hilltop Children's Center

### Your Turn

Take some time to review ways you could expand the possibilities for your teaching, whatever the restrictions you experience. On a large piece of paper, create three columns. Write "Current Practice" at the top of the left-hand column, "Intent in this Practice" at the top of the middle column, and "Other Possibilities" at the top of the right-hand column.

In the left-hand column, make a list of the current practices and requirements that you feel are constraining your teaching. Next to each item in your list, in the middle column, write your understanding of the intent behind this practice. For instance, if you are required to turn in lesson plans a month in advance, in the middle column you might write, "Make sure teachers are planning for children's learning." In the right-hand column, consider other possibilities for meeting this intent. Here you might write, "Put brief observation notes with a question and next step for further exploration." Once you have identified some options for expanding the possibilities for your teaching, choose one as a goal to work on. Identify who you need to talk with about this possibility. Who might offer you support, encouragement, or resources? What reservations might you expect and how will you address those? Plan your changes incrementally.

- What could you shift on Monday morning?
- What changes might you have in place in the next four months?
- How do you want to start the new school year differently in September?

### •PRINCIPLE•
## Document Everyday Experiences That Meet Standards

With the growth of state-funded preschool programs, early childhood teachers find themselves increasingly required to work with prescribed standards and learning outcomes. Gone are the days when the standards for early childhood programs were primarily focused on health and safety. Wider educational trends, along with our own efforts to professionalize our field, now require teachers to be more knowledgeable about learning domains, working with diversity and second language learners, and a host of other considerations requiring expertise. This is not inherently bad, but it certainly is complex. In the absence of a clearly defined set of values and educational philosophy, teachers can easily be swept into teaching practices that aren't meaningful for children or for teachers. On the other hand, standing on a firm philosophical and pedagogical foundation, teachers should be eager to gain clarity about learning domain content.

Numerous resources are now available to assist teachers in understanding standards and how to integrate them into curriculum practices (Seefeldt 2005; Gronlund 2006). In selecting the approach you want to take, ask yourself, "How can I nurture children's imaginations and intellectual growth while integrating specific content into curriculum experiences?" The challenge of meeting standards can become an excuse for not approaching curriculum in a more emergent, child-centered way. However, when you see yourself as capable of innovation and draw on teacher actions in the curriculum framework *Learning Together with Young Children* describes, you'll find many possibilities for documenting how standards and learning outcomes are being met.

Marsie, a teacher in a program funded for low-income families through Title I in a public school, offers several examples of how her teaching approach meets her state's math standards. Do you see the important role of close observation and documentation in her success?

*Marsie y Marta su compañera de trabajo. Desarrollaron una mesa con "un bocadillo matemático" después de leer un articulo titulado "Math at the Snack Table" por Linda Meriwether, los estudiantes de Meriwether eran de kindergarten, pero Marsie y Marta esteban confiadas en que sus estudiantes de cuatro años del preescolar podían comprometerse con esto como una experiencia de aprendizaje extendida a través de todo el año. Ellas sintieron que esto podría cubrir los estándares de matemáticas que requiere el estado y al mismo tiempo ofrecer múltiples oportunidades no solamente para contar, si no para resolver problemas, aprender a reconocer grupos de hasta cinco objectos sin contar, y enfrascarse en socializar conversando acerca de lo que están haciendo. Así como también ayudándose unos a otros. Los bocadillos están disponibles diariamente dentro del salón. Usamos una tarjeta para el "menú" donde los niños pueden "leer" para aprender la cantidad y tamaño del bocadillo ofrecido. Las maestras facilitan y apoyan la "lectura" del menú al principio del año por varias semanas facilitando en la lectura del menú. Cuando los niños empiezan a aprender el concepto del menú, las maestras les pasamos el proyecto a ellos, incluyendo decidir la cantidad diaria de cada bocadillo, y escribir el menú. Las maestras piden voluntarios para escribir el menú. A menudo los niños se toman su tiempo para dibujar con lujo de detalles y escoger los colores cuidadosamente. Algunos de los voluntarios eran niños que usualmente no escogían escribir durante otras actividades. En representaciones simbólicas ellos estaban en una etapa muy temprana. Los dibujos de las galletas algunas veces eran líneas algo circulares y algunos garabatos a través del papel. Esta experiencia evoluciono al punto que los niños podían pararse a un lado de la mesa de los bocadillos y interpretar sus dibujos para los demás. Los niños pasaban la información unos a otros y se abrían a la diversidad de formas para representar ideas en estos menús. Los niños que escribían estos menús se sentían capaces y querían hacer menús en las siguientes semanas. Conforme lo hacían ellos empezaban a sostener el lápiz con tres dedos y comenzaron a escoger escritura en otras áreas del salón. Conforme el año avanzaba varios reconocieron grupos de hasta 5 cosas sin tener que contar. Esta experiencia autentica ofrece practica en dibujar círculos, cuadrados, y triángulos. Algunos de los niños escribían los números en los menús. También pudieron tener muchas experiencias midiendo. Un niño que no puede contar usa su mano izquierda para sostener la parte de arriba de la tarjeta que muestra 10 uvas. El después usa su mano derecha para poner una uva en su plato. Él mueve su mano izquierda a la siguiente uva y con la derecha agrega otra uva hasta que tiene 10. La sonrisa en su cara conforme mira su plato lleno muestra confianza y satisfacción "Si, yo lo puedo hacer!"*

•

*Marsie and her coworker, Marta, developed a "math snack" table after reading an article by Linda Meriwether entitled "Math at the Snack Table." In the article, Meriwether's students were kindergarteners, but Marsie and Marta were confident their four-year-old preschool students could engage with this as an extended learning experience throughout the year. They felt it would address their state's standards for math while offering multiple opportunities not only to count, but to problem solve, learn to recognize sets of up to five objects without counting, converse socially about what they were doing, and help each other.*

*Snack is an everyday choice in this classroom. They use a "menu" card that the children "read" to count out and to measure their snack. The teachers worked with the children supportively for several weeks at the beginning of the year, facilitating the "reading" of the menu. As the children began to understand the concept of the menu, the teachers turned the project over to them, including allowing them to decide on the amount of each snack item for the day, and writing the menu. The teachers asked for volunteers to write the menu. Many children took time to draw the menu in great detail, carefully choosing their colors. Some of the volunteers were children who did not usually choose to write. They were in the very early stages of symbolic representation. Their menus were, for the most part, an attempt at a circle with lines drawn across the page. These children would stand at the snack table and interpret the amounts of the snacks to take to the other children. Children would pass the information along to each other and were very content to read the more difficult menu that the children had made. The children who wrote these menus felt successful in their experiences and wanted to make menus in the following weeks. They began to use the pencil with a correct grip and started to choose the writing area to work in.*

*As the year progressed, many children recognized sets of up to five without having to count. Within a meaningful context, they practiced drawing circles, squares, and triangles. Some children were writing the numbers on the menus. The children also had many experiences with measurement. One child who could not count used his left hand to pinch the top of the card displaying ten grapes. He then used his right hand to put one grape on his plate. He would then move his left hand to the next grape on the card and, with the right hand, add another grape to his plate until he had ten grapes on the plate. The smile on his face as he looked at his full plate showed self-confidence and a sense of "Yes, I can do it!"*

Manzo PACE Preschool

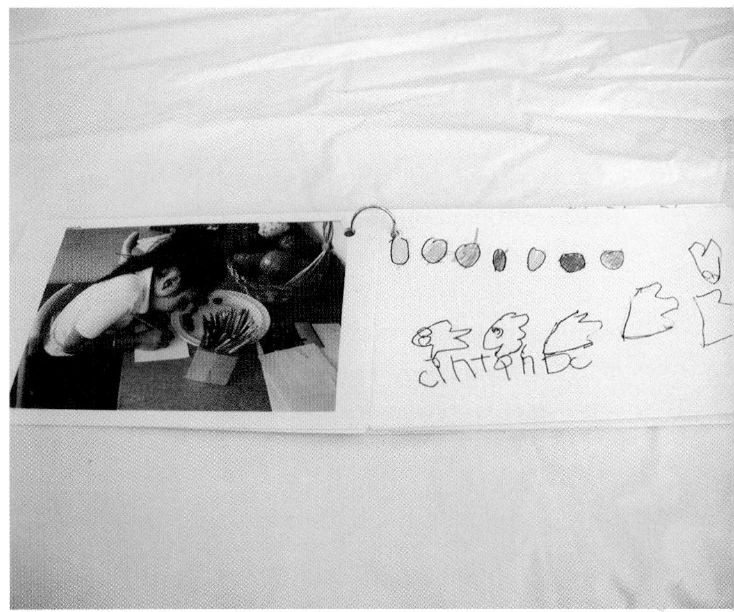
Manzo PACE Preschool

Manzo PACE Preschool

## *Escuchen a Marsie*

"Nuestro programa se esfuerza para traer las ideas de Reggio Emilia a niños de bajos recursos económicos, donde la mayoría hablan español. Los estándares y regulaciones pudieran sentirse como barreras pero, si nosotros creemos que el niño es competente y en nosotras como maestras, podemos ofrecer experiencias que pueden ser usadas a lo largo de la vida y ofrecerlas en el aprendizaje diario. Esto puede implicar el juego autodirigido, invitaciones que como maestras brindamos, o la forma en que arreglamos la rutina diaria en el salón. Nosotros nos deleitamos al descubrir lo entusiasmados que los niños están y lo creativos que pueden ser en su pensamiento. Comer bocadillos es un tiempo para que todos socialicen, incluyendo a las maestras. Nosotros consideramos esto como una extensa y profunda experiencia que ofrece interminables posibilidades. Que forma tan grata de cubrir los estándares de matemáticas, literatura y lenguaje, desarrollo social y emocional, y ciencias. Y, si, al final del año los niños pudieron usar los números correspondientes 1 por 1 para contar hasta 5 cosas de los bocadillos ofrecidos y algunos contaban hasta el 20.

"Hemos documentado las experiencias acerca de la mesa de los bocadillos matemáticos con fotografías, paneles de documentación y con libros que incluyen series de fotografías, en una página los niños están escribiendo el menú y en el lado opuesto esta el menú original que ellos escribieron. Nosotros usamos estos menús a través del año. El libro de menús se pone parado sobre la mesa de los bocadillos para que los niños lo lean. Escribimos 2 páginas resumiendo todos los estándares que cubrimos con esta experiencia. Los administradores y padres inmediatamente pueden ver el aprendizaje que se lleva acabo y los estándares que estamos cubriendo."

### *Listen to Marsie*

"Our program strives to bring the ideas of Reggio Emilia to low-income children, most of whom are Spanish speaking. Standards and regulations can feel like a barrier, but if we believe in the competent child and in ourselves as teachers, we can come up with meaningful experiences and embed them in everyday learning. This may involve self-directed play, invitations we bring as teachers, or the way we set up ongoing routines in the room.

"We were delighted to discover how enthusiastic the children were and how creative they could be in their thinking. Snack is a very social time for everyone, including teachers. We find it a broad, deep experience that offers endless possibilities. What a great way to meet standards in math, literacy and language, social and emotional development, and science. And yes, at the end of the year the children could all count from 1 to at least 5 and many to over 20. We have documented our math snack experiences with photos, documentation panels, and a menu book in a ring binder showing a photo of the child writing the menu on one page and the actual menu on the opposite page. We use these menus a number of times throughout the year. The books stand up on the math snack table for the children to read. We wrote a two-page summary of all the standards we are meeting with this experience. Administrators and parents are immediately able to see the learning that is taking place and the standards we are meeting."

### *Reflect*

The story of math snacks reveals an almost seamless relationship between everyday activities and meeting learning objectives. This accomplishment stems from the teachers' high regard for children's abilities; their relaxed, easygoing schedule full of self-directed choices, including snacks; and their recognition of all the learning that unfolds when children are given meaningful tasks to do. When they put documentation of the children's process of making menus alongside the menu itself, the teachers are demonstrating they value the process as well as the final product. Taking the time to write a two-page summary of how this activity addresses standards awakened other adults in the room to the learning that is taking place. It also strengthened their own ability to connect what they are seeing to the professional data on math as a learning domain. ■

## •PRINCIPLE• Make Assessments Relevant and Meaningful

Assessing children's learning has become a significant focus of attention in today's early childhood programs. As with resources on meeting standards, you can find any number of tools to guide the assessment process (Gullo 2004; Gronlund 2003). Most assessment tools include some kind of developmental continuum or checklist. Tools that rely on portfolio collections and anecdotal records to interpret development progress claim to be "authentic assessment" because a work sampling system (Meisels et al. 1994) draws on a range of experiences children have with everyday curriculum, rather than relying on a periodic, out of context test to assess children's competencies.

From our point of view, developmental checklists are of limited value because they fail to acknowledge the complexity of the learning process. Similarly, teachers tend to narrow portfolio collections of work samples without including documentation of the learning process itself. For assessments to genuinely represent whether young children are meeting learning standards, they need to paint a picture of how children are playing and working, with specific indicators of their thinking in their action. Teachers must sharpen their understandings of how children acquire the dispositions and skills of academic learning so that they can plan for this and assess progress accordingly.

## Felipe's Car Makes Daily News

Children bring a range of experiences and interests to their early childhood programs. Sometimes children are far more passionate about an activity or investigation than the curriculum teacher's plan. Learning to shift your focus to what engages children can provoke you to find new avenues to engage them in academic pursuits. As you read Pauline and Marsie's story, do you see how they took advantage of Felipe's fascination with fast cars to document his grasp of math concepts? Notice the meaning their daily journal has for the children's families.

*Con el apoyo del administrador en una escuela del distrito, en un salón de educación preescolar para niños de bajos recursos económicos. Pauline, una maestra de arte y recursos, Marsie, la maestra líder, y Marta la ayudante, crearon un ambiente hermoso en el salón que incluye una área que ellas le llaman un "estudio". Notando que Felipe estaba muy interesado en los autos, Pauline le ofreció un libro de referencias de autos que mostraba muchas marcas y modelos de autos. Felipe estaba fascinado con las diferentes velocidades que alcanzaban varios autos. El notó en cada página donde estaban escritos los números de las millas que cada auto alcanzaba por hora y empezó a buscarlos cada vez que volteaba de página en el libro. Trabajó para figurar si el número era más pequeño o mayor que el anterior. Pauline lo invitó a dibujar algunos de los autos que le gustaban. Juntos Felipe, Pauline, y Marsie crearon un libro acerca de sus dibujos e ideas. El regreso al libro de referencias en el transcurso de varios meses dibujando más páginas y mirando en el libro de referencias comparando detalles del libro con sus trabajos. Esta experiencia cubría muchos de los estándares de matemáticas, lenguaje, literatura, y socio emocional conforme el compartía el libro con familiares y amigos el desarrollaba un fuerte sentido de identidad propia y confianza. Otros padres y administradores que visitaron pudieron ver en esta documentación del proceso del libro de Felipe y en el diario del aprendizaje que está pegado en la pared.*

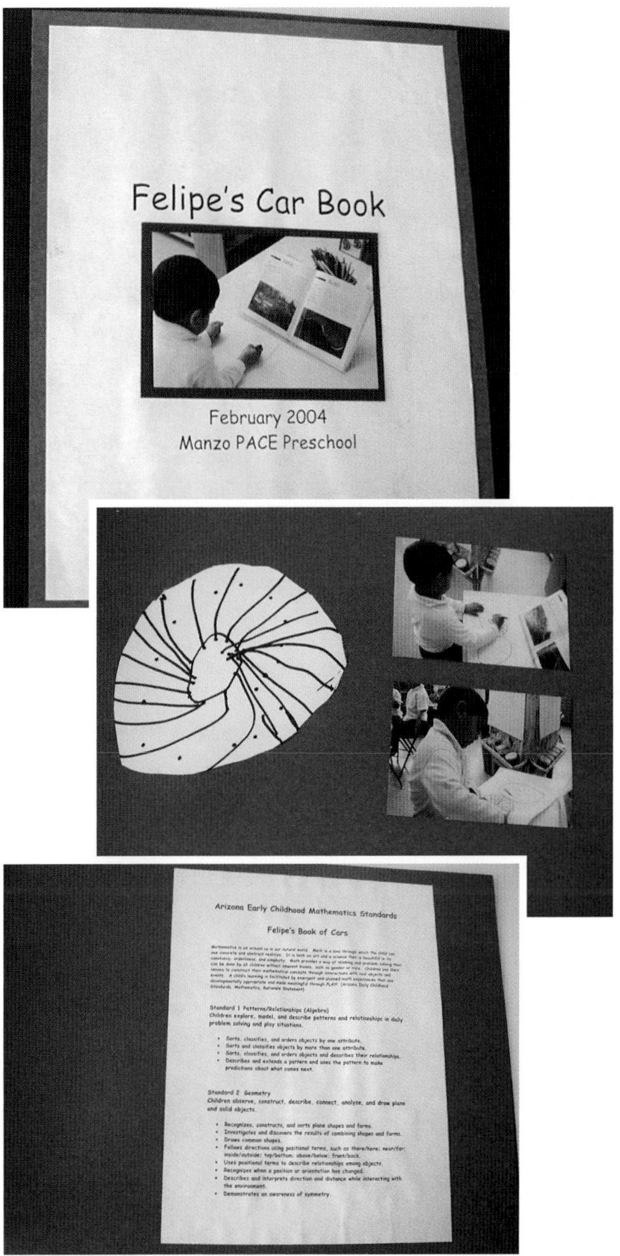


Manzo PACE Preschool

*With support from their administrator in a school district early childhood classroom for low-income children, Pauline (a studio and resource teacher), Marsie (a lead teacher), and Marta (a co-teacher) created a beautiful classroom environment that included an area they call a "studio." Noticing Felipe's interest in cars, Pauline offered him an adult reference book about cars featuring many makes and models of sports cars. Felipe was fascinated by the difference in speed of the various cars. He noticed where the numbers for miles per hour were located on each page and began to look for them as he turned the pages. He worked to figure out if a number was smaller or larger than previous numbers.*

*Pauline invited him to draw some of the cars he liked. Together Felipe, Pauline, and Marsie created a book about his drawings and ideas. He went back to his book over the course of many months, drawing more pages and looking at the resource book (expository text), comparing details in it to his own work. This experience met many math standards, language and literacy standards, and social emotional standards as he shared the book with his family and friends and built a strong sense of self-identity and self-confidence. Other parents and visiting administrators were able to see standards being met with the documentation of this process in Filipe's book and in the daily journal posted on the bulletin board.*

### Escuchen a Marsie

"La historia de Pauline iniciando una investigación extensa con Felipe es un ejemplo de cómo nosotros creemos que proveyendo experiencias significativas para los niños continuamos alcanzando los estándares que el estado nos pone enfrente. El aprendizaje de Felipe era evidente en su libro, y así lo mostramos en nuestro diario del aprendizaje.

"Nuestro Diario del aprendizaje empezó después de que visité una escuela preescolar inspirada en Reggio, esto fue en otro estado, ahí vi los diarios de sus clases. Sentimos que un diario del aprendizaje pegado a la pared enfrente del lugar donde se firma seriá una gran manera de comunicarles a nuestras familias acerca del aprendizaje de cada día. Nosotros usamos fotografías que diariamente tomamos con una cámara digital y escribimos en ingles y español acerca de las experiencias que ahí se están llevando acabo. Nuestro diario es escrito a mano con él fin de que mi asistente Marta y yo lo mostremos lo más pronto posible, usualmente al siguiente día. Ingles es mi primer idioma entonces si yo lo escribo en casa conforme edito las fotografiás, podría resultar en una versión de ingles impresa mientras la versión de español seria escrita a mano por Marta. Nosotros queríamos que los dos idiomas tengan la misma importancia y no que la versión en ingles pareciera más oficial así que decidimos escribir todo a mano.

"Siempre nos emociona mucho cuando vemos que las familias leen el diario conforme llegan o cuando recogen a sus niños. Frecuentemente ellos traen a otros miembros de la familia para que vean las fotografiás y también lean el diario. Los niños se ven en las fotografías y le piden a los adultos que les lean lo que ahí esta escrito. Esto produce muchas reflexiones de las experiencias de aprendizaje y conversación acerca de lo que aremos enseguida. Esto refuerza la identidad de nuestros estudiantes que están aprendiendo el idioma ingles y también los hace estudiantes competentes. Conforme los días van pasando, ponemos los diarios en una carpeta de argollas y desplegamos los diarios nuevos. Los familiares que no pueden venir muy seguido al salón, pueden sentarse y leer la carpeta del diario y saber lo que ha estado pasando. Los visitantes y administradores también leen los diarios. Ellos pueden ver que nuestro aprendizaje inspirado en Reggio promueve pensar profundamente y cubre todos los estándares de aprendizaje del estado para la niñez temprana."

### Listen to Marsie

"The story of Pauline launching an extended investigation with Felipe is an example of how we believe we can provide meaningful experiences for children and still meet the standards our state puts forth. Felipe's learning was clearly evident in his book, and we also highlighted it in our daily learning journal.

"We began our daily learning journal after I visited a Reggio-inspired program in another state and saw their daily journal posted on the classroom wall. We felt that a daily learning journal posted at the sign-in board in our classroom would be an excellent way to communicate with our families about the learning taking place each day. We use daily photos, taken with a digital camera and developed each night, and write in both Spanish and English about the learning experiences taking place. Our journal is handwritten so that my assistant, Marta, and I can get it posted as speedily as possible, usually the following day. English is my first language, so typing the journal at home, as I edited the photos, would result in a typed English version, whereas the Spanish version would be handwritten by Marta. Since we wanted the two languages to be equal in importance and not have the English version appear more official, we have chosen to write it all by hand.

"We are always very excited to find the families reading the previous day's journal as they pick up or drop off their children. Frequently they bring in other family members to read the journal as well. The children see the photos and ask to be read what is written. This produces a lot of reflection on learning and conversation about what we might do next. It strengthens our English language learners' identities as competent learners as well. As the days progress, the previous week's journals are put in a notebook as new postings are made. Family members who are not able to come into the room often are able to sit and read the notebook journal and catch up on all that has been going on. Visitors and administrators also read the journals. They can see that our Reggio-inspired learning promotes deeper thinking and meets standards."

### *Reflect*

Pauline and Marsie used Felipe's interest in cars to engage his learning at a deeper level. Rather than just giving him cars to play with, they took his interest seriously by offering him an adult reference book. They invited him to draw the cars he liked and gave him this opportunity again and again so that he could keep developing his ideas. Recognizing not only the math standards that were being met in this activity, but also the literacy and social/emotional domains, they spread this news to others via their daily learning journal board.

And notice the care Marsie takes to honor the home language of Felipe and most of his classmates. They post things in Spanish as well as English and make sure that these languages are portrayed with equal value. ■

Manzo PACE Preschool

Pauline and Marsie's daily learning journal brings alive what Margaret Carr (2001) calls "learning stories." Carr developed this narrative form of assessment to address the Aotearoa/New Zealand government's requirement that teachers provide documentation that demonstrates their knowledge and understanding of each child and their individual plan for learning outcomes. In their learning stories, teachers capture significant moments throughout their days with children and then use photos to tell the story of the child's learning. Each story focuses on and tries to make learning visible from a very small snapshot of what the child is engaged in at the time. However, as you read through each child's portfolio, a clearer picture starts to evolve as the stories weave together and unravel the particular context and background for that learner.

As we saw in the story of Felipe's engagement with the book of his drawings and ideas, learning stories helps create a positive identity for children as they return to them, often on a daily basis, and share the stories with their friends and family.

Another important aspect of New Zealand's learning stories is the way they nurture relationships between the children and their parents. Parents are invited to contribute learning stories to their children's portfolios by adding their perspective on a story, perhaps offering a related story from home. These contributions are often referred to as "Parent Voice" in the portfolio.

## Grasping Water

In writing learning stories, teachers may weave questions into the stories, for both the child and the parents. With no pretense of being objective, learning stories not only describe the children's actions, but make the teacher's feelings and interpretations visible as well. Notice in the following story how Fran writes to Henry in the first person, describing what she has seen and what she thinks about it. You'll often find that parents do the same in return.

*Henry often likes to share with others the discoveries that he has made while exploring the Tots garden. He seems to have an affinity with nature, noticing how falling rain appears to change the color of concrete, the intricate details of small creatures, and how the wind moves the leaves in the puriri tree.*

*Today Henry came over to his teacher who was watering a fern, to chat and offer his assistance. While watering the agave plant by the steps, Henry made an important discovery.*

*"Look, Fran, the water is running down the plant like a fountain."*

*Henry reached out his hands to gather the water that was trickling down the leaves of the agave. He noticed that the flow and quantity of the water was greater than the volume that he could hold in his hands and he searched the nearby area to see what could aid in the water collection. A container from the sandbox was used to capture the water. Henry soon made other discoveries.*

*"The leaves are like the pipes that we use in the water trough and I'm recycling all the water."*

*Henry continued with this interest, transporting the collected water to other areas of the garden helping to care for the Tots environment.*

### Listen to Fran

"Henry, your interest in the natural world amazes me! You take notice of the smallest things, investigating, testing out theories, and using the wealth of knowledge that you already have to make further discoveries. Thank you for sharing your special interests with me."

### Reflect

Fran's posted learning story about Henry's interest in the natural world appears on the next page. As you can see, Fran is keen on sharing her reflections of the dispositional learning inherent in Henry's story. She reviews the dispositional outcomes their curriculum delineates and then describes the indicators teachers and parents can be alert to in individual learning stories.

**Curriculum Outcome: Well-being**
Developing the disposition of trust and playfulness.
*We look for the child being involved.*

**Curriculum Outcome: Belonging**
Developing the disposition of courage and curiosity.
*We look for the child taking an interest.*

**Curriculum Outcome: Communication**
Developing the disposition of confidence.
*We look for the child expressing a point of view or feeling.*

**Curriculum Outcome: Contribution**
Developing the disposition of responsibility.
*We look for the child making a contribution.*

**Curriculum Outcome: Exploration**
Developing the disposition of perseverance.
*We look for the child persisting with difficulty, challenge, and uncertainty.*

# The Natural World

Teacher Fran April 2005

**Well-being :**
Developing the disposition of trust and playfulness.
We look for the child being involved.

**Belonging :**
Developing the disposition of courage and curiosity.
We look for the child taking an interest.

**Communication :**
Developing the disposition of confidence.
We look for the child expressing a point of view or feeling.

**Contribution :**
Developing the disposition of responsibility.
We look for the child taking responsibility.

**Exploration :**
Developing the disposition of perseverance.
We look for the child persisting with difficulty, challenge, and uncertainty.

Henry often likes to share with others the discoveries that he has made while exploring the Tots garden. He seems to have an affinity with nature, noticing how falling rain appears to change the colour of concrete, the intricate details of small creatures and how the wind moves the leaves in the puriri tree.

Today while I was watering the fern and succulent garden Henry came over to chat and offer his assistance. While watering the Agave plant by the steps Henry made an important discovery.

*"Look Fran the water is running down the plant like a fountain."*

Henry reached out his hands to gather the water that was trickling down the leaves of the Agave. Henry noticed that the flow and quantity of the water was greater than the volume that he could hold in his hands and he searched the nearby area to see what could aid in the water collection. A container from the sandpit was soon used to capture the water. Henry soon made other discoveries.

*"The leaves are like the pipes that we use in the water trough and I'm recycling all the water."*

Henry continued with this interest, transporting the collected water to other areas of the garden helping to care for the Tots environment.

**Teacher Reflections** **Henry, your interest in the natural world amazes me!!! You take notice of the smallest things, investigating, testing out theories and using the wealth of knowledge that you already have to make further discoveries. Thank you for sharing your special interests with me.**

Fran's recognitions invite dialogue with the children's families, and indeed, with the children themselves. Because Fran includes some direct comments to Henry in the learning story, his parents are prompted to re-read the story to him. "Look, Henry, Fran wrote about you being a scientist today with your investigations of water in the garden." Thus, the teacher, the family, and the child are all engaged in the assessment process, recognizing and delighting in how learning is unfolding. ■

## Your Turn

Whether or not you are required to assess children with a particular tool, you will want to be following their learning and development process. To make this more relevant and meaningful for you, the children, and their families, spread out before you some collected documentation. Invite at least one colleague or classmate to join you in analyzing your collection from different points of view. Use the questions below, which are adapted from *The Art of Awareness: How Observation Can Transform Your Teaching* (Curtis and Carter 2000).

### WHAT'S THE IMPORTANT STORY TO TELL?

**The Child's Story**
***What the Child Did and Said***

List descriptive words with specific details about the tone of voice, body language, what was done, said, created.

**The Learning and Development Story**
***What the Child Was Learning***

What experiences, ideas, questions, and understandings is the child developing or expressing?

What learning domains is the child working on? For example:

- language/literacy
- social/emotional
- numeracy/math
- scientific inquiry
- creative expression
- symbolic thinking
- critical thinking/antibias
- physical development

**The Teacher's Story**
***What You Are Thinking***

What are you curious about?

What do you value in this?

What do you want to offer next and why?

**The Family's Story**
***What Ideas Does the Child's Family Have about This?***

Have they seen the child engage in this sort of play or exploration at home?

Does this activity fit with or challenge the family's beliefs, values, or practices?

What do they hope for here?

## •PRINCIPLE•
## Seek Different Perspectives to Inform Your Planning

If you work in a program with a diversity of families, children, or coworkers, use this diversity to enrich your perspectives and planning. When teachers begin to study their documentation for possible curriculum projects, they often identify a number of topics or learning outcomes they could pursue with the children. This is a critical juncture, because too often a teacher's agenda can take over and obscure what a child is actually curious about or the ideas he is exploring in his play. You might also be overlooking the different viewpoints and contributions parents can offer. Before jumping in with a series of plans and resources for the children, take the time to explore different perspectives on the meaning of what your documentation has captured.

First and foremost, try to find the children's perspective. You can show them some piece of your documentation and invite them to say more about its meaning. You can engage in dialogue with your coworkers and the children's families. Their perspectives can illuminate yours. If you like using the Internet, find a related listserv or chat room, or launch a blog where other early childhood professionals are eager to discuss and explore the meaning in children's conversation and play. As you plan, take one step at a time, with a focus of discovering more about the children's thinking, so that you can determine what scaffolding is needed. Your plan should be shaped around inquiry, some form of research or investigation for you *and* the children.

### Don't Bug Me

*Linda's initial efforts at using an emergent approach to curriculum have been based on trying to develop curriculum plans around "themes" the children seem interested in. For instance, when they noticed the children interested in bugs, she and her team developed an extensive curriculum plan centered on different kinds of bugs, with activities related to this theme.*

Lakewood Co-op Preschool

*Recently, as she thought more about the idea of looking for what was really capturing the children's attention, Linda realized that they had totally overlooked a little girl's close interest in the wings of a ladybug. The child was investigating how the wings were sometimes hidden and then appeared. But at the time, Linda and her coworkers didn't pay attention to this and just focused on the idea of bugs in general. "We totally missed it!" she exclaimed in hindsight. It was a great relief to her to hear that this is common for teachers who are just starting to think in new ways about deeper curriculum experiences for children. She realized that even teachers she admired and held up as role models once struggled with what to do. "Sometimes I see someone so advanced, and I don't think about the fact that they had to learn how to do this too."*

### Follow Their Hearts

Rukia, a child care teacher, discovered the power of studying her observations for new perspectives. As you read her story, look for Rukia's desire to be responsive to the parents' perspective about school readiness, even as she seeks their son's perspective on the meaning of his block play.

*Peter, a child in Rukia's room, lives with his two dads, who are very keen on ensuring that his teachers are getting him ready for school. Rukia noticed that Peter's main interest is building with blocks, and he prefers to do this above anything else. She decided to observe this block play more closely, hoping to get more insight into Peter's fascination. Initially, she wondered if his talk about creating big dinosaurs was a fascination with issues of power. But as she watched further, she noticed Peter was carefully creating small piles of blocks all around his big dinosaurs. Rukia was hesitant to post her documentation, concerned that Peter's dads would think she wasn't moving him into more academically oriented activities. Seeking some action to take, she gathered the photos she wanted to display and took her notes to meet with her director. As they examined each of the photos, they concluded Rukia should try to find out more about the little piles of blocks Peter was consistently making from day to day. Rukia returned to Peter with photos of the little piles of blocks and told him she was so curious about them.*

*Peter: "Those are eggs. And (pointing to the bigger block structures) these are dinosaurs who want to be daddies."*

*Rukia: "Tell me more about these eggs."*

*Peter (shaking his head slowly as if lost in thought): "They just have to follow their hearts."*

*When she returned to share her documentation of this conversation with her director, Rukia realized that Peter's perspective was obviously grounded in the context of his family and adoption; his block representations had deep meaning for him. She felt his dads would appreciate her documentation now and, indeed, they did. They were touched and appreciative of her close attention to their son's play. Rukia used their conversation as an opportunity to also describe more about how she sees Peter as on track for school readiness and the ways she intends to support his continued learning.*

Clifton School

Clifton School

**Reflection & Action**

***What details stand out that I can make visible for further consideration?***

*

***What in my background and values is influencing my response to this situation and why?***

*

***How might issues of culture, family background, or popular media be influencing this situation?***

*

***What values, philosophy, and goals do I want to influence my response?***

### *Listen to Rukia*

"One of the most profound changes that I have made as a professional is in my image of the child, and thus my image of the teacher. My work with young children has evolved and my effort to honor the perspectives of Peter and his dads is an example of that. I think my role as a teacher is to support, to challenge, to research, and to give hugs. Peter's ongoing fascination with blocks made me curious, but at the same time, I wanted his fathers to know that I heard their concerns and I, too, wanted him to be successful in school.

"At first I thought my task was to document and show his dads all the learning Peter was engaged in as he played with blocks. I was also looking for where I could introduce some learning concepts in a developmentally appropriate way. I believe children can benefit from that. However, as I observed with learning goals in mind, I realized my research approach was flawed. I needed to understand what Peter was doing from his point of view, not from our adult goals for him.

"Getting my director's perspective helped me focus in on those little piles of blocks he was making. I might have missed that, assuming the dinosaur theme or some academic learning was what I should pursue. At the core of my evolution in teaching has been listening to and connecting with my children, and then talking with others about possible meanings for what I am seeing. I was so moved by Peter's words that the eggs 'just have to follow their hearts.' He was thinking so deeply about how he came to his family. Children are capable of exploring complex ideas and emotions. I never want to minimize them with some teaching agenda I have."

### Reflect

This story provokes opportunities to enhance a curious disposition. Where does Peter's phrase "follow their hearts" come from? Is it language his dads have used or is this his own expression? Either way we get a glimpse into how loved Peter knows he is. When parents are quick to emphasize their academic goals for their children, play-oriented teachers may think they need to educate the parents about developmentally appropriate practice. Because they are the educators, teachers may think they know more than the parents. But Peter's words remind us to seek both his point of view and that of his dads. Even if parent perspectives provoke tensions for teachers, you must keep in mind that they want the very best for their children.

Rukia is a responsive teacher, using the perspectives of the children, their families, and other professionals to challenge her own thinking. Because she was attentive to details in gathering documentation and took time to study them with her director, Rukia was able to suspend her teacher agenda and discover what was really significant for Peter and ultimately for his dads. She didn't, however, suspend her goals of ensuring Peter will be ready for school. She will continue to be alert to opportunities to teach content and skills in developmentally appropriate ways. ■

## •PRINCIPLE• Learn from Conflicting Ideas

Many teachers who want to start teaching differently struggle to negotiate new ideas with their coworkers. A teaching approach that attempts to follow the lead of the children can be challenging on many fronts. When you aren't working with a scripted or scope-and-sequence curriculum you are always doing a dance. And sometimes you step on toes, especially when there are different ideas about who should be leading and what steps to take. Teachers love working with colleagues when the dance is simpatico and they see eye to eye on most things. However, even compatible teachers have perspectives that eventually bump into each other, often ruffling feathers and raising tensions. How do you shape these moments as occasions for learning rather than judging?

Our Canadian colleague and author Carol Anne Wien reminds us that "emergent curriculum requires a toleration of error as teachers feel their way to creative solutions. Such ways of working require all the authentic and fruitful resources of thinking and feeling that teachers can bring to the classroom: the result is that teachers demonstrate vitality, energy for learning, and remarkable new ideas."

Wien brought the following story about Bobbi and Annette to us (extracted from an as yet unpublished manuscript called *The Sculpture Project*) when we raised the question with her: "What do you see teachers do when they don't share the same idea about a strategy to try with children?" She tells this story from her perspective as a weekly educational consultant and participant observer in the Peter Green Hall Children's Centre in Halifax, Nova Scotia, where Annette is the art specialist and assistant director and Bobbi is the teacher in a classroom for four-year-olds. We zero in on one small feature of the story to introduce how one teacher's idea of discovery is another's fear of contamination.

## Discovery or Contamination?

Inevitably there are times in the life of a project investigation when it is not clear what to do next, or how to resolve a dilemma. In such instances, when solutions are generated, no one is sure how they will work, or whether they are in fact "the right" moves that support the children's developing sense of an idea and how they might participate in it. In the following story, notice the interaction between Bobbi and Annette as they negotiate what materials to use and the role of the teacher. What do you see as the source of their emerging tensions?

*One day in the four-year-old classroom, Ahmed made an offhand comment about playdough being "sculpture." Bobbi, his teacher, wondered about this, talked to the children about their ideas, and found them very interested in pursuing the idea of sculpture. As a result, she provided more playdough, which led to more sculpture—mostly little lumpy animals. Bobbi was concerned by the children's frustration with the playdough, which kept breaking, drying out, and preventing them from getting the detail they wanted. She consulted with Annette, an art specialist in the program, but was skeptical when Annette suggested using Plasticene. Bobbi had previously found Plasticene unpliable and unresponsive to children's efforts to mold it. In this instance, the debate between Bobbi and Annette centered on different understandings: the experience of the material told Annette that Plasticene was a solution, and Bobbi's previous experience with the children told her it wasn't.*

Peter Green Hall Children's Centre

*They agreed to try the Plasticene, and Bobbi was pleasantly surprised to find that on this occasion it was the right material. The children settled into producing "sculpture" with increased focus, more details, and a wider range of subject matter, from human figures to sunflowers. Then a new problem emerged. Bobbi noticed the children's ongoing concern that their objects wouldn't "stand up." Annette interpreted this as the classic problem of struggling to move from two dimensions to three dimensions and suggested that she demonstrate what artists might do, using clay and a wire armature wrapped around a rock. The children were fascinated, enjoyed bending the wire into lively shapes, and produced very effective sculptures by pressing lumps of clay around their bent wire. Annette did two demonstrations with different children during small group times, and she and Bobbi then provided lots of rocks, wire, and clay on the art shelves for the children to use when they wanted sculptures to "stand up."*

*These materials, however, were not touched. Bobbi and Annette were perplexed. What had gone wrong? The children were still interested in sculpture, enjoyed the display of what they had made, but continued to choose Plasticene—thus repeating of the problem that things wouldn't stand up—rather than the new materials on the shelf. Annette thought perhaps they had missed a step, that the children needed a chance to explore wire by itself to understand it more as a medium with its own "language," as Reggio educators would say (Edwards, Gandini, and Forman 1998). So Annette invited the children to draw squiggles on paper, and to bend wire to match their squiggled lines. Several children grew intrigued with the possibilities of wire and created marvelous sculptures, such as one called "the dancing mammoth." Still, no one returned to the wire armatures waiting on the shelves. Bobbi and Annette let it go.*

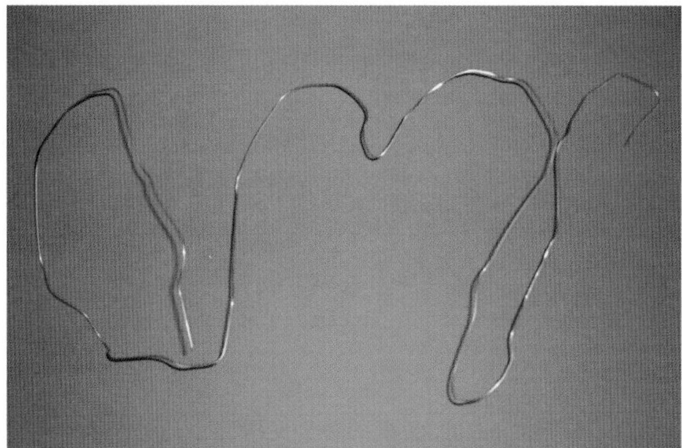

Peter Green Hall Children's Centre

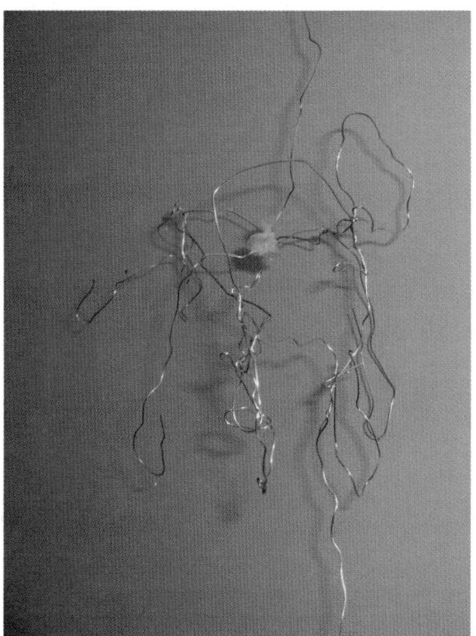

Peter Green Hall Children's Centre

*The children continued to engage in different sculpture activities, such as taking walks to discover sculpture in the community and looking at art books of sculpture, but the problems of working vertically persisted. One day Bobbi walked in after an interview with a parent and found Annette showing the children how to wrap a wire shape with paper and tape on the wrapping board to create three-dimensional forms. "What are you doing?" Bobbi asked, horrified, because she thought the demonstration too directive, bypassing possible discovery and research on the children's part. She thought the children might lose their capacity to discover connections on their own as they explored sculptural processes. She did not think the children were ready for this sort of move and saw it as "a disconnect." She and Annette had not had time to discuss Annette's activity beforehand due to the practical realities of scheduling many activities in a complex organization. Bobbi's comment "stopped Annette cold" and she wondered if she'd "blown it." Annette was afraid she had "really screwed up badly." She finished the activity with the children and put the materials away, but she really regretted her enthusiasm to teach the technique so quickly.*

Peter Green Hall Children's Centre

### Listen to Carol Anne

"I pondered the source of the apprehensions here. Both Annette and Bobbi struggle constantly in their work with the tension between letting children discover (but not have to 'reinvent the wheel') and something they call 'contamination.' By contamination, they mean reducing the children's confidence in their own ideas, in their capacity to figure things out, and to express their understanding in their own ways. To them, a child who asks an adult to draw something for her because she can't do it is someone whose confidence has been 'contaminated.' Simultaneously, they believe that techniques in using materials need to be demonstrated to children, so they have some possibility of using various media with competency. They find the line between demonstrating a technique to increase children's sense of possible moves with a material, and the worry that children's ideas will be hampered or 'put down,' a frequent source of tension. Our ongoing discussion about this tension is a reminder that uncertainty always resists easy resolution, and new spirals of thought continuously open out."

### *Reflect*

It isn't possible, nor really desirable, for teachers to always agree on a course of action. Does your perspective resonate more with Annette or with Bobbi? Teachers must negotiate different ideas, just as children do. This story brings us a challenge: rather than being intimidated by differences or, conversely, feeling your ideas are the "right" ones, you can use conflicts as opportunities to reexamine your image of children and the role of a teacher with them. Teaching is a dynamic process and learning often involves disequilibrium. You learn to teach by reflecting on your own ideas and thinking hard with other people. Be curious about what others are thinking and invite conversations around differences. When you have to name your experiences, what you know and believe to be true, your own understandings are strengthened. Trying on other perspectives furthers your growth as well. ■

### Your Turn

Having read a number of examples of ways teachers are using our principles to guide them in adapting our curriculum framework for their context, which of these do you want to take on in earnest as a next step for yourself? Review the list of principles at the beginning of this chapter again and make a plan for yourself. Consider these questions to take up this challenge.

- What change in your attitude holds the most promise for changing your practice?
- How can you expand possibilities for using your documentation?
- Where do you see openings for more flexibility in interpreting regulations and performance standards?
- Who among your colleagues offers the most fruitful challenges to your thinking?

# Claim Your Responsibility to Live Fully and Teach Well

*Teaching as an ethical enterprise goes beyond presenting what already is; it is teaching toward what ought to be. It is walking with the mothers of children, carrying the sound of the sea, exploring the outer dimensions of love . . . Teaching of this kind might stir people to come together as vivid, thoughtful, and yes, outraged . . . The fundamental message of the teacher is this: You can change your life. Whoever you are, where you've been, whatever you've done, the teacher invites you to a second chance, another round, perhaps a different conclusion. The teacher posits possibility, openness, and alternative; the teacher points to what could be, but is not yet. The teacher beckons you to change your path.*

**BILL AYERS**

Getting inspired by new ideas can bring on a rush of excitement and an initial flurry of activities. Perhaps you are the kind of person who dives in and spends an extraordinary amount of time and energy trying to implement a number of changes. Or, you might be someone who feels cautious, overwhelmed, or uncertain about where to begin in applying what you are learning. If you are to move forward with the curriculum framework proposed in this book, you must create a sustainable plan for yourself, one that keeps you learning and agitating for change. Sustainability is a key word here. You will need nourishment and companions on the journey.

When you seek ongoing professional development for yourself, carefully judge what will offer sustenance and renewal. Consider forming a study group focused on the theoretical framework or pedagogy you are pursuing, or the leadership skills you want to advance in yourself. Seek out programs to visit where there is an established practice of the approach you are interested in. Find a mentor and become involved in mentoring others. Each time you consciously extend yourself to help an adult or a child learn something, you become more cognizant of the dynamics involved in teaching and learning.

As we witness in children, early childhood educators who embark on lifelong learning alternately feel exhausted and invigorated, discouraged and inspired, afraid and courageous. When you make a commitment to refuse less than children, families, and you deserve, you become part of a tradition of warriors for justice and champions for change. To claim your responsibility to live fully and teach well, study these principles and draw inspiration from the spotlight stories this book offers.

- Find colleagues to support your learning
- Take risks to try new things
- Visit inspiring programs
- Explore the question "Why?" to challenge thinking
- Take leadership for change

## •PRINCIPLE•
## Find Colleagues to Support Your Learning

Ideally you want to be working in tandem with coworkers in your program, but if you find that slow going, make connections with other early childhood professionals who share your passion. Consider going to a workshop or conference focused on the ideas and practices you are pursuing, and make it a point to try to find someone interested in an ongoing dialogue. Explore other programs or organizations in your community where you can find colleagues and form alliances. It is not uncommon for early childhood organizations to be dominated by people who aren't practicing teachers or home providers, so you may need to challenge these groups to reach out to those on the floor with children. There are many online groups and resources, but there is no substitute for face-to-face meetings where you can practice the risk-taking that often accompanies a dialogue across different perspectives. Being an educator or change agent requires ongoing learning, refining of your vision, and leadership skills.

### Create a Lifeline

*Julie, a Head Start coordinator, took action to overcome her isolation as the only one in her agency with a different vision for what children and families deserve.*

*"I moved to this city to take a job as a coordinator of a newly built, Reggio-inspired site that I hoped would become a model program. Immediately I found myself isolated because no one in my agency had the exposure or experience with the ideas that I had, and I had a big vision guiding my work. To connect with others I put out a flyer calling people to join me in a Reggio Roundtable where we could study and talk together, visit each others' sites, and offer each other support. The response was really good. People in this Roundtable group were my lifeline when I found myself drowning in a sea of paperwork, pressures, and lack of understandings about my vision back at my agency. When that stuff gets you down, you have to reach out to others. You need that to keep growing and not fall back yourself."*

Martin Luther King Jr. Day Home Center

Puget Sound ESD Head Start

### Your Turn

If you find yourself working in isolation, try to answer these questions for yourself.

- Who would be interested in hearing about an observation that puzzled me?
- Who might share in my excitement about what just happened with the children's investigations?
- Who would challenge me with a different perspective on what I'm seeing or thinking?
- What book would I like to study and discuss with others?

Then, using your answers to these questions, contact some of these folks and propose a monthly get-together, or set up a blog to regularly share your observations and questions and get other perspectives and challenges.

### Play a Few Chords

*Consider this simple, yet bold, risk that Billie, a family provider, took with the children in her care.*

*"After years—decades actually—of wanting to learn to play the guitar, I am finally taking lessons and being brave about my clumsy, awkward efforts in front of my kids. For so long I have been the teacher and although I certainly have learned a great deal from the children, I never quite 'got' the feelings that come with being the 'learner,' at least not since college many years ago. Letting myself trust these little ones with my ineptitude and fear has been so freeing and has created a new kind of bond between us. When I try to play a few chords of 'Go Tell Aunt Rhody,' they give me a standing ovation and their support is sincere. When I get frustrated because I can't get a chord to sound right, they remind me that it just takes practice and that I'll get it sooner or later. How often could I have been more patient with a child who didn't understand a concept that seemed so obvious to me? Now I get it! Being a learner right along with them has made me more aware of how often we 'direct' children rather than trust them to figure out what works best for them. I am so thankful for their patience as I figure this out in my own time. Being part of this community of learners has made me a better teacher." —Billie*

Heart and Home Family Child Care

## •PRINCIPLE•
## Take Risks to Try New Things

As you continue to develop, you will discover how taking risks can enhance your understanding of the teaching and learning process, as well as help you form closer relationships with others. What do you know about yourself as a risk taker? Who could serve as a role model for you? It might be someone you know, or one (or more) of the providers and teachers who have contributed stories to this book. Taking risks on behalf of something you really want to learn or accomplish nearly always enhances your self-confidence, and often your humility, whether or not you feel completely successful.

### Your Turn

Reflecting on Billie's story, consider something you have been longing to do but haven't yet worked up your courage to begin. Considering the risks involved, what part of this might you share with the children? Next, take some time to assess yourself as a risk taker. When it comes to trying some new actions, which of the following statements feels most like you?

- I avoid taking risks and tend to put my head in the sand when something new is required.
- When there's something new I want to learn, I'm willing to go through the discomfort to learn it.
- When I feel something really needs changing, I'm willing to stick my neck out.
- I'm always ready to challenge the status quo, to speak up, or advocate for something that obviously needs changing.

Are you satisfied with your current relationship to risk-taking? Do you want to make any changes?

## •PRINCIPLE•
## Visit Inspiring Programs

Visits to other programs are viable professional development opportunities. You get a first-hand look at how others are translating their philosophy and values into practice, and often forge new relationships for ongoing dialogue. You can learn from but never replicate what others are doing. Each program has its own context, resources, and challenges.

### ¡Si se puede!

*Linda Irene has been teaching for over twenty years and is always in search of new ideas and professional development for herself. Hearing about a bilingual program in another city making a shift away from traditional, theme-based curriculum, she arranged to visit them. Over the course of two days she observed in the classrooms, attended a professional development training they were holding, and met with individual teachers and the director. These experiences helped her reflect on her current practice and struggles in her teaching and she returned to her program with new energy and ideas to offer.*

José Martí Child Development Center

### *Eschuchen a Linda Irene*

"En contraste con lo que sucede en mi centro educativo, donde nuestro director da libertad a los profesores para elegir su propio currículo. En el centro educativo que visité todos parecían estar enfocados en la misma dirección. Por lo que todos estuvieron muy emocionados en recibir invitaciones. Cuando caminé, desde los salones de clase pasando por la bodega, para la reunión con el personal pude observar el contraste de la transición que iba ser llevada a cabo, es decir, desde materiales dirigidos a un aprendizaje tradicional para la niñez temprana hacia materiales más creativos y culturalmente vibrantes. Ellos dijeron que usar las ideas de invitaciones los había dispuesto más a compartir tanto materiales como ideas. Ellos parecían tener más confianza en poder desenvolver este plan acerca del currículo en una manera más significativa, y no sólo convertirlo en simple papeleo.

"Aprendí mucho hablando con una maestra acerca de cómo ella integra sus valores con esta idea de invitaciones. Ella identificó sus valores como sus raíces indígenas, sus valores familiares, la unidad, la paz y la libertad, el respeto y la educación. Yo pude observar cuando ella demostraba eso con los niños. A ella le gusta trabajar con frases o dichos como ¡Si se puede! Ella ha observado cómo estableciendo invitaciones con los materiales permite que los niños aprendan mientras juegan. Ella siempre incluye opciones relacionadas con escritura porque quiere que los niños obtengan esas habilidades tan importantes, pero quiere que esto suceda de una forma natural.

"Su director les ha brindado el apoyo para estos cambios y ella ha realizado los preparativos necesarios para enviar a los maestros semanalmente a reuniones de desarrollo en su centro educativo. Ella esta animando a todos los profesores para continuar con su educación. Los que carecen de habilidades o educación del idioma Inglés obtienen ayuda, no solo a través de clases, sino también con un ambiente de apoyo brindado por sus colegas. Ella reconoce que los maestros más capaces pueden guiar a los otros, de este modo ella expande la base de liderazgo.

"Regresando a mi centro educativo ahora tengo mucho en que pensar en términos de innovar ideas. Estoy tan inspirada con mi visita y ahora tengo ideas acerca de cómo salir adelante. Yo sé que se puede hacer. ¡Si se puede!"

### *Listen to Linda Irene*

"Unlike my center, where our director gives teachers freedom to chose their own curriculum approach, everyone at the center I visited seems to be on the same page. And they are so excited about setting up invitations. When I walked from their classrooms to their storage room to the staff meeting, I could see the contrast from where they've been to how they are making this transition away from traditional early childhood learning materials to more creative, culturally vibrant ones. They said that using the ideas of invitations has made them more willing to share both materials and ideas. They seem to have more confidence that they can figure out how to do this curriculum thing in a meaningful way and not just have it be about filling out paperwork.

"I learned a lot from one teacher about how she integrates her values with this idea of invitations. She identified her values as her indigenous roots, her family values, unity, peace and liberty, respect, and education. I could see her demonstrate those with the children. She likes working with slogans or mottos like ¡Si se puede! (Yes we can!). She sees how setting up invitations with open-ended materials allows the children to learn while they are playing. She always includes options related to writing because of wanting the children to get those important literacy skills, but this happens in such a natural way.

"Their director is so supportive of these changes, and she has made accommodations to get teachers to weekly professional development meetings in their center. She is encouraging all her teachers to continue their education. Those who lack English language skills or education are getting help, not only by going to classes, but from the supportive environment of their coworkers. She recognizes that the stronger teachers can mentor the others, so she is expanding the leadership base.

"Going back to my center I now have a lot to think about in terms of making changes. I'm so inspired from my visit and now I have ideas about how to move ahead. I know it can be done. ¡Si se puede!"

### *Reflect*

Do you have moments of discouragement or confusion in your current setting? When this happens, many teachers begin griping, blaming, or burning out. Linda Irene avoided the temptation of falling into a rut or negative mindset about the struggles she was having in her own program. Instead, she took the bold step of using her professional development hours to visit another program known for its excellence in bilingual education and openness to new ideas and practices. As a result, both her heart and mind were nourished. ■

### •PRINCIPLE•
## Explore the Question "Why?" to Challenge Thinking

If you are on the teaching staff of an early childhood program trying to implement the ideas of *Learning Together with Young Children*, sooner or later you will want these practices to go beyond your own room. When your supervisor is on the same track, you'll probably have support for what you are doing, but if your room is to be more than an anomaly in your program, you'll want to provide more leadership in transforming your whole organization. You start, of course, by modeling with your own work, the translation of a philosophy and set of values into everyday living and learning with children. And, you invest time in building relationships with the children's families, your coworkers, and your administrators. The more you "think out loud" with them, the better they'll understand the "why" behind what you are doing. If you decide to change your approach to daily routines (for example, no longer focusing circle time on the calendar or enforcing rules that limit how many children can play in a particular area), explain the values or philosophy these changes reflect and what you are trying to accomplish.

### Thinking Together

*Working with an assistant who had more traditional views of the teacher's role, Deb found that continually asking "why?" in their planning meetings prompted some new understandings and practices that then spread to other teachers in her program.*

*"This year, Kirsten, my new coteacher, had a traditional approach to curriculum planning. She was eager to plan entertaining, 'cute and fun' activities for the children. Rather than squishing her enthusiasm, I used her suggestions as an opportunity for us to think together. When she wanted to make a rain forest and hang it from the center of the room. I asked, 'Why would we want to do this? Where does the idea come from?' I wanted us to practice the thinking we need to do underneath the activities we planned.*

*Kirsten was unsure of her role in an emergent approach to curriculum. I gave her a clipboard and pen and set her to work observing the details of children's play. I steered her toward children she didn't feel a connection with. In our discussions we explored the 'why' or meaning of what the children were doing. I suggested she show children the photos and sketches she had of what they were doing and ask them 'why?' I knew this coaching role was giving Kirsten a framework for thinking when I overheard her having a conversation with another teacher in our building. She was asking why they didn't do documenting and storytelling with the children like we did in our room. Kirsten had made this practice her own and was now coaching others to explore the 'why' of their practice."*

Burlington Little School

### •PRINCIPLE•
## Take Leadership for Change

The ideas in *Learning Together with Young Children* stand firmly in the tradition of progressive educators who have come before us, who believe as we do that education should be a vehicle for social transformation, not perpetuation of the status quo. If this is true for you, consider ways you can become a stronger leader for change.

## Dissolving Boundaries

*Judy, a community college instructor, tells a remarkable story of five child care providers who agitated for more meaningful education to enhance their professional development. Their actions not only resulted in a new structure of improved education for themselves, but ultimately benefited other students who were eager to become bilingual as well.*

*"We have to use bridges to dissolve boundaries. The demographics of our communities are changing. This means our current assumptions must change. Five Spanish-speaking child care providers approached our department with a request for training to improve their understanding of developmentally appropriate practice and state licensing regulations. We established a cohort for primarily mono-Spanish speakers; eleven have successfully completed courses that meet CDA competencies. Because others wanted to be bilingual as well, we have recently opened the cohort to include mono-English speakers. . . . We are now in the second year of providing Early Childhood and Family Study college courses with a bilingual format of instruction. It has been exciting to participate in a safe learning environment where people are sharing and discovering ways to communicate and discuss common interest topics."*

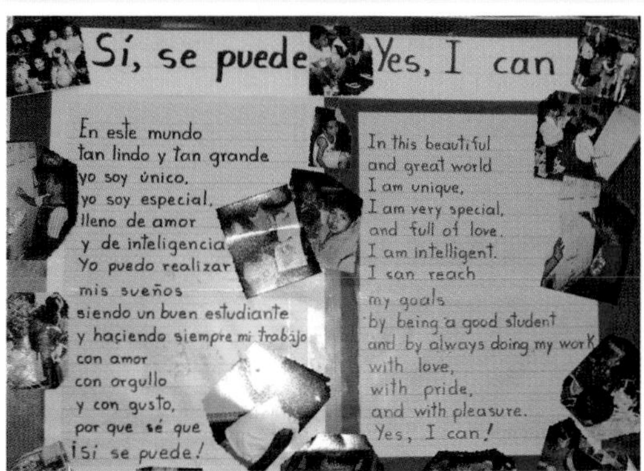


José Martí Child Development Center

José Martí Child Development Center

Transformation must start within each of us and then ripple out to wider and wider circles. There are attitudes, practices, organizations, and policies to be changed. Each of us has a role to play in creating this paradigm shift. Rebecca New (1997) reminds us that "organizational principles, physical environments and pedagogical strategies all combine to play an overt advocacy role for young children's rights." She further states that "the heightened emphasis on leadership and advocacy among American early childhood professionals reflects a sense of heightened need—not for resources, but for resolve. The contrast between our nation's ability and its will to care for its youngest citizens has never been so clear."

New's words are reminiscent of Loris Malaguzzi's description of the history of the remarkable schools of Reggio Emilia that have inspired the world. Describing the early years in the late 1940s when they began to re-create schools out of the disasters of fascism and war in their region of Italy, Malaguzzi (1998) says: "Finding support for the schools in a devastated town, rich only in mourning and poverty, would be a long and difficult ordeal, and would require sacrifices and solidarity now unthinkable. . . . Some of the schools would not survive. Most of them, however, would display enough rage and strength to survive."

So the task before us is to mobilize our resolve and display enough rage over the current lack of attention to the rights of children, the current trends and policies that are devaluing and standardizing their childhoods, and robbing them of more meaningful educational experiences. Simultaneously, we must display our strength, individually and collectively, in ways we have yet to imagine.

As of the writing of this book, many thinkers, leaders, and groups have raised challenges to the status quo and regressive trends in early childhood education. Our hope is that you will join in these efforts, first through your own professional practice with children and families, and also by becoming an advocate and agitator for change. Consider joining efforts like any of the following.

- Become a teacher researcher, nurturing your own development through inquiry, while contributing to an expanded view of children and the teaching and learning process. Perhaps you will go on to publish your work, in the tradition of Vivian Paley and Karen Gallas, or perhaps in "Voices of Practitioners," the Beyond the Journal Web page of *Young Children,* online at www.journal.naeyc.org/btj/vp/.

- Join one of the World Forum Working Groups and dialogue with others around the world on issues such as nature education for young children, peace building with young children, men in early childhood education, early childhood in Africa, children with HIV/AIDS, and many more. Connecting with people outside of your own country greatly expands your perspectives. Visit www.childcareexchange.com/wf/projects/.
- Launch or join a campaign to refocus current directions in early childhood education. One such example comes from an early childhood group of colleagues in California who worked to develop a manifesto to declare their right and intention to challenge the trend toward the misuse of standards and assessments. See appendix D for more information.
- Consider working with a group formed to go beyond challenging the standards and assessments movement, de-emphasizing "quality" and, instead, proposing a set of values and principles to guide the work of early childhood education. One such group, Early Education Advocates, describes their mission as "stimulating a broad discussion of the deeply felt human values that underlie our work and the formulation of a statement of social and political commitment." Samples of their beliefs about children and a statement of values and commitments are in appendix D and on their Web site at http://earlyeducationadvocates.org/.
- Study grassroots initiatives for financing community child care programs. One example is Sound Child Care Solutions, a nonprofit consortium with an innovative approach to collective management of child care. The consortium creates a structure that allows high quality centers to join together, sharing office functions to streamline and strengthen business practice but retain their community and family identity. See appendix D for their concept or visit www.soundchildcaresolutions.org.

Our hope is that knowing many early childhood educators around the world are joining together to provide stronger leadership for social change will both inspire and spur you into action. Together we are more powerful than we may imagine. Remembering the words of Terry Tempest Williams, let's mobilize our imaginations and our resolve to keep democracy alive.

> *Democracy is a way of life: the right to be educated, to think, discuss, dissent, create, and act, acting in imaginative and revolutionary ways. The human heart is the first home of democracy. It is where we embrace our questions. Can we be equitable? Can we be generous? Can we listen with our whole beings, not just our minds, and offer our attention rather than our opinions? Our future is guaranteed only by the degree of our personal involvement and commitment, as we engage the qualities of inquiry, intuition, and love.*

APPENDIX A

# Tools to Help Clarify Your Current Perspectives and Foundations

*Before beginning any new curricular approach, it's helpful to evaluate what's happening now in your program, what values and theoretical framework are already driving your work with children, and what new thinking you might need to undertake. Appendix A contains two resources that will help you consider your starting points as a teacher or a team, and examine the relationship between your values, theory, and what you do in the classroom.*

## SELF-ASSESSMENT TOOL

We created the following assessment to help you think about the resources and thinking you already possess, and what new development and support might be necessary to adopt the curriculum approach of *Learning Together with Young Children.*

### ASSESSING YOUR FOUNDATION FOR IN-DEPTH CURRICULUM WITH CHILDREN

#### CLARIFYING YOUR BELIEFS AND VALUES

To consider whether you have developed your vision and teaching practice for in-depth curriculum work, please list three words or phrases you typically use to describe children.

________________________________________

________________________________________

________________________________________

In light of these words, please write a brief paragraph for each of your answers to these questions.

- What do you believe children are capable of and deserve?
- What values do you want to shape children's lives in your program?
- How do you demonstrate you value childhood?
- What process have you used to clarify your beliefs and values as an individual and a program?

#### ASSESSING YOUR FOUNDATION FOR IN-DEPTH CURRICULUM WITH CHILDREN
**Designing an Engaging Environment with Interesting Materials**

To consider how well you have prepared your environment for in-depth curriculum work, write a brief paragraph for each of your answers to these questions.

- How have you designed your environment to reflect your beliefs and values?
- How does your environment reflect the lives of the children and their families and the community in which they live?
- What materials do you offer children to
  a) encourage them to make things from their understandings and imagination?
  b) provide for sensory exploration and transformation?
  c) evoke a feeling of magic, wonder, and curiosity?
  d) allow them to feel powerful and active in their bodies?
  e) explore different ways of seeing and being in the world?
- How does your environment give attention to order, aesthetics, and the natural world?

## ASSESSING YOUR FOUNDATION FOR IN-DEPTH CURRICULUM WITH CHILDREN

### Using Observation and Documentation Skills

To reflect on your current view of the role of observation and documentation in your work, choose which of the following sentences is most true for you. Describe why the statement you chose is closest to your experience.

- Most of the time I do the documentation required, but I honestly don't find it useful.
- I think the process of documentation is very important and useful for my understandings and planning.
- I gather lots of documentation, but I don't know what to do with it.
- I think of documentation as a delightful treasure hunt with many treasures to be found.

What system do you use to gather and analyze your observations of the children?

How do you use your observations in planning for the environment and curriculum activities?

## ASSESSING YOUR FOUNDATION FOR IN-DEPTH CURRICULUM WITH CHILDREN

### Creating a Classroom Culture for In-Depth Curriculum with Children

To consider how your daily schedule and use of time support in-depth curriculum, write down your daily schedule, noting the specific amounts of time allocated for each component of the schedule. Add up the exact time for each of the following:

- Child-initiated and child-directed time (children select their own materials and activities to work with alone or with others)
- Teacher-initiated and teacher-directed time (teachers direct children's choices and attention to an activity, including transitions and routines such as meals, sleep, and so on)
- Teacher-led time (teachers offer children choices among activities)
- Teacher coaching time (teachers coach and demonstrate the use of materials, tools, and processes)

Are you satisfied with the balance of time in your schedule? What changes might be indicated?

What strategies do you use to help children and their families make the transition between home and your program, and how do you make them feel connected during the day?

How do you encourage families to collaborate with you in shaping curriculum experiences for the children?

In what ways do you encourage children to notice different perspectives and points of view?

How are children given ownership of your environment and activities?

How are relationships and children's pursuits respected, made visible, and celebrated?

## VALUES, THEORY, AND PEDAGOGY

The following chart shows the connection between values, theory, and pedagogy in the classroom. The left column offers four possible perspectives/values that could guide your thinking. Follow each row across to see the theoretical assumptions, outcomes, pedagogy, and record keeping consistent with each perspective. Use it as a model for creating your own document showing your values about children and teaching, the theory that supports you, and the teaching that results from both.

### CLARITY ON VALUES AND THEORETICAL PERSPECTIVES AND THEIR OUTCOMES IN PRACTICE

| Perspective/ Values | Theoretical Assumption | Practical Outcomes | Pedagogy | Record Keeping |
|---|---|---|---|---|
| **Readiness/ Preparation for the future** | Behaviorism (Skinner 1965) | Preparation for school. | Teacher directs and controls outcomes. | Checklists |
| **Developmental/ Protection** | Developmental psychology (Piaget 2001) | Notion of universal child moving through predetermined set of developmental milestones. Teachers plan experiences to meet these. | Teacher guides children through verbal and physical support. Helps with conflict resolution.<br><br>Teacher facilitates, providing experiences with time and space to extend and challenge children's interests. | Use of child observations linked directly to planning learning experiences. |
| **Foster group and individual identity** | Sociocultural theories (Vygotsky 1978; Brofenbrenner 2006; Rogoff 2003; Carr 2001) | Children construct own knowledge through interaction with others. | Teacher scaffolds learning and complexity through play. | Collections of samples of children's work in portfolios with documentation that explains learning goals. |

| Perspective/ Values | Theoretical Assumption | Practical Outcomes | Pedagogy | Record Keeping |
|---|---|---|---|---|
| **Critical reflection; Multiple perspectives and meanings** | Post-modern and post-structuralist, critical science (Dahlberg, Moss, and Pence 1999; Dahlberg and Moss 2005) | Learning happens in particular social and cultural context.<br><br>Reciprocal relationships with families and communities.<br><br>Children are cocreators with adults; explore issues of power, social justice, equity in democracy. Many ways of viewing the world and multiple pathways to learning. | Adults and children negotiate and collaborate in the learning process.<br><br>Educators reflect, question, and challenge their practice by documenting and analyzing children's experiences and learning. | Variety of approaches, including family and children's input into documentation process and meaning making. |

Adapted with permission from *Building Waterfalls: A Living and Learning Curriculum Framework for Adults and Children (Birth to School Age)*, Queensland, Australia: C&K 2006.

APPENDIX B

# Sample Curriculum and Assessment Statements

*The following are statements about curriculum and assessment from the Mid-America Head Start, Kansas City, Missouri; Puget Sound ESD Head Start, Burien, Washington; Aotearoa/New Zealand Ministry of Education; and a national U.S. group, Early Education Advocates. Use them as models of what is possible for your program.*

## MID-AMERICA HEAD START CONSTRUCTIVIST CURRICULUM PLAN

The following document, from Mid-America Head Start in Kansas City, Missouri, demonstrates a possible way to justify a curriculum such as *Learning Together with Young Children* within the confines of a restrictive set of requirements. Rather than purchasing an established curriculum for their entire agency, this Head Start program developed their own "Constructivist Curriculum Plan," drawing on sound learning theory and credible research. Their collaborative work to unify their philosophical approach to curriculum deepened their own understanding and improved their professional development efforts for staff. Only the table of contents and introduction are reproduced here.

### OVERVIEW OF MID-AMERICA HEAD START CONSTRUCTIVIST CURRICULUM PLAN

The Constructivist Curriculum Plan is the result of a collaborative process by managers, educators, and parents involved with our Head Start agency. The plan was written by Carol Bolz, Ann Camey, Brenda Loscher, Carolyn McIntire, Barbara Otto, and Brenda Sottler.

Barbara Otto led the Curriculum Committee, whose members spent many hours researching, planning, reading, discussing, and writing the Constructivist Curriculum Plan. The following people participated in the committee process during the 2000–2001 program year: Brenda Sottler, Carolyn McIntire, Theresa Owens, Carol Bolz, Brenda Loscher, Lisa Matthews, Wadandra McBride, Pegi Stamps, Jill Kroenke, Mindy Mikesell, Willie Burke, Melissa Smitson, and Liz Smith. The following experts were contracted to consult with the Curriculum Committee: Dr. Ed Greene and Dr. Jacqueline Jones.

A number of others have worked to update, revise, and implement the Constructivist Curriculum Plan in the years since it was introduced in 2001. Those people include: Joyce Taylor, Ann Camey, Lisa Johnston, Anita Gomes-Stewart, Keri Young, and Aileen Murphy-Swift.

Liz Smith, education manager, has made significant contributions in overseeing and facilitating the creation, implementation, and revision of the Constructivist Curriculum Plan.

This is an overview. The full document is available upon request.

#### TABLE OF CONTENTS

## INTRODUCTION

Head Start was founded in 1965 as part of President Lyndon Johnson's War on Poverty. Sergeant Shriver was put in charge of the effort. He formed a committee that included educators, child development experts, pediatricians, social workers, psychologists, and administrators who designed Head Start as a comprehensive child and family development program with national standards and local options. It was decided that the goal for the program would be to help children develop competence in social and school settings.

Since Head Start's inception, a tension has existed between those educators and policymakers who emphasize child development and social competence goals, and those who emphasize IQ gains, learning, and school readiness goals (Zigler and Muenchow 1992).

Early research on the effects of Head Start showed IQ gains in children. Subsequent research showed that the IQ gains faded out after several years. Various longitudinal studies published during the 1970s and 1980s concluded that children who attended Head Start grew up to be more likely to finish school and be employed, and less likely to be placed in special education, to have a criminal record, or to experience teen pregnancy (Zigler and Styfco 1993).

In the 1990s, a trend toward accountability in education began. The National Education Goals Panel—which included state governors, members of the United States Congress, state legislators, and advisors—set the following goal: "By the year 2000, all children in America will start school ready to learn" (National Education Goal Panel 1991).

In 1993 and 1994, legislation was passed calling for greater accountability and quality improvement based on further assessment for all federal programs. Head Start responded with the Head Start Program Performance Measures Initiative in 1995. This initiative established a framework for helping children meet the goals of social competence and school readiness.

In 1997–1998, Head Start conducted a very large national study—the Family and Child Experiences Survey—to assess the outcomes of participation in Head Start for children and families. Results indicated that Head Start improves children's social skills and narrows the gap between disadvantaged children and all children in vocabulary and writing skills (U.S. Department of Health and Human Services 2000).

The National Research Council (1998) published a report from the Committee on the Prevention of Reading Difficulties in Young Children stating that large numbers of children have difficulty learning to read; and poor children, nonwhite children, and nonnative speakers of English are more likely to be among them. Many recommendations were made for providing language and literacy experiences for children and families during the early childhood years.

In 1998, the United States Congress reauthorized Head Start and required that the Head Start Performance Standards be expanded to include thirteen specific child outcomes in the areas of literacy, language, and numeracy. Head Start programs would be required to gather and analyze data on these child outcomes in order to make decisions about program quality.

Head Start responded by building upon the framework of the Program Performance Measures to develop the Head Start Child Outcomes Framework. The framework was issued by the Administration for Children and Families (2000) along with information about using child outcomes in program assessment.

In December 2000, the National Head Start Child Development Institute was offered to Head Start managers and educators to support them in identifying a curriculum approach that is consistent with Performance Standards and is based on sound child development principles about how children grow and learn. Each Head Start program is required to have a written plan that includes:

- the goals for children's learning and development
- the experiences through which they will achieve these goals
- the role of staff and parents in helping children achieve these goals
- the materials needed to support the implementation of the curriculum

A group of managers, education consultants, and education coordinators from our Head Start agency attended the National Head Start Child Development Institute. Upon their return to Kansas City, a Curriculum Committee was formed and charged with the task of developing a written curriculum plan for the agency. Education Coordinator Barbara Otto was assigned to lead the work of the committee. Education Manager Liz Smith was asked to oversee the process. Early childhood education experts Dr. Ed Greene and Dr. Jacqueline Jones were contracted to work as consultants for the Curriculum Committee.

During preliminary committee meetings, it was noted that our agency was very large and diverse. Our program options included Head Start, Early Head Start, Center-Based or Home-Based Services, Family Child Care, Partnership Sites, and the Kansas City, Missouri School District and Independence School District Delegate Agencies. At the time, education staff members from these various program options were utilizing several different curriculum models.

The Curriculum Committee discussed the possibility of identifying a single curriculum model for the entire agency. That option was rejected because there was no single model whose curriculum domains and goals for children lined up with the Head Start Child Outcomes Framework. Neither was there a single curriculum model whose assessment system would allow our agency to gather all needed information for analyzing child outcomes. Also, the Curriculum Committee did not want to disregard the choices made by partners, delegates, and the family child care program as to which curriculum model was most effective for them. Neither did the committee want to waste the time, effort, and funds that had been invested in training and developing educators in the implementation of the various curriculum models.

Therefore, the committee decided to write a curriculum plan for the agency that would have as its foundation a philosophical approach to early childhood education. The Curriculum Committee identified the "constructivist" approach, based on cognitive developmental theory, as the philosophical foundation of the plan. It was decided that educators would be able to draw from several curriculum models—all of which shared the constructivist philosophical foundation—to guide them in their practice. However, the Goals for Children and the Assessment and Outcomes System would be locally designed.

This "Constructivist Curriculum Plan" is the written curriculum plan for our Head Start agency. It was originally introduced in August 2001. Since then, an accompanying curriculum plan has been written for Early Head Start. Constructivist Curriculum Institutes have been developed and presented to introduce the plan. The plans and the institutes have been updated regularly in order to stay current with the Head Start program and the field of early education, and to remain meaningful and useful to our practitioners.

## REFERENCES

National Education Goals for America, The. 2000. *From America 2000: An Education Strategy.* Rev. ed. Washington, D.C.: U.S. Department of Education.

Snow, C. E., M. S. Burns, and P. Griffin, eds. 1998. *Preventing Reading Difficulties in Young Children: National Research Council.* Washington, D.C.: National Academy Press.

U.S. Department of Health and Human Services. 2000. *Head Start Child Outcomes Framework.* Log No. ACYF-HS-IM-00-18. Washington, D.C.: Administration of Children, Youth and Families.

U.S. Department of Health and Human Services. 2000. *Head Start Family and Child Experiences Survey: FACES Findings; New Research on Head Start Program Quality and Outcomes.* Washington, D.C.: Administration on Children, Youth and Families.

Zigler, E., and S. Muenchow. 1992. *Head Start: The Inside Story of America's Most Successful Educational Experiment.* New York: Basic Books.

Zigler, E., and S. J. Styfco, eds. 1993. *Head Start and Beyond.* New Haven, Conn.: Yale University Press.

## PUGET SOUND ESD HEAD START CURRICULUM STATEMENT

Puget Sound ESD Head Start in Burien, Washington, offers another example of an agency addressing current Head Start requirements to name the research-based curriculum they use. Puget Sound ESD wanted their teachers to use an emergent curriculum approach and developed the following statement for their curriculum.

### PUGET SOUND ESD HEAD START CURRICULUM STATEMENT

Puget Sound ESD Head Start sees every child as a whole person who is capable, intelligent, resourceful, experienced, and a learner. We use a locally designed, emergent curriculum drawn from the ideas and practices embedded in *Authentic Childhood* (Fraser and Gestwicki 2002), *Reflecting Children's Lives* (Curtis and Carter 1996), and *The Creative Curriculum* (Dodge, Colker, and Heroman 2002). Curriculum encompasses experiences and environment (physical space, social interactions, and daily routines and rituals) designed and arranged to foster learning and development.

#### GOAL

The optimal development of the whole child: social-emotional, language/literacy, cognitive, physical, and creative domains.

#### THE ROLE OF THE FAMILY

- Families are a valuable source of information and share insights about their child's interests, abilities/skills, strengths, and needs.
- Families and teachers collaborate to create individual learning goals to be incorporated into the environment, materials, experiences, and daily routines.

#### THE ROLE OF THE TEACHER

- Teachers develop supportive relationships with children that foster positive social and emotional development: empathy, problem-solving, camaraderie, self-regulation, confidence, persistence, resilience, and self-esteem.
- Teachers respect children's emerging interests and inquiries and develop them into topics for discussion, exploration, and group projects.
- Teachers provide opportunities for children's multiple learning styles in the environment, experiences, and materials.
- Teachers use a range of strategies and tools to support and extend the learning goals based on the objectives outlined in the ECEAP/Head Start Early Learning document.
- Based on the elements of the Portfolio System of Assessment (observations/work samples and the Developmental Profile Checklist) and family contributions, teachers plan, implement, and individualize for children and the classroom community.
- Teachers incorporate planned health, nutrition, and safety experiences, and a personal safety curriculum, "Talking About Touching," into the child development program.

## THE ROLE OF THE ENVIRONMENT

- The cultures and languages of children and families are reflected by the materials chosen to create a richly diverse environment.
- Both the indoor and outdoor environments are provisioned and planned to provide a variety of opportunities for active learning, creativity, and social interactions.
- The environment conveys the unique personality and values of the children, families, and staff.
- The design and arrangement of the environment evolves in response to the changing interests and growth of the children and to stimulate ongoing development.

## ASSESSMENT FOR LEARNING IN AOTEAROA/NEW ZEALAND

With thanks to the Aotearoa/New Zealand Ministry of Education we have extracted a portion of its description of the early childhood exemplar books, which offer examples of assessments that make visible learning the Ministry defines as valued, and reflect the philosophy and four principles of New Zealand's curriculum Te Whāriki. These examples illustrate how assessment can help the learning community develop ongoing and diverse learning pathways. Assessment sits inside the curriculum, and assessments do not merely describe learning, they also construct and foster it.

### KEI TUA O TE PAE—ASSESSMENT FOR LEARNING: EARLY CHILDHOOD EXEMPLARS

#### HAVING CLEAR GOALS

Assessment for learning implies that we have some aims or goals for the children's learning. Te Whāriki provides the framework for defining learning and what is to be learned. The goals and indicative learning outcomes are set out in strands.

**Well-being/Mana Atua**

The health and well-being of the child are protected and nurtured. Children experience an environment where their health is promoted, their emotional well-being is nurtured, and they are kept safe from harm.

**Belonging/Mana Whenua**

Children and their families feel a sense of belonging. Children . . . experience an environment where connecting links with the family and the wider world are affirmed and extended; they know that they have a place; they feel comfortable with the routines, customs, and regular events; they know the limits and boundaries of acceptable behavior.

**Contribution/Mana Tangata**

Opportunities for learning are equitable, and each child's contribution is valued. Children experience an environment where there are equitable opportunities for learning, irrespective of gender, ability, age, ethnicity, or background; they are affirmed as individuals; they are encouraged to learn with and alongside others.

**Communication/Mana Reo**

The languages and symbols of their own and other cultures are promoted and protected. Children experience an environment where they develop nonverbal and verbal communication skills for a range of purposes; they experience the stories and symbols of their own and other cultures; they discover and develop different ways to be creative and expressive.

### Exploration/Mana Aotūroa

The child learns through active exploration of the environment. Children experience an environment where their play is valued as meaningful learning and the importance of spontaneous play is recognized; they gain confidence in and control of their bodies; they learn strategies for active exploration, thinking, and reasoning; they develop working theories for making sense of the natural, social, physical, and material worlds.

There are particular dimensions for considering Māori educational advancement, which are outlined in the document.

## DOCUMENTING ASSESSMENT

Some assessment will be documented, but most of it will not. There should be a balance between documented and undocumented interactions, and the two kinds of interactions should be in tune with each other.

The phrase "assessment for learning" implies an assumption that we develop ideas about "what next?" and the exemplars include many examples of planning from assessments. Usually the child will decide "what next?" For example, a child may decide whether to repeat an attempt on a jigsaw puzzle that was successfully completed yesterday or to try a more difficult one. Teachers, often in negotiation with a learner, will also make decisions about "what next?" and how to respond to what the learner does. Most teachers' decisions or negotiations will be undocumented and spontaneous, but there are good arguments for documenting some of the possible next steps.

## ASSESSMENT FOR LEARNING

### Noticing, Recognizing, and Responding

Assessment for learning is described as "noticing, recognizing, and responding," a description from Bronwen Cowie's work on assessment in science classrooms. These three processes are progressive filters. Teachers notice a great deal as they work with children, and they recognize some of what they notice as "learning." They will respond to a section of what they recognize.

Mary Jane Drummond's definition of assessment adds more to this description of assessment for learning: "[the] ways in which, in our everyday practice, we [children, families, teachers, and others] observe children's learning [notice], strive to understand it [recognize], and they put our understanding to good use [respond]."

The early childhood exemplar books use the term "assessment for learning." Many writers call this "formative assessment." Philippe Perrenoud says that "any assessment that helps the pupil [child] to learn and develop is formative," and adds, "development and learning depend on countless factors that are often interrelated. Any assessment that helps to optimise one or more of these factors, to however small a degree, can be considered formative."

Perrenoud includes children's motivation, their social identities as learners, their views about learning, and the learning atmosphere among these "countless factors."

One important connection between assessment and learning is feedback. Research tells us that feedback to learners improves learning. Some of this feedback will be through documentation (such as assessments that families and teachers can read back to children and photographs that children can "read" themselves). Some of it will be verbal. Some of it will be nonverbal (through a gesture, a nod, or a smile). Feedback tells the learners what outcomes are valued in the learning community and how they are doing, and it acknowledges the goals that children set for themselves.

Teachers share stories as well as feedback and this enriches their noticing, recognizing, and responding.

**Everyday Contexts**

Assessments are carried out in everyday contexts. A major purpose of documentation is that it will inform everyday, undocumented, interactive teaching and spontaneous feedback, making children's interactions richer and more reciprocal. The curriculum is at its best when activities and conversations are sited in meaningful contexts.

**Protecting and Enhancing the Motivation to Learn**

Assessment for learning will protect and enhance children's motivation to learn. In 2002, Terry Crooks, one of New Zealand's leading commentators on assessment, set out some requirements for effective learning. He emphasizes motivation: People gain motivation and are most likely to be learning effectively when they experience success or progress on something they regard as worthwhile and significantly challenging.

**Acknowledging Uncertainty**

The phrase "assessment for learning" suggests that we know what an appropriate next step might be, and for complex learning we don't always know.

**Listening to Children**

One way of responding to the inevitable uncertainty is to get to know the children well, to listen and observe carefully, and to respond appropriately. One of the exemplar books demonstrates how children can comment on their own learning, set their own targets, and do their own assessing.

**Collective Assessments**

This curriculum emphasizes the critical role of socially and culturally mediated learning and of reciprocal and responsive relationships for children with people, places, and things. Children learn through collaboration with adults and peers, through guided participation and observation of others, as well as through individual exploration and reflection. Thus, the documented assessments are both collective and individual and are often dictated by the children.

**Keeping a View of Learning as Complex**

Worthwhile educational outcomes are often complex, especially if they are about relationships and participation. Te Whāriki states that "the outcomes of a curriculum are knowledge, skills, and attitudes" and that they "combine together to form a child's 'working theory' and help the child develop dispositions that encourage learning." A focus on learning dispositions, accompanied by the aspiration that children should be secure in their sense of belonging and in the knowledge that they make a valued contribution to society, foregrounds children's strengths and achievements. Assessment notes what children can do when they are "at their best."

Recognizing complexity means viewing assessment as something much more complex than assigning marks or checking boxes. No one format is "right," but the Te Whāriki principles provide four evaluative criteria:

- Is the identity of the child as a competent and confident learner protected and enhanced by the assessments?
- Do the assessment practices take account of the whole child?

- Do the assessment practices invite the involvement of family and whanau [extended family]?
- Are the assessments embedded in reciprocal and responsive relationships?

In the assessment documentation or "learning story," annotations follow a standard question-and-answer format:

- What is happening here?
  *The answer gives a brief description of what is happening.*
- What aspects of the area specified does this assessment exemplify?
  *The answer explains why this assessment was chosen.*
- How might this documented assessment contribute to developing the area specified?
  *The answer suggests how this assessment might be used to support learning and development in the relevant area.*
- What might this tell us about informal noticing, recognizing, and responding in this place?
  *The assessment process is part of the pedagogy that occurs in the context of reciprocal and responsive relationships in each setting.*

## ASSESSMENT FROM THE CHILD'S PERSPECTIVE

The New Zealand approach to assessment asks teachers to consider questions from the child's voice as centers begin their journey of ensuring accountability through evaluation and assessment. These questions are built on the principles of their Te Whāriki curriculum, which provides the framework for defining learning and what is to be learned. Their goals are based on clearly defined values and reflect the following strands:

| | | |
|---|---|---|
| **Belonging** | Do you appreciate and understand my interests and abilities and those of my family? | Do you know me? |
| **Well-being** | Do you meet my daily needs with care and sensitive consideration? | Can I trust you? |
| **Exploration** | Do you engage my mind, offer challenges, and extend my world? | Do you let me fly? |
| **Communication** | Do you invite me to communicate and respond to my own particular efforts? | Do you hear me? |
| **Contribution** | Do you encourage and facilitate my endeavours to be part of the wider group? | Is this place fair for us? |

From Podmore, V., H. May, and M. Carr. 2001. The Child's Questions. In *Programme Evaluation with Te Whāriki Using "Teaching Stories,"* p. 9. Published by the Institute for Early Childhood Studies, Victoria University of Wellington, New Zealand.

## EARLY EDUCATION ADVOCATES

To challenge current trends in defining outcomes for early childhood education, a U.S. professional group, Early Education Advocates, drafted this statement of "capabilities desired." Consider doing something similar in your community.

### FIFTEEN CAPABILITIES DESIRED FOR CHILDREN AS OUTCOMES FOR EARLY EDUCATION

Here is a way to describe more important qualities in children than "academic readiness" or the ability to pass a knowledge test for entry into elementary school.

When children leave early childhood to enter common school they can:

- Participate as a member of an interdependent community
- Care for themselves, others, and the community
- Treat others with love and compassion
- Cooperate with other children to accomplish group goals
- Celebrate group accomplishments
- Laugh and play with a tangible sense of joy
- Express many human emotions in language and art
- Be inquisitive
- Initiate new ideas and invent solutions to problems
- Stick with difficult tasks or come back to them later in order to succeed
- Run, hit, catch, throw, kick, and tumble
- Sing and dance with exuberance
- Paint, draw, sculpt, and construct objects of beauty
- Maintain the community's spaces in cleanliness and order
- Greet guests with courtesy and charm

These are all natural acquisitions for children from all cultures when they are (1) treated as capable human beings, (2) listened to, and (3) trusted. Provisions for young children that offer opportunity to be with other children can create the kind of community in which all children achieve these fifteen capabilities. Imagine all children by age six being this way.

Then imagine being a kindergarten teacher and having children with these fifteen capabilities enter the room at the beginning of the year. There would be no "behavior problems." These children would be responsive and eager to learn. The teacher could get right to work, listening to the children's interests and finding out what aspect of the world they wanted to explore. If that topic were spiders, for example, children would be eager to examine, write about, read about, draw, create poetry about, listen to music about, create scientific displays about, research, count, and mathematically represent spiders. Because they shared this love of learning with others, they would exceed all the academic standards by far. Experience in a culture of a learning community is true "readiness" for school, because all the children come to view themselves as capable and competent, not just a few.

The fifteen capabilities are durable. The following school year the first grade teacher would inherit those same children, eager and happy to be at school, not like the browbeaten, destroyed children we often see in schools today.

It is up to every one of us who considers himself or herself a contributor to the early experience of our children—as an elementary or early childhood teacher, principal, or parent—to examine what we really want for our children and advocate for it with politicians, leaders, and our friends. The fifteen capabilities are what we want for all our children.

Right now the dominant discourse is about remediation for some of our children, the poor ones, the underprivileged ones, the ones that are "at risk." When community leaders and politicians want children to be "ready" for school they are speaking about poor children. Rather than offering resources, they are offering tests and standards. The implication in the dominant discourse is that certain children are deficient and need remediation.

Actually, these children and their families need good places to be and grow with adequate resources and staff who earn a family support wage, so all our children are not destroyed by the cultures of poverty and racism. All our children can achieve the fifteen capabilities that can transform our society, reduce poverty, and make our towns and cities better places to live.

Two actions we can take right now can help:

1. Never accept talk about the problems of education as residing in the children or their families. The children are who they are, capable and strong from the time of their birth. Every here and now offers possibilities for new ways of being. That's what we do in school. That's our job as early educators of children and families.

2. Talk about the fifteen capabilities rather than academic readiness as the outcome we all desire for our children and for childhood.

For more ideas, visit http://earlyeducationadvocates.org.

APPENDIX C

# Sample Planning Forms

*Included here are examples of forms that reflect an integrated approach to planning curriculum for children. Adapt them to work for your program as you begin to use the* Learning Together with Young Children *framework.*

# Planned Possibilities

**BURLINGTON LITTLE SCHOOL PRESCHOOL CURRICULUM, BURLINGTON, WASHINGTON**

**Week of** ______________________________

**Important Events**—What is happening this week? (School events, family activities, parent nights, etc.)

**Morning work tables**—Self-directed, focused tasks to introduce children to new materials and concepts

| Table 1 | Table 2 | Table 3 |
|---|---|---|
| | | |

**Process time activities**—Teacher-led activities for coaching and teaching skills

| Monday | Tuesday | Wednesday | Thursday | Friday |
|---|---|---|---|---|
| | | | | |

**Focused interests and coexplorations:** What observations do we have that show us the children's interests? What are the children excited about? What are we excited about?

**Next step for focus:** What next steps can we offer children to pursue their interests? What are the underlying values and lessons we would like the children to learn? What new materials, process time activities, or books and games for circle can we offer to extend their interests? What questions will guide our documentation?

**Educational display:** What documentation displays will help the children continue to investigate and pursue their interests?

**Documentation display:** What can we display to showcase our recent activities to families and visitors?

**Materials needed:** What do we need to gather and prepare for our focus of study? Who will do what?

## Toddler Play School Planned Possibilities

(from last week's notes)

Week of ______________

Sensory/Art

Dramatic Play

Construction/Problem Solving

Music/Movement

Books/Rhymes

Relationships/Identity Development

| Notes: What did we observe today? How does what we observed relate to the ongoing work of the children? What other meaning might we make of what we are seeing? |
|---|
| **Monday notes** |
| **Tuesday notes** |
| **Wednesday notes** |
| **Thursday notes** |
| **Friday notes** |
| **Continuing focus**—What next steps do we want to plan for individuals and the group based on this week's observations and notes? |

## Planning for Possibilities

### Puget Sound ESD Head Start, Burien, Washington

Week of ______________________

Reflections/summary from last week:

Intent/hopes for children's learning this week:

| **Materials and environmental aspects to support children's learning** (social-emotional, language/literacy, cognitive, physical, creative) | | |
|---|---|---|
| | | |
| | | |

| **Planned activities to support children's learning** | | | | |
|---|---|---|---|---|
| Monday | Tuesday | Wednesday | Thursday | Friday |
| | | | | |

**Transition ideas/changes to routine or schedule to support children's learning:**

Color code planned health and nutrition experiences. Indicate "Talking About Touching" and lesson number.

Note ILP goals using children's initials.

# Planning for Possibilities

## Puget Sound ESD Head Start, Burien, Washington

Week of ______________________________

Reflections/summary from last week: Where did children spend time? What were children interested in? What was the underlying meaning or developmental theme of the play? How can I learn more about the reason/needs behind the children's interest?

Intent/hopes for children's learning this week: What is the group goal for the upcoming week? i.e., establishing routines, building community, working on cooperation, further explore or extend interest in ____________.

| **Materials and environmental aspects to support children's learning** (social-emotional, language/literacy, cognitive, physical, creative) |
|---|
| How can I set the stage for children? How can the environment support/promote each developmental area? How can the available materials and environment support/extend the reflections noted from last week? |
| How can the available materials and environment support the intent/hopes for this week? How can individual children's ILP goals be supported through available materials and the environment? (Indicate goals using children's initials.) |

**Planned activities to support children's learning**

| Monday | Tuesday | Wednesday | Thursday | Friday |
|---|---|---|---|---|
| i.e.: large group activities, small group activities, cooking projects, large motor, songs/stories, health activities, nutrition activities, TAT lessons, etc. . . . | How can the planned activities support/extend the reflections noted from last week? How can the planned activities support this week's intent/hopes? How can individual children's ILP goals be supported through planned activities (Note ILP goals using children's initials). | | | |

**Transition ideas/changes to routine or schedule to support children's learning:**

Describe plans for transitions and changes to the routine or daily schedule.

How can the whole day, including transitions and routines, be utilized as learning opportunities? How can transitions, routines and the schedule support/extend reflections notes from last week? How can transitions, routines, and the schedule support this week's intent/hopes? How can individual children's ILP goals be supported through transitions, routines, and schedule? (Note ILP goals using children's initials.)

Color code planned health and nutrition experiences. Indicate "Talking About Touching" and lesson number.

## Planning for Future Possibilities

### Puget Sound ESD Head Start, Burien, Washington

| Children excited about/interested in: | New challenges to support: |
| --- | --- |
| Ideas from parents/families: | Ideas to revisit: |
| Ideas for parents/families: | Ideas for volunteers: |

**Each child is capable, intelligent, resourceful, experienced, and a learner.**

# Planning for Future Possibilities

## Puget Sound ESD Head Start, Burien, Washington

| Children excited about/interested in: | New challenges to support: |
| --- | --- |
| Note what you observe children doing. It may be individuals, small groups of children, or the whole group. Consider what might be behind the interest. | From your observations, note what children may need more practice with or need more opportunities to experience. |
| **Ideas from parents/families:** | **Ideas to revisit:** |
| Note ideas you have gathered from families' Consent agenda & minutes. Opportunities to learn this include talking with family support staff, attending parent gatherings, listening for more clues in conversations with parents, and posing questions and providing input opportunities for parents. | From your observations, note experiences, skills, or concepts it may be appropriate or interesting to revisit to reinforce, expand, or extend. |
| **Ideas for parents/families:** | **Ideas for volunteers:** |
| What are ways to involve families?<br>How can connections/communication between home and the center be promoted?<br>How can I acknowledge what parents are doing?<br>How can I invite parents to be part of the plans? | How can I utilize volunteers?<br>Are there specific times volunteers will be available?<br>How can I help "unexpected" volunteers feel welcome and helpful?<br>How can I help volunteers feel appreciated? |

**Each child is capable, intelligent, resourceful, experienced, and a learner.**

# Planning Form

## Harvest Resources, Seattle, Washington

| Observation summaries/Teacher reflections | | | | |
|---|---|---|---|---|
| Brainstorm possibilities; then choose one or two to pursue | Ideas and hypotheses about children's perspectives to explore | Planned activities | Learning domains | Prep/materials needed |
| Individualized Plans | | | | |

# Learning Together with Young Children

## Reflecting, Planning, and Taking Action

As you develop plans for children's learning, reflect on one or more of the questions below.

- What details stand out that I can make visible for further consideration?
- What in my background and values is influencing my response to this situation and why?
- How might issues of culture, family background, or popular media be influencing this situation?
- Where do I see examples of children's strengths and competency?
- How do I understand the children's point of view in this situation?
- How are the environment and materials impacting what's unfolding and what changes could be made?
- How are teacher actions impacting this situation?
- What learning domains are being addressed here and what other domains could be addressed?
- What theoretical perspectives and child development principles could inform my understandings and actions?
- What values, philosophy, and goals do I want to influence my response?

Summary of curriculum goals from reflections on questions considered:

Drawing on the principles of the core practices in *Learning Together with Young Children,* explore the possibilities related to your curriculum goals and then choose one or two actions to focus your planning. As you take actions, return to observing and reflecting so your next steps will be relevant and take learning deeper.

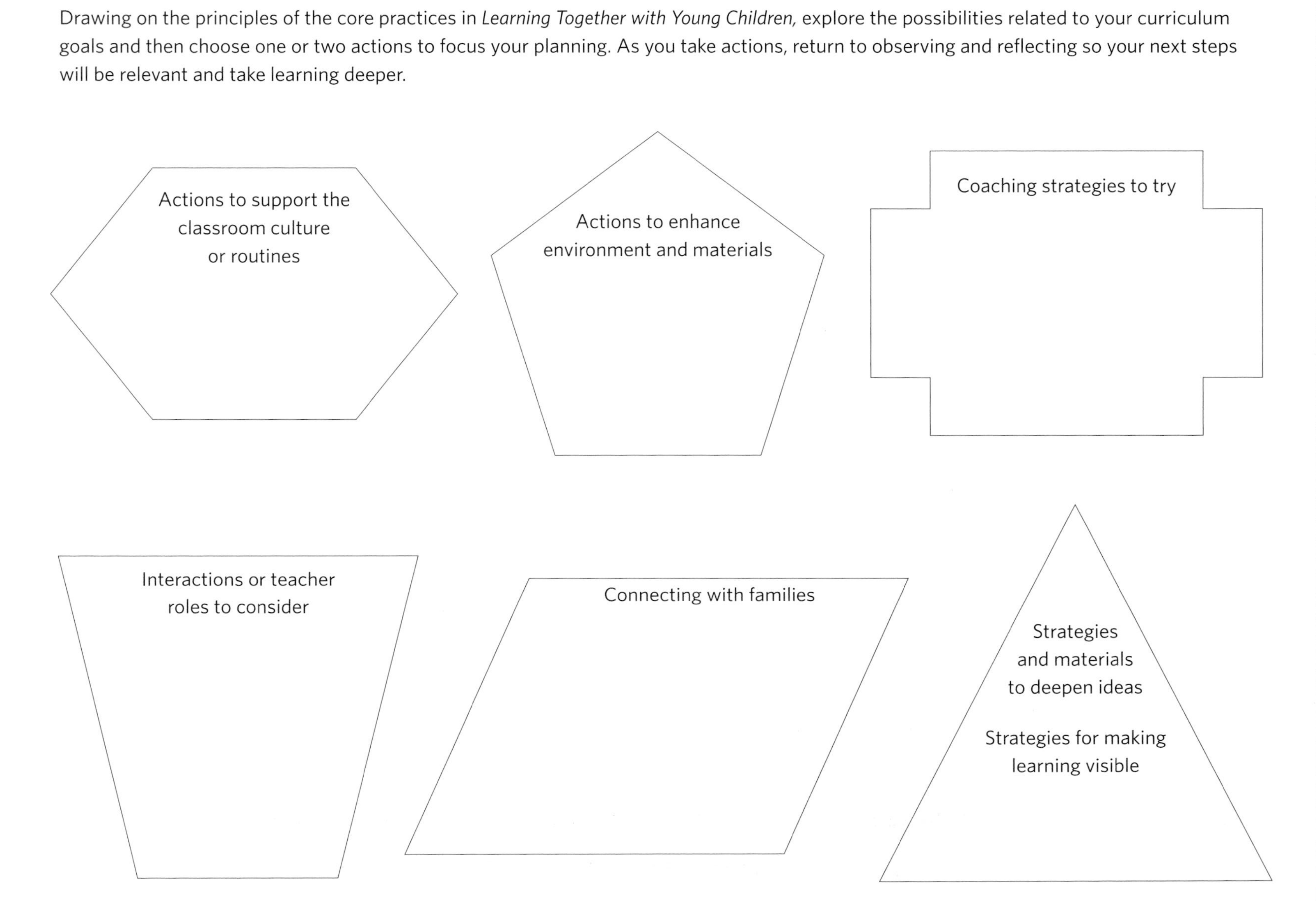

# Experimental Curriculum Planning Form

## New Hampshire Technical Institute Child and Family Development Center, Concord, New Hampshire

Zone (area of room) ______________________ Week of ______________________

| | Monday | Tuesday | Wednesday | Thursday | Friday |
|---|---|---|---|---|---|
| Observation | | | | | |
| Teacher thinking | | | | | |
| Activity/ Scaffolding for tomorrow | | | | | |

APPENDIX D

# Sample Advocacy Efforts

*The following three statements show how some early childhood teachers around the country are responding to the increasing pressure for standardized curricula and assessment. Read them as inspiration and a call to action, and then consider writing your own. What do you stand for? What do you believe about young children and education? What is your foundation?*

## A MANIFESTO
**(Developed by early childhood professionals in California)**

### A MANIFESTO: EARLY CARE AND EDUCATION LEARNING STANDARDS FOR CHILDREN 0 TO 5 YEARS OF AGE

A manifesto is a public declaration of intentions. We, as early care and education (ECE) professionals, are the defenders of developmentally appropriate practices as they pertain to young children (ages 0 to 8 years of age). These young children are among our society's most vulnerable members, particularly in the realm of public policy. For these reasons, we hereby execute our rights to declare our collective intent to uphold developmentally appropriate practices as they apply to young children in our society.

The word *manifesto* was selected on the basis of our strong beliefs regarding this issue and our commitment to a public and unapologetic declaration of our support for the nature and rights of childhood.

For the purposes of this document, the term "young children" shall apply to those children 0 to 5 years of age and not yet in kindergarten.

The trend toward determining standards and administering assessments to young children has descended upon the early care and education (ECE) field. For the most part, this trend has its genesis from outside the ECE profession. The threat of misuse of and/or misunderstanding of standards is real. The consequences are grave and already apparent to many of us.

School performance is under attack as student attitudes toward school and learning suffer under the new pressures presented by the No Child Left Behind (NCLB) legislation. Teacher motivation suffers as the curriculum is increasingly taken from their hands and replaced with predetermined activities, lessons, and reading lists. Individualized learning is under assault by lockstep curricula demanding that all children in entire districts are on the same page on the same day.

Childhood diabetes, stress, and obesity are all on the upswing. Active lifestyles, once the norm for young children, have given way to sedentary lifestyles dominated by media influences as schools increasingly turn to expensive technology-driven software to document learning in computer program–generated reports. Also contributing to declining child health is the reduction and even elimination of nonacademic aspects of school-day schedules.

Consequently, this trend is of great concern to us in the ECE profession. As professionals bound by the National Association for the Education of Young Children (NAEYC) Code of Ethical Conduct and guided by principles set forth in the International Association for the Child's Right to Play (IPA), we, the undersigned, collectively issue this declaration of intent and purpose.

#### I.

We, the undersigned, recognize that beyond learning standards exists an additional realm. This realm of implementation or engagement is crucial to the success of any endeavor to apply workable learning standards to young children.

Therefore, our Manifesto, unapologetic in its defense of the child's right to be a valued part of the family and community, and of both the child's right to play and the inherent value of play, declares the following to be non-negotiable items:

We will *only* support learning standards that in their implementation:

- Systematically include families as integral components of the program, deserving of ongoing and open two-way communication, opportunities for participation, and include families as partners in the school community and learning process, at such times and places where families shall be able to participate
- Systematically recognize, encourage, and support community involvement in the curriculum (e.g., community helpers, parks, libraries, other community resources, businesses, etc.)
- Actively encourage and support male involvement and seek out intergenerational and peer participation
- Systematically address the child's need for social and emotional engagement with her or his peers
- Include the outdoor environment as an integral and valued part of the program
- Implement child-directed, active learning and play-based learning opportunities as an integral, valued part of the program
- Systematically address the many domains of the whole child (details regarding these domains are addressed below)

And because a young child's mastery of skills is often dynamic and fluid, and because a young child's motivation to exhibit mastery of skills does not exist outside of the context of social interaction and play, we will *not* support learning standards that in their implementation:

- Require children to "perform in" or be assessed within an artificial learning environment. An artificial learning environment is typically purposefully removed from social and play contexts, and is therefore inherently limited in its ability to identify skills which a child may possess and which that child may reveal only within the context of play and social interactions. In addition, artificial learning environments remove children from the healthy cultural constructs of language and identity so necessary to accurately assess immigrant and second generation students.

## II.

Furthermore, and for the many reasons stated, we, the undersigned, understand that results-driven standards pose a special jeopardy to children. We understand that assessments which fail to accept children as individual learners with individual strengths, opportunities, challenges, and histories are destined to generate inaccurate pictures of the very children that they purport to evaluate, as well as inaccurate accounts of the learning environment, the educational team, and the learning process itself. Therefore,

We will *not* support learning standards that evaluate their success based upon:

- Young children performing timed tests
- Formal assessment measures alone (We support the right of teachers to utilize informal observation-based assessments and "child work portfolios" as appropriate alternatives to more formal assessment tools and strategies.)
- Criteria, assessments, or tests limited to a language other than the child's first language
- The expectation that all children in a given age group perform the same task at the same time
- A focus upon child deficits rather than child strengths (These strengths shall include child interests, learning modalities, and creative and expressive skills.)

**III.**

Therefore, be it known that we, the undersigned, are in agreement that implementation and engagement standards shall demonstrate inclusion of and respect for:

- The Child's Right to their Home Language:
  English language learners shall not be segregated from the other children except to the very limited degree that this segregation is strictly for the purposes of enhanced learning opportunities within the Cognitive Domains.
- The Child's Right to Reasonable Accommodation and Inclusion:
  Children with special needs shall not be segregated from the other children except to the very limited degree that this segregation is strictly for the purposes of enhanced learning opportunities within the Cognitive and Physical Health and Development Domains.
- The Child's Right to Individualization:
  Children will receive instruction and support in a way that respects their individual pace, learning styles, abilities, and needs.
- The Child's Rights to Play:
  Children shall have regularly scheduled daily opportunities to engage in child-initiated play, both indoors and out of doors.

And because the mind of the infant or young child is qualitatively different from the school-age child in terms of representational intelligence and other related cognitive abilities, we will only administer learning standards that have been designed specifically for the young child by acknowledged child development professionals and experts. And because a young child's cognitive development is built upon a foundation of basic needs that include social and emotional well-being, we will only administer learning standards that address the whole child. These standards shall include the following six domains:

- Cognitive development
  Language Arts
  Science and Inquiry
  Mathematics
  Literacy
- Physical Health and Development
  Fine and Gross Motor Skills
  Nutrition, Health, Safety, and Body Image
  Anti-bias and Inclusion
  Active Lifestyle, including Outdoor Environments
- Social and Emotional Development
  Self-Concept
  Self-Control
  Cooperation
  Social Relationships, including Anti-bias and Nonviolence
  Self-Esteem and Empowerment

- Creativity
  Art
  Dramatic Play
  Problem-Solving, including use of Outdoor Environments
- Play
  Teacher-directed and Child-directed
  Indoor and Outdoor
  Physical and Social
  Existing in significant blocks of time daily
- Approaches toward learning
  Engagement and Persistence
  Reasoning and Problem-solving
  Initiative and Curiosity
  Risk and Challenge

## IV.

And finally, because the quality of the adult-child relationship is fundamental to the learning process, Learning Standards implementation strategies must address the need for the continued professional growth and development of the caregiver and the continued education of family members in matters of child growth and development, advocacy, and community resources.

In support of the principles and standards set forth in this Manifesto, we, the undersigned, cite the following:

- *Code of Ethical Conduct and Statement of Commitment,* NAEYC, 1998
- Play Under Siege, *Children's Play: The Roots of Reading,* Edward F. Zigler, Sandra J. Bishop-Josef, Zero to Three Press, Washington, DC, 2004
- IPA and the Declaration of the Child's Right to Play, *The Great Outdoors: Restoring Children's Right to Play Outside,* Mary S. Rivkin, NAEYC, Washington, DC, 1995

Our strong beliefs are based on the importance of our children's early care and education, and supported by research.

Our strong stand is necessary to counteract the unrelenting drive toward a standardization of learning and test-driven assessment that often fails to match the goals and guidelines of a developmentally appropriate early learning experience.

Our commitment in this matter is solely to the well-being of young children, and not to any institution or organization.

# A DECLARATION OF VALUES

## EARLY EDUCATION ADVOCATES TAKING ACTION

At this critical time in our history, millions of people in the United States are particularly energized to take concrete action for children. It is time to combine our efforts to advocate for children and reconstruct our vision of childhood. For more information or to make contributions, visit our Web site: www.earlyeducationadvocates.org.

### OUR MISSION

We gather to define and promote democratic, participatory, and diverse early education provisions for children birth to common school age, for the United States. We wish to stimulate a broad discussion of the deeply felt human values that underlie our work and the formulation of a statement of social and political commitment.

### A DECLARATION OF VALUES TO UNDERLIE PROVISIONS FOR EARLY EDUCATION

Our cooperative effort to draft a set of guiding values promotes learning processes based on the values of human dignity, participation, openness to uncertainty, and democracy. We continually reflect on and revise this declaration of values and welcome input.

#### Belonging

We offer children opportunities to belong to multiple, diverse, and caring communities.

We ensure that whatever the situation children and adults find themselves in, they feel comfortable. Children feel included.

#### Well-being

We offer children provisions to insure their well-being in mind, body, and soul.

We have a responsibility and a commitment to care and be cared for in all dimensions of human health. We enable groups and individuals to think critically and question commonplace assumptions to repair our world.

#### Wholeness

We view children as whole, competent, and powerful human beings, connected to adults and other children.

Children, their families, and members of their communities are capable and not incomplete. We appreciate them for who they are and for who they will become. Children are valued as whole, complete human beings.

#### Reciprocity

We become and change ourselves in our relationships with others.

We are willing to be disturbed and have our beliefs changed by what others think and who others are. Children are our allies in action. We learn from them and they from us. In the exchange with others, we disarm power and privilege. Vital to diversity is the presence of reciprocal, mutual, equitable relationships.

**Respect**

We treat children with honesty, encouragement, and compassion in ways that honor their uniqueness and experience.

We have a responsibility and a commitment to care and be cared for in responsive and mutual relationships with people and the environment. We thrive in the beauty of being together.

**Participation**

We invite the participation of all in creating our possibility and defining our opportunities through our interactions.

We offer physical spaces, social spaces, languages, means of expression, time, and organizational systems that are open and somewhat indefinite to be created with and responsive to the participants. Through interaction and cooperation, children benefit from and contribute to an array of experiences and languages. School is a form of community life.

**Trust**

We convey our faith in children with the expectation that human goodness and growth are emerging possibilities at all times.

We stay truthful ourselves. We listen carefully. Children are trusted and receive trust so they learn to cooperate and communicate openly. We are trustworthy when we treat others fairly and responsibly. Responsibility emerges through trust, truth, and experience.

**Joy**

We treasure the spontaneity, laughter, richness, wonder, curiosity, movement, playfulness, vibrancy, and energy of children.

We preserve the joy of childhood in our interactions with children and each other. We seek the courageous expression of one's true being.

## CHILD CARE BUSINESS STRUCTURE—A NEW MODEL

### SOUND CHILD CARE SOLUTIONS— A CONSORTIUM OF CENTERS, BETTER TOGETHER

**www.soundchildcare.org or www.seattleconsortium.org**

Running a child care center requires two completely different skill sets: It is a business, and has to keep the doors open, but it's also an intimate partner in the important work of educating children. It's often difficult for a child care center to be excellent in both arenas.

Imagine an organization where these two functions are smoothly interwoven and of equal priority. Imagine a community of teacher-learners where children come first, their families are important, and children from all economic backgrounds have an opportunity to participate in a wonderful learning environment. Imagine a non-profit where the use of technology and cutting-edge business tools frees funds to continue improving the quality of early learning.

Sound Child Care Solutions (SCCS) creates a structure whereby strong child care centers can join together, sharing office or administrative functions to streamline and strengthen business practice, but retaining their community and family identity. We see an opportunity to make a generational leap in service delivery. Usually centers are small businesses, unable to gain advantages of economies of scale, but comfortable for families with their accessible size. By uniting across centers and combining the most cutting-edge tools to support early childhood education and small business, we free resources to improve teacher and director practice and serve more low income children.

The goal of Sound Child Care Solutions is to create a consortium structure whereby centers can gain:

- The economic strength of being a part of a larger organization, enabling the merged centers greater opportunity to weather economic and enrollment ebbs and flows
- Financial discounts that come from economies of scale in business functions like payroll, benefits management, banking, janitorial, food services, and purchasing
- Higher quality early childhood education (ECE) that comes with a more stable financial and organizational structure and a comprehensive approach to professional development
- Technology tools to streamline business and help teachers individualize teaching

Centers joining the consortium have a commitment to high quality ECE, culturally relevant antibias practices, and some stable source of funding in addition to tuition, such as employer subsidies, public funding, or free or reduced rent. Centers choose to join us, retaining their name, their unique community identity, and their board. Center staff become SCCS employees, center boards become center advisory boards, and center directors become SCCS corporate officers. Each center director leads education at his or her center while sharing in the consortium's major operational and financial decisions. All funds are pooled and managed as one entity. Staff and center directors work together to strengthen all centers in SCCS administratively and programmatically. Ongoing professional development, career pathways, and supports like a substitute pool strengthen centers, ensuring stability and consistency for children and families, and a respectful, healthy work environment for teachers and directors. Effective use of technology improves quality and helps teachers best individualize teaching.

Technology supports noninvasive outcomes tracking, generating data to continuously improve classroom, site, and administrative quality.

Research has consistently found that high quality outcomes for children and families are dependent upon strong center administrative practices like the ones offered by the consortium. SCCS will eventually expand to ten to fifteen centers, at which time we expect to spin off a new consortium. Built on national research pointing to the importance of strengthening child care economically, this new model takes the further innovative step of creating an opportunity for centers to choose to come together, rather than be "taken over" by a for-profit chain or large nonprofit, or forced to merge out of desperation. It generates value through economies of scale while preserving the unique culture that each center creates within its community. It returns all savings to the children rather than to shareholders or a big organization. It is a sustainable and replicable model.

# References


Berk, Laura, and Adam Winsler. 1995. *Scaffolding Children's Learning: Vygotsky and Early Education.* Washington, D.C.: National Association for the Education of Young Children (NAEYC).

Bodrova, E., and D. Leong. 2004. Chopsticks and Counting Chips. In *Spotlight on Young Children and Play,* ed. D. Koralek. Washington, D.C.: National Association for the Education of Young Children (NAEYC).

Bredekamp, S., and C. Copple, eds. 1997. *Developmentally Appropriate Practice in Early Childhood Programs.* Rev. ed. Washington, D.C.: National Association for the Education of Young Children (NAEYC).

Bredekamp, S., and T. Rosegrant, eds. 1995. *Reaching Potentials through Transforming Curriculum, Assessment, and Teaching.* Vol. 2. Washington, D.C.: National Association for the Education of Young Children (NAEYC).

Brofenbrenner, U. 2006. *The Ecology of Human Development: Experiments by Nature and Design.* Cambridge, Mass.: Harvard University Press.

Brookes, M. 1996. *Drawing with Children.* New York: Penguin Putnam, Inc.

Brosterman, N. 1997. *Inventing Kindergarten.* New York: Harry N. Abrams, Inc., Publishers.

Carr, Margaret. 2001. *Assessment in Early Childhood Settings: Learning Stories.* Thousand Oaks, Calif.: Sage Publishing.

Carter, M., and D. Curtis. 1998. *The Visionary Director.* St. Paul, Minn.: Redleaf Press.

Cronin, S., and E. Jones. 1999. *Play and Cultural Differences. Beginnings Workshop. Child Care Information Exchange* 127, no. 1. Redmond, Wash.: Exchange Press.

Cronin, S., and C. Masso. 2003. *Soy Bilingue: Language, Culture, and Young Latino Children.* Seattle, Wash.: Center for Cultural and Linguistic Democracy.

Curtis, D., and M. Carter. 1996. *Reflecting Children's Lives.* St. Paul, Minn.: Redleaf Press.

Curtis, D., and M. Carter. 2000. *The Art of Awareness: How Observation Can Transform Your Teaching.* St. Paul, Minn.: Redleaf Press.

Curtis, D., and M. Carter. 2003. *Designs for Living and Learning.* St. Paul, Minn.: Redleaf Press.

Dahlberg, G., and P. Moss. 2005. *Ethics and Politics in Early Childhood Education.* London: Routledge.

Dahlberg, G., P. Moss, and A. Pence. 1999. *Beyond Quality in Early Childhood Education and Care: Postmodern Perspectives.* London: Routledge.

Day, Carol Brunson. 2006. Personal communication reflecting on "Reconsidering Early Childhood Education in the United States: Reflections from Our Encounters with Reggio Emilia." In *The Hundred Languages of Children.* 1998. eds. C. Edwards, L. Gandini, and G. Forman. Greenwich, Conn.: Ablex Publishing.

Delpit, L. 2006. *Other People's Children.* New York: The New Press.

Dodge, D., L. Colker, and C. Heroman. 2002. *The Creative Curriculum.* Washington, D.C.: Teaching Strategies, Inc.

Duckworth, E. 1996. *The Having of Wonderful Ideas and Other Essays on Teaching and Learning.* New York: Teachers College Press.

Edwards, B. 1979. *Drawing on the Right Side of the Brain.* Los Angeles: JP Tarcher, Inc.

Edwards, C., L. Gandini, and G. Forman, eds. 1998. *The Hundred Languages of Children: The Reggio Emilia Approach; Advanced Reflections.* 2nd ed. Greenwich, Conn.: Ablex Publishing.

Elkonin, D. [1971] 1977. Toward the Problem of Stages in the Mental Development of the Child. In *Soviet Developmental Psychology,* ed. M. Cole. White Plaines, N.Y.: M. E. Sharpe.

Forman, G. 1996. *Negotiating with Art Media to Deepen Learning. Beginnings Workshop.* No. 108. Redmond, Wash.: Exchange Press.

Fraser, S., and C. Gestwicki. 2002. *Authentic Childhood.* Albany, N.Y.: Delmar.

Freire, P. 1970. *Pedagogy of the Oppressed.* New York: Herder and Herder.

Gallas, K. 1994. *The Languages of Learning: How Children Talk, Write, Dance, Draw and Sing Their Understanding of the World.* New York: Teachers College Press.

Gandini, L., and C. Edwards. 2001. *Bambini: The Italian Approach to Infant/Toddler Care.* New York: Teachers College Press.

Gardner, H. 1993. *Frames of Mind: The Theory of Multiple Intelligence.* New York: Basic Books.

Gardner, H. 1999. *Intelligences Reframed: Multiple Intelligences for the 21st Century.* New York: Basic Books.

Gatto, J. 2002. *Dumbing Us Down: The Hidden Curriculum of Compulsory Schooling.* Gabriola Island, BC, Canada: New Society Publishers.

Gibbs, J. 2000. *Tribes: A New Way of Learning and Being Together.* Windsor, Calif.: CenterSource Systems.

Goleman, Daniel. 1995. *Emotional Intelligence.* New York: Bantam Books.

Greenman, J. 2006. *Caring Places, Learning Spaces.* Redmond, Wash.: Exchange Press.

Gronlund, Gaye. 2003. *Focused Early Learning: A Planning Framework for Teaching Young Children.* St. Paul, Minn.: Redleaf Press.

Gronlund, Gaye. 2006. *Making Early Learning Standards Come Alive.* St. Paul, Minn.: Redleaf Press.

Gullo, Dominic. 2004. *Understanding Assessment and Evaluation in Early Childhood Education.* New York: Teachers College Press.

Hoffman, E. 2004. *Magic Capes, Amazing Powers: Transforming Super Hero Play in the Classroom.* St. Paul, Minn.: Redleaf Press.

Hohmann, M., B. Banet, and D. Weikart. 1979. *Young Children in Action.* Ypsilanti, Mich.: High/Scope Press.

Horm-Wingerd, D. 2002. The Reggio Emilia Approach and Accountable Assessment in the United States. In *Teaching and Learning: Collaborative Exploration of the Reggio Emilia Approach.* eds. V. Fu, A. Stremmel, and L. Hill. Upper Saddle River, N.J.: Pearson Education, Inc.

Hunter, T. 2004. *Still Growing.* Bellingham, Wash.: Song Growing Company (compact disc). www.tomhunter.com

Intrator, Sam, and Megan Scribner. 2003. *Teaching with Fire.* San Francisco: Jossey Bass.

Johnson, J., J. Christie, and T. Yawkey. 1987. *Play and Early Childhood Development.* Glenview, Ill.: Scott, Foresman & Co.

Johnston, J. S. 2006. *Inquiry and Education: John Dewey and the Quest for Democracy.* Albany, N.Y.: New York Press.

Jones, E. 2004. Playing to Get Smart. In *Spotlight on Young Children and Play,* ed. D. Koralek. Washington, D.C.: NAEYC.

Jones, E., and G. Reynolds. 1992. *The Play's the Thing: Teacher's Role in Children's Play.* New York: Teachers College Press.

Katz, L. 1993. *Dispositions: Definitions and Implications for Early Childhood Practices.* Urbana, Ill.: ERIC Clearinghouse on Elementary and Early Childhood Education.

Katz, L. 1998. What Can We Learn from Reggio Emilia. In *The Hundred Languages of Children: The Reggio Emilia Approach,* eds. C. Edwards, L. Gandini, and G. Forman. Greenwich, Conn.: Ablex Publishing Company.

Kolbe, U. 2005. *It's Not a Bird Yet: The Drama of Drawing.* Byron Bay, NSW, Australia: Peppinot Press.

Louv, R. 2005. *Last Child in the Woods: Saving Our Children from Nature Deficit Disorder.* Chapel Hill, N.C.: Algonquin Books.

MacNaughton, G., and G. Williams. 1998. *Techniques for Teaching Young Children.* Frenchs Forest, NSW, Australia: Addison Wesley Longman Australia.

Malaguzzi, L. 1998. History, Ideas, and Basic Philosophy. In *The Hundred Languages of Children: The Reggio Emilia Approach,* eds. C. Edwards, L. Gandini, and G. Forman. Greenwich, Conn.: Ablex Publishing Company.

Malaguzzi, L., ed. 1996. *The Hundred Languages of Children: Narrative of the Possible.* Reggio Emilia, Italy: Reggio Children.

McGhee, P. 2003. *Understanding and Promoting the Development of Children's Humor: A Guide for Parents and Teachers.* Dubuque, Iowa: Kendall/Hunt Publishers.

Meier, D., and B. Henderson. 2007. *Learning from Young Children in the Classroom: The Art and Science of Teacher Research.* New York: Teachers College Press.

Meisels, S. J., J. R. Jablon, D. B. Marsden, M. L. Dichtelmiller, and A. B. Dorfman. 1994. *The Work*

*Sampling System.* Ann Arbor, Mich.: Rebus.

Meriwether, Linda. 1997. Math at the Snack Table. *Young Children* 52, no. 5.

Momaday, N. February 7, 2007. Weekday radio broadcast. Seattle, Wash.: KUOW, National Public Radio.

Mooney, C. 2000. *Theories of Childhood: An Introduction to Dewey, Montessori, Erikson, Piaget and Vygotsky.* St. Paul, Minn.: Redleaf Press.

NAEYC. 2007. Beyond the Journal: Voices of Practitioners. www.journal.naeyc.org/bti/vp/.

Neugebauer, B., ed. 1999. *Play and Culture: Beginnings Workshop* 127, no. 1. Redmond, Wash.: Exchange Press.

New, R. 1997. Next Steps in Teaching "the Reggio Way." In *First Steps toward Teaching the Reggio Way,* ed. J. Hendrick. Upper Saddle River, N.J.: Merrill/Prentice Hall.

Paley, V. 1990. *The Boy Who Would Be a Helicopter.* Cambridge, Mass.: Harvard University Press.

Palmer, P. 1998. *The Courage to Teach.* San Francisco, Calif.: Jossey-Bass.

Patterson, C., A. Fleet, and J. Duffie. 1995. *Learning from Stories: Early Childhood Professional Experiences.* Sydney, NSW, Australia: Institute of Early Childhood, Macquarie University.

Pelo, Ann. 2007. *The Language of Art.* St. Paul, Minn.: Redleaf Press.

Phillips, C. B., and Sue Bredekamp. 1998. Reconsidering Early Childhood Education in the United States: Reflections from Our Encounters with Reggio Emilia. In *The Hundred Languages of Children,* eds. C. Edwards, L. Gandini, and G. Forman. Greenwich, Conn.: Ablex Publishing.

Piaget, J. 2001. *Language and Thought of the Child.* New York: Routledge Classics.

Project Zero and Reggio Children. 2001. *Making Learning Visible: Children as Individual and Group Learners.* Reggio Emilia, Italy: Reggio Children.

Rinaldi, Carlina. 1998. Projected Curriculum Constructed through Documentation—Progettazione. In *The Hundred Languages of Children,* eds. C. Edwards, L. Gandini, and G. Forman. Greenwich, Conn.: Ablex Publishing.

Rogoff, B. 2003. *The Cultural Nature of Human Development.* New York: Oxford University Press.

Ruef, K. 2005. *The Private Eye: Looking and Thinking by Analogy.* Lyle, Wash.: The Private Eye Project.

Seefeldt, Carol. 2005. *How to Work with Standards in the Early Childhood Classroom.* New York: Teachers College Press.

Senge, P. 2000. *Schools That Learn: A Fifth Discipline Book for Educators, Parents, and Everyone Who Cares about Education.* New York: Doubleday.

Shonkoff, J. P., D. Phillip, and the Committee on Integrating the Science of Early Childhood Development. 2000. *From Neurons to Neighborhoods: The Science of Early Childhood Development.* Washington, D.C.: National Research Council, Academy of Science.

Shore, R. 1997. *Rethinking the Brain: New Insights into Early Development.* New York: Families and Work Institute.

Skinner, B. 1965. *Science and Human Behavior.* New York: Free Press.

Small, M. 1999. *Our Babies, Ourselves: How Biology and Culture Shape the Way We Parent.* New York: Anchor Books.

Vygotsky, L. 1978. *Mind in Society: The Development of Higher Psychological Processes.* Cambridge, Mass.: Harvard University.

Wagner, Tony. 2002. *Making the Grade: Reinventing America's Schools.* New York: Routledge Falmer.

Whitney, T. 1999. *Kids Like Us: Using Persona Dolls in the Classroom.* St. Paul, Minn.: Redleaf Press.

Wien, C. 1995. *Developmentally Appropriate Practice in Real Life.* New York: Teachers College Press.

Wien, Carol Anne. 2004. *Negotiating Standards in the Primary Classroom.* New York: Teachers College Press.

Wien, C. A., and B. L. Keating. *The Sculpture Project.* (unpublished manuscript).

Williams, L., and Y. De Gaetano. 1985. *Alerta: A Multicultural, Bilingual Approach to Teaching Young Children.* New York: Addison-Wesley.

Wood, Chip. 1999. *Time to Teach, Time to Learn.* Turner Falls, Mass.: Northeast Foundation for Children.

# Index